D0430786

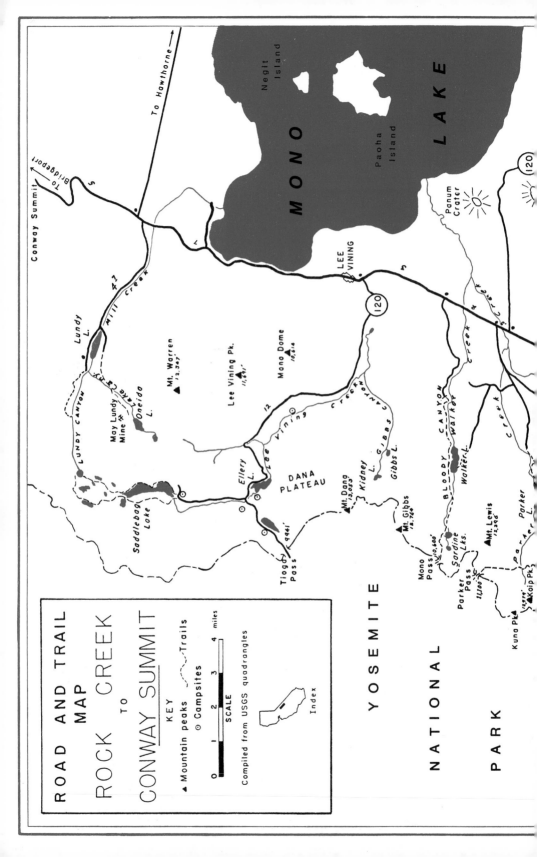

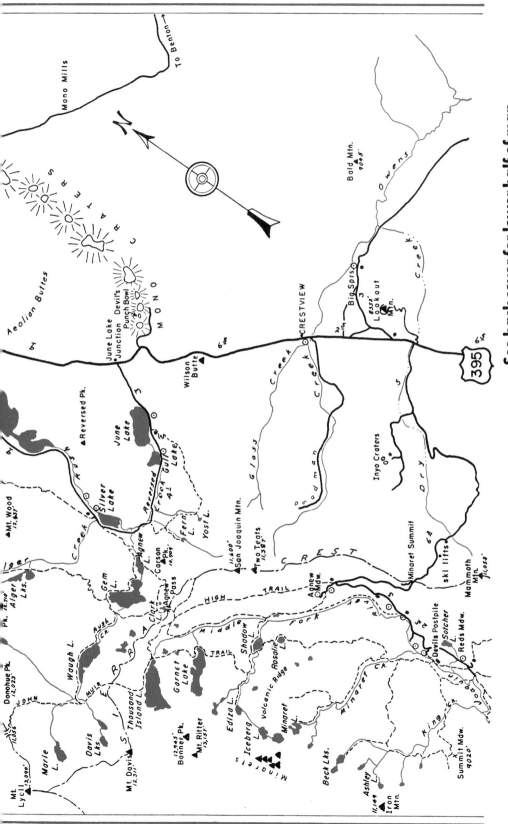

See back cover for lower half of map.

Mammoth

Lakes Sierra

A handbook for
roadside and trail

Dean Rinehart, Elden Vestal, Bettie E. Willard

Edited by Genny Smith

Illustrated by Susan Rinehart

Sixth Edition, 1993

GENNY SMITH BOOKS ❧ MAMMOTH LAKES, CALIFORNIA

Book and cover design and production by David Mike Hamilton

Photo layout by Stephanie Furniss

Front cover photo, Lake Mary and Crystal Crag, by Stephen H. Willard

Mammal drawings by Elden Vestal

Maps by Dean Rinehart

Historic photographs from the collections of Adele Reed, Genny Smith, Laws Railroad Museum, Eastern California Museum

Photographs by Ed Cooper, David J. Dunaway, LaMoine R. Fantozzi, Philip W. Faulconer, Robert C. Frampton, Don Gibbon, Philip Hyde, T J Johnston, J. W. MacBride, H. W. Mendenhall, Edwin C. Rockwell, Tom Ross, Gerhard Schumacher, John S. Shelton, Julius Shulman, Bev Steveson, Stephen H. Willard, Billy Young

Library of Congress Cataloging in Publication Data

Rinehart, C. Dean (Charles Dean), 1922-
    Mammoth Lakes Sierra : a handbook for roadside and trail / by Dean Rinehart, Elden Vestal, and Bettie E. Willard ; edited by Genny Smith ; illustrated by Susan Rinehart. — 6th ed.
        p. cm.
Includes bibliographical references (p.) and index.
ISBN 0-931378-13-3
    1. Mammoth-High Sierra Recreation Area (Calif.)—Guide-books. 2. Mammoth Lakes Region (Calif.)—Guide-books. 3. Trails—California—Mammoth-High Sierra Recreation Area—Guide-books. 4. Natural history—California—Mammoth-High Sierra Recreation Area—Guide-books. I. Vestal, Elden. II. Willard, Beatrice E. III. Smith, Genny IV. Title.
F868.S5R46 1993   93-1250
917.94'4—dc20   CIP

First edition, May 1959
    Second printing, October 1959
    Third printing, August 1961
Second edition, July 1964
Third edition, June 1969
    Second printing, August 1971
Fourth edition, June 1976
    Second Printing, May 1980
Fifth edition, August 1989
Sixth edition, July 1993
Manufactured in the United States of America

Contents

The Sixth Edition, 1993

A wealth of new information has been gathered during the last fifteen years, and the best part of it is that interest and research in the eastern Sierra is flourishing. The most significant changes in this edition come from recent research on this region's history, wildlife, geology and on Mono Lake. Thanks to Gary Caldwell's research on the Mammoth Mining Company, published in 1990 under the title *Mammoth Gold*, we have a far more detailed and accurate assessment of the mining days—and the true stories are even better than the tall tales. Thanks to Tod Fletcher's research on the history of the Bodie-Mono Lake area, published as *Paiute, Prospector, Pioneer,* we know much more about the early miners and ranchers there. Particularly important, his review of documents relating to Jedediah Smith, Joe Walker and Lt. Tredwell Moore clears up a lot of misinformation on who went where and when.

Thanks to wildlife biologists, we are learning much more about the local deer herds and about the bighorn sheep and the pronghorn, which they have recently transplanted to their historic ranges. DWP scientists and independent scientists of many disciplines have converged on Mono Lake the past fifteen years. Along with two landmark studies—one by the National Academy of Sciences, one by the Community and Organization Research Institute of the University of California—they have brought us an understanding of the lake's ecology and its importance. Thanks to geologists from many institutions, notably the US Geological Survey, we know much more about the region's recent geologic past and have some clues to its future.

The back country hasn't changed and the trails have changed little. But our approaches to the trails have changed considerably, with better parking areas at road ends, some roads re-routed and some new bridges at important and dangerous stream crossings. Some bridges have washed out and will not be replaced.

Don't be surprised if some of our text differs markedly from signs and articles and other books, including our own previous editions. After all, we wouldn't have bothered to bring out a new edition if the old one were still adequate. Our information is as accurate and up to date as we could make it. We welcome corrections, additions and suggestions. Send them to the editor, PO Box 1060, Mammoth Lakes, CA 93546.

Genny Smith
Mammoth Lakes, July 1993

Mount Ritter and Banner Peak   *J. W. MacBride*

Discovery!

This book is mainly about wild places and the wild things

you may discover there. That is, if you are lucky you will discover them, for the essence of wild things is that they appear and disappear for reasons of their own, not because we whistle a call. They live in their world in *their* way. They may give us a glimpse now and then of that world, and the thrill of those unexpected moments, those brief encounters, may linger always.

So in this guide there is no attempt to tell you "all about" the wild places of the eastern Sierra. Their secrets will become yours only as you wander about and discover them yourself. We want to help you form a comfortable acquaintance with the landmarks, the plants, the rocks, and the animals, but we can only open doors. You are on your own—to choose, or not, to walk through some of those doors, to explore, to discover.

Thousand Island Lake   *Stephen H. Willard*

T.J. Lake   *Stephen H. Willard*

Old Mammoth   *Stephen H. Willard*

Stephen Willard discovered the Sierra a lifetime ago.

Wintering in the desert and summering here, Willard devoted most of his life to photographing scenic landscapes. He and his wife Beatrice opened a studio in Mam- moth in 1924 and operated it until her death in 1977. We are privileged to publish a selection of photographs from his life's work. You will find them scattered through- out the photo sections. Contact prints from his eight-by-ten negatives were made espe- cially for this edition.

Lake George, Crystal Crag   *Bev Steveson*

Wild Places, Wild Things

This is mainly a book about the wild places in the Mammoth Lakes Sierra and the things you may discover there. We can't guarantee that you will find them, though, for the essence of wild things is that they live in their world in their way on their own time schedule, not ours. They appear and disappear for their own reasons, not because we whistle a call. The brief encounters, the unexpected moments—these are thrills remembered a lifetime. You may go for weeks without ever seeing an alpine columbine or a mountain quail or a pika, without ever hearing a hermit thrush. Then one day on a boulder slope that looks no different than a hundred others you have passed, a pika scurries over the rocks, carrying wildflowers in its mouth and spreading them out to dry for hay. If you care to, you can learn about him and his boulder-world, how he manages to survive nine-month winters, who his neighbors are, what he feeds on and who feeds on him. The next time you hear a pika's nasal call, the experience may then be a deeper one and you may feel more at one with the pika, realizing that you are a creature at his boulder slope, briefly in *his* wild place.

And what's happening in the Sierra's wild places? Something of a miracle has happened to keep them wild at all. Few would there be if all the sheepmen, lumbermen, road-builders, miners and developers had had their way.

If no one had objected to their doings, your favorite Sierra campsite would be far from wild today.

Reds Meadow and the San Joaquin's Middle Fork valley, for example—in a broad, dramatically beautiful canyon of forest and meadow, popular for family camping—would no longer be quiet and pristine. Instead we would see lumbering and lumber trucks in the valley and on the entire slope to the east, sheep stripping the meadows of flowers and grass, motorcycles on the trails, ski tows stretching from the top of Mammoth Mountain to Reds Meadow and wide swaths cut for ski trails through the red fir forest, a road to Shadow Lake, and a high-speed trans-Sierra truck route coming down from Summit Meadow and climbing over Minaret Summit. Each one of these activities was seriously proposed and advocated strenuously for years by one group or another. If no one had objected, where then would we go today for serenity and wildness?

Fortunately for us, John Muir and his friends began objecting a century ago and we have them to thank for Yosemite Park. Others have continued to object, so that today we have a glorious strip of wild land along the Sierra crest where one can hike for more than two hundred and fifty miles without ever seeing a road and hearing road noises. Its wildness is firmly protected by law in national parks and national forest wilderness areas. The newest is the Ansel Adams Wilderness, established in 1984 after thirty years of opposition from Madera and Fresno counties and their allies, notably lumbermen.

By a strange twist, another threat to the High Sierra today comes from the very people who love it the most—the hikers and fishermen and backpackers. Around some favorite lakes there have been just too many of us. During the short summer season, in the Inyo Forest wilderness, overnight campers alone accounted for half a million visitor days of recreation use in 1988; add to that the uncounted numbers of day hikers, fishermen and riders. During the 1960s, as back-country use multiplied, a few botanists and ecologists noticed changes and scars at some of the most heavily used lakes such as Bullfrog, Shadow and Desolation, but no one paid much attention to their warnings. It wasn't until around 1970 that the danger signals became so glaring that few people could miss them—plants obliterated by too many trampling feet, water polluted, down-wood scarce. Shadow Lake, a famous campsite on the John Muir Trail in one of the most beautiful settings of all the Sierra, is a good example. Owing to years of camping near its inlet, the lakeshore was hard packed, denuded of grass and flowers, and covered with charcoal and blackened stones. And there is still another dimension to consider. How close together can people hike the same trail and camp around the same lake before their very closeness destroys the quiet and wildness they came for?

ea ea ea

If all this sounds grim, don't be disheartened. If you hear the Sierra is crowded, don't believe it. There is solitude and wildness for the finding even in the Sierra, especially on weekdays and in the off-season. There is lots of it a quarter-mile off any trail, and more of it up those canyons with no trails that I hope no one ever writes a guidebook about. And there are encouraging signs that more and more of us are learning how to walk softly in the wilderness, to think of each meadow, each lakeshore as a high mountain garden we would no more trample than we would our own garden. And so remarkable is the ability of plants and soil to recover from abuse that a few years of rest are already working their wonders. Within the short time backcountry rangers have been diverting campers from damaged areas, grass and flowers are returning to the shore of Shadow Lake.

Too, there's an awareness, more keenly felt these days, that the world is a very small planet—a small but wondrous creation inhabited by plants and animals so numerous and varied we don't yet know them all. Since we alone hold the power to annihilate our brother creatures—and have—the more reason for us to assume responsibility for their welfare. In this perspective the protection of wild creatures and their living space needs no other justification. We need wild places because wild things are on this earth along with us. That is reason enough.

–G. S.

The Mammoth Lakes Sierra

Una gran sierra nevada

Writing in his journal from a hill near San Francisco Bay and looking to the northeast, Pedro Font, a Franciscan missionary, described an immense treeless plain "into which the water spreads widely, forming several low islets; at the opposite end of this extensive plain, about forty leagues off, we saw a great snow-covered range [una gran sierra nevada] which seemed to me to run south-southeast to north-northwest."

Over the crest of that great snowy range, directly east of San Francisco Bay where Pedro Font stood in 1776, lies a superbly beautiful portion of the 400-mile-long Sierra Nevada, the Mammoth Lakes Sierra. Six hours north of Los Angeles and three hours south of Reno, this 50-mile portion of the eastern Sierra slope extends from Rock Creek canyon to Lundy Canyon. Its magnificent mountains tower more than six thousand feet above two desert valleys to the east—Mono Basin with its huge lake, and Long Valley—both around 6500 feet in altitude.

In a broad opening in the steep mountain front, below a mile-wide lakes

9

basin, lies the resort town of Mammoth Lakes. Although Mammoth Mountain is lower than neighboring peaks, its great hulk dominates the landscape for miles around. Into the mountain front north and south of Mammoth, water and ice have cut the deep-gashed canyons of Hilton, McGee, Convict, Parker, Walker, Lee Vining, and Mill creeks. Rock Creek drains a much longer canyon; Little Lakes Valley, at its head, cradles more than two dozen small lakes. Rush Creek drains a broad basin below the Sierra crest and empties into Silver Lake, below the dramatic vertical face of Carson Peak. There the village of June Lake clusters around Silver, Gull and June Lake.

The Sierra Nevada's steep eastern slope is a world apart from the lands to the west. In contrast to the Sierra's western slope that rises gradually for seventy miles, from sea-level in the fertile Great Valley up to its snowy crest, the eastern slope drops abruptly thousands of feet to arid valleys below. Akin to the desert lands eastward, the land is spacious and open to the sky, the views immense. In contrast to west slope rivers and dense forests, east slope streams are small, the forests sparse with little underbrush; little moisture from Pacific rain clouds reaches these lands east of the mountains.

In the Mammoth Lakes region, however, at the center of the generally arid eastern Sierra, two low passes on either side of Mammoth Mountain funnel Pacific storms over the Sierra crest, across Mammoth Pass and Minaret Summit. Winter storms bring heavy snows and a long ski season to Mammoth Mountain and June Mountain. They water the Jeffrey pine forest that extends miles to the east and account for late-lying snowbanks that water unexpected meadows and pockets of wildflowers. If you are surprised that we consider these 9000-foot passes low, you will be astonished to learn that you must look a hundred miles south or seventy-five miles north to find a lower pass. Along this central portion of the Sierra Nevada, stretching from Lake Tahoe south, few gaps breach its crest. Most of its passes stand ten, eleven and twelve thousand feet high, little lower than its peaks.

Even the rocks of the Mammoth Lakes Sierra are unusual. Instead of only gray Sierra granite, here more ancient rocks display a hundred shades of maroon, red-gold, dark brown, blue-gray, pink-tinged purple and bright rust. Younger volcanic eruptions have splattered the region with red cinder cones, pinkish-tan flows, whitish pumice, and black obsidian.

The abrupt changes in altitude, from 13,000-foot peaks to 6500-foot valleys, account for an extraordinary diversity of plant and animal life within short distances. Alpine willow covered by nine-month snowbanks flourish only a few miles west of desert sagebrush; the white-tailed jackrabbit in summer inhabits the mountain forests, only a few miles from his black-tailed low-country cousin.

As if all these glories were not enough for one region, a few miles west rise

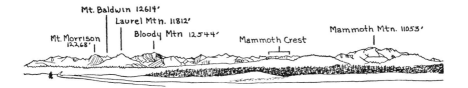

The Sierra crest, looking south from Deadman Creek Road.

two more grand ridges, the Silver Divide and the Ritter Range, with the tantalizing glacier-spangled peaks of the Minarets, Mount Ritter and Banner Peak rising two thousand feet above the Sierra crest. And on the horizon to the east stand the White Mountains, higher than Mammoth Mountain by three thousand feet. With all these variables, each canyon, each campsite, each trail is a unique combination of views, of colors, of flowers, forest, birds and furry creatures.

Unlike most high mountains, the eastern Sierra welcomes campers and mountaineers with long summers that are relatively warm and dry. It is also readily accessible—by scheduled airline, by bus and by good roads. Eleven highways cross the Sierra, though some are closed in winter. From any of them you can link up with US Highway 395, surely one of the most scenic highways in all the west, which hugs the base of the Sierra Nevada for almost its entire length, from Susanville south to Ridgecrest. From 395, dozens of sideroads wind far up the canyons while others head east into the desert—all lead to countless surprises and magnificent viewpoints. From the road ends, good trails lead farther into the mountains and over the passes. Miles of joy and endless days of wonder are yours for discovering.

Some Basic Information

The Inyo National Forest

Most of the land described in this guidebook lies within the Inyo National Forest, administered by the US Forest Service. Adjoining the Inyo Forest along its western boundary are the Sierra National Forest and Yosemite National Park; on its northern boundary, the Toiyabe National Forest. It's all glorious mountain country regardless of which agency administers it, although there are some important differences between national park and national forest regulations. Firearms, dogs even on leash and other pets are prohibited on all national park trails. They are allowed on all Inyo National Forest trails.

The Inyo Forest has an extensive program of evening talks, exhibits, guided tours and self-guiding nature trails. Inquire at ranger stations for schedules of events, for maps, books, wilderness permits, and information on just about everything—campgrounds, trail conditions, weather. They are listed below with the mountain areas they administer.

White Mountain Ranger Station, 798 N Main St., Bishop 93514. Rock Creek, Hilton and McGee Creeks.

Mammoth Ranger Station, PO Box 148, Mammoth Lakes 93546. Convict Creek, the Ritter Range, Reds and Agnew Meadows, Mammoth Lakes area.

Mono Lake Ranger Station, PO Box 429, Lee Vining 93541. June Lake, Rush Creek, Lee Vining Creek canyon, Saddlebag Lake, Lundy Canyon.

Bridgeport Ranger Station, Bridgeport 93517. Toiyabe National Forest. From Virginia Lakes north.

Or write or telephone: Inyo Forest Supervisor's Office, 873 N Main St., Bishop 93514

Maps

An original map with trail and road information updated for this edition is included in this guidebook on the end papers. For a larger scale map that covers the entire Inyo National Forest, we highly recommend the Inyo Forest Visitors Map. The California State Automobile Association/Automobile Club of Southern California also publishes a fine map, Guide to Eastern Sierra, that covers the country between Lone Pine and Bridgeport.

Forest Visitors Map, Inyo National Forest, 1993, 30 x 40 inches, color. Scale: ½ inch = 1 mile. This is by far the best of the maps that cover the entire area. Road and trail information is as up to date as you will find. This map covers the entire Inyo National Forest, from its southern boundary near Owens Lake north to Mono Lake, and from its western boundary near the Sierra Nevada crest to the eastern slope of the Inyo and White Mountains. Available at all ranger stations.

Mountain Bikes and Motorcycles

Over three hundred miles of back roads offer rides that range from easy to very difficult, all with spectacular views of dramatic mountain scenery. Don and Réanne Douglass's book, *Mountain Biking the High Sierra: Guide II, Mammoth Lakes and Mono County*, 1992, will guide you to the best of them. Available locally and by mail from Fine Edge Productions, Rt 2, Box 303, Bishop 93514. Guide I covers Owens Valley and Inyo County. Riding cross-country damages the terrain and is prohibited. Some narrow mountain trails that are heavily used by horses, pack trains, backpackers and hikers are not suitable for riding; to avoid serious accidents, riding on certain trails is prohibited. Check in at ranger stations for current information on which trails are designated for riding.

Winter

Although this guidebook dwells on where to go and what you may discover in summer, some day you will want to come in winter, if you haven't already. A totally different, shimmering white, snow-covered world awaits you. There are many lifts for downhill skiing and several hundred miles of signed, groomed trails for cross-country skiing and for snowmobiling. Other winter sports include dogsledding, sleighriding and bobsledding. Most of the organizations listed below under "sources" can supply you with winter information, in addition to these: June Mountain Ski Area, PO Box 146, June Lake 93529; Mammoth Mountain Ski Area, PO Box 24, Mammoth Lakes 93546.

Sources of More Information

Besides the natural wonders this guidebook describes, Mono communities offer events of many kinds. Parades, music festivals, picnics, arts and craft fairs, barbecues, air shows. A triathlon, a motocross, fishing derbies. Events for cyclists, mountain bikers, water skiers, tennis players, runners. And every year something new. Call the Mammoth Lakes Visitors Bureau (1-800-367-6572) for current road and weather conditions and for county-wide information, winter and summer. See the local newspapers for details: *Mammoth Times*, PO Box 3929 and *Review-Herald*, PO Box 110, Mammoth Lakes 93546. Listed below are some important sources of information.

Bodie State Historic Park, PO Box 515, Bridgeport 93517.

California Department of Fish and Game. Maps and information at the office, 407 W Line St., Bishop 93514.

Eastern High Sierra Packers Assoc., 690 North Main St., Bishop 93514. Pack trips, day rides, spring and fall horse drives, horses, mules, burros. Eight pack outfits serve the area.

Interagency Visitor Center, at the junction of Hwy 136 and US 395, a mile south of Lone Pine. Loaded with information on just about every aspect of the eastern Sierra, including current road, trail and weather conditions. Maps, pamphlets and an exceptional selection of books.

Los Angeles Dept. Recreation and Parks, 200 N Main St., Los Angeles 90012. Information on: Crowley Lake fishing and boating regulations, storage and rentals; family camping at Camp High Sierra.

Mammoth Lakes Visitors Bureau, PO Box 48, Mammoth Lakes 93546. Accommodations, services, maps, self-guided tours of Mono County attractions, and information on events winter and summer.

Mono Basin National Forest Scenic Area Visitor Center, USFS, just north of Lee Vining, opened in 1992. Its dramatic structure crowns a magnificent site overlooking Mono Lake. Outstanding hands-on exhibits, an exceptional film *Of Ice and*

Fire, ranger talks, two art galleries—all focused on the wonders and mysteries of Mono Lake.

Mono Lake Tufa State Reserve, PO Box 99, Lee Vining 93541. Information, maps, guided trips.

Mono Lake Committee Information Center and Bookstore, PO Box 29, Lee Vining 93541. Nature walks, canoe trips, advice on roads, trails, points of interest. Fine selection of regional and environmental books. Headquarters for the fight to preserve Mono Lake and for news on how you can help protect the lake and all its creatures from slow death. Operated by the non-profit Mono Lake Committee.

Museums. Hours vary, inquire locally. *Mammoth Museum,* Mammoth Lakes. Located in a 1930s log cabin on Mammoth Creek. Exhibits on mining, skiing and local history; self-guided tours. *Mono County Museum,* Bridgeport. Extensive collections of historic photographs, Paiute baskets and other items from the early days of Mono County. Located in the 1880 elementary school building. Picnic area adjacent. *Schoolhouse Museum,* Lee Vining, next to Hess Park. Focused on Mono Basin history.

Non-profit groups offering local field trips. The following are volunteer organizations offering field trips to points of interest year-round: Bristlecone Chapter, California Native Plant Society; Eastern Sierra Audubon Society; Toiyabe Chapter, Sierra Club. Although they have no permanent phone numbers or offices, you can probably locate them through ranger stations, the Bishop *Inyo Register* newspaper and the Interagency Visitor Center listed above. They also welcome support for their efforts on behalf of eastern Sierra wildlife, wilderness and land-use decisions that will ensure a healthy environment.

Youth Hostels. Hosteling—a simple, low-cost way of outdoor recreation and traveling throughout the world, for those young in spirit regardless of age—has reached the eastern Sierra. Hilton Creek Hostel opened in 1989: Rt 1, PO Box 1128, Crowley Lake 93546. For membership and information write: American Youth Hostels, 733 – 15th St. NW, Suite 840, Washington D. C. 20005.

Roadsides

You can drive from Sherwin Summit to Conway Summit, the section of US Highway 395 described in this guidebook, in less than two hours. Yet so many scenic and interesting roads and trails lie between these two summits that a two-week vacation allows only a beginning acquaintance with all there is to see and do.

In the following pages you will find descriptions of points of interest along Highway 395, as well as along most of the sideroads branching east and west. The material is arranged from south to north, beginning at Sherwin Summit 21 miles north of Bishop and ending at Conway Summit 13 miles south of Bridgeport. Both summits, appropriately, are named after pioneer settlers. For more details on the points of interest, turn to the relevant sections that follow: trails, geology, trees, flowers and shrubs, mammals, fish, birds and history.

Although most people focus on the dramatic Sierra canyons to the west, there is another, different world east of Highway 395—the high desert. The cool seasons and cool summer evenings are choice times to wander this tan, arid world. Forests of pinyon and Jeffrey pine, groves of aspen and, in spring, carpets of lavender lupine and magenta mimulus make it far less bleak than it may seem at a distance. Although many of the roads are pumice, they are safe for passenger cars if you observe a few precautions—have a full gas tank, take water with you, make sure someone knows where you are going and *stay in the road tracks*. Pumice is as treacherous as sand. Venturing into pumice on little used side roads, even with 4-wheel drive, is asking for trouble.

US 395. Highway 395 was first known as "El Camino Sierra," a romantic name probably inspired by El Camino Real, the old road connecting the California missions. East of the Sierra, from earliest times trails had linked the Indian settlements; other trails crossed Sierra passes to neighboring Indians on the west slope. These were the trails the first prospectors followed, as their feverish search for gold led them from the played-out placers of the Mother Lode to the land east of the Sierra. The cattlemen, farmers, merchants and soldiers who came next followed the same well-worn paths and then tramped new ones to the mining camps. With use, the trails widened into "roads," which were adequate for slow, large-wheeled wagons, but not for speedy, thirty-mile-per-hour automobiles, which began traveling them in the early 1900s.

California voters approved the first bond issue to construct a state highway system in 1910. With pressure from the Inyo Good Road Club, El Camino Sierra (260 miles between Mojave and Bridgeport) was included in the state's first highway plan. The first segment to be worked on was the old wagon road up Sherwin Hill. In 1916 almost a thousand people attended the barbecue in Rock Creek canyon celebrating completion of ten miles of graded, oiled road. Something to celebrate, indeed—the long trip from Bishop to Mammoth Lakes could now be made in two and a half hours! Bit by bit the entire route, two ruts through sand and sagebrush, was paved or oiled. Since cars often sank to their axles in the loose pumice of Deadman Summit and in the sand near Division Creek, these two projects were next; then bridges across some of the creeks; then a graded road over Conway Summit. Finally in 1931 a hard-surface road was completed all the way from Bishop to Los Angeles. Today's four-lane highway up Sherwin Grade was completed in 1956.

US 395 Sherwin Summit to Mammoth Lakes

As you climb Sherwin Grade, take the time to stop at some of the turnouts and look back to the south. The airplane-like views are spectacular—into Pine Creek and Bishop Creek canyons, down the length of the Sierra crest, and across to the White-Inyo mountains.

As you drive up the grade, you can't help but notice the sparkling pink and pale gray roadcuts in the volcanic rock known as *Bishop tuff*. It is one of

Morgan Pass   Bear Creek Spire   Mt. Dade   Mt Abbot 13715'   Mt Mills 13468'

Pyramid Pk.

Little Lakes Valley

many indications of volcanic activity that you see all the way to Mono Lake. This tuff—150 cubic miles of it—exploded long ago from vents now buried beneath the floor of Long Valley Caldera. Its surface has weathered to the rosy tan color you see on both sides of the highway. Since the tuff is relatively soft and easily quarried, it was used as a building stone by some of the early settlers.

Just north of Sherwin Summit, 7000 feet, watch for the first glimpse (northwest) of the Ritter Range's thirteen-thousand-foot peaks. As the road drops from the summit to cross Rock Creek, the old Sherwin Grade road branches off to the left, leading to lower Rock Creek and rejoining 395 in Round Valley. It follows the general route of the historic Sherwin Toll Road, built during the 1870s by James L. C. Sherwin. In 1859, lured by tales of the fabulous Comstock Lode, Sherwin and his bride from Kentucky had come west to Virginia City. Eventually Sherwin homesteaded in Round Valley at the foot of the grade bearing his name, and in 1874 built a wagon road up to his sawmill in lower Rock Creek canyon. Several years later, during the rush to the Mammoth mines, Sherwin extended his wagon road to the top of the grade and operated it as a toll road. It is hard today to imagine the dangers of that road. Wagons going down the steep grade occasionally went out of control and crashed, killing the horses. A huge boiler being freighted to the Mammoth Mining Company's mill broke loose and rolled all the way to the bottom of the grade.

Sideroad to Rock Creek Lake and Little Lakes Valley. Rock Creek Road branches left (W) from the highway to follow noisy, splashing Rock Creek upstream to the campgrounds along the creek and to the resort, store and pack station near Rock Creek Lake. The gray-green trees dotting the lower brush slopes are pinyon pine; a few large, light reddish brown Jeffrey pine tower above them. Along the creek grow copper birch, cottonwood, willow, and the quaking aspen that turn brilliant colors in late September, making this road in fall a glorious drive through a golden forest. At 10,300 feet, the trailhead at the end of the road is the highest in the Sierra and 350 feet higher than Tioga Pass. A short walk up the trail reveals a stunning view of Little Lakes Valley and the great 13,000-foot peaks clustered around its upper end. Weeks could be spent exploring just this one canyon, for it has over fifty lakes within half a day's hike.

Sideroads to Toms Place and Owens Gorge. The turnoff to Rock Creek connects with Crowley Lake Drive, which leads to several resorts off the freeway. The first of them is Toms Place, named for Tom Yerby, who opened a fishing resort with a store and cabins in the early 1920s. East of US 395, the Owens Gorge Road crosses Long Valley Dam, leads to the southeast tip of Crowley Lake, and joins a network of dirt roads leading east toward Casa Diablo Mountain and north toward Benton Crossing. The Owens Gorge is a 700-foot-deep gash cut by the Owens River into the Bishop tuff. Part of the gorge is inaccessible; part of it is busy with hydro plants. However, it is possible to see a similar one close up by hiking the gorge cut by Lower Rock Creek. See Trails chapter.

US 395 resumed. The highway skirts the lower edge of Little Round Valley, whose meadows have long provided summer pasture for sheep and for Owens Valley cattle. On the upper side of the road, among the squat, symmetrical pinyon pine, you may notice some mountain mahogany—large angular shrubs that in late summer have a silky, silvery appearance caused by fuzzy, spirally twisted "tails" on the seeds. Mountain mahogany is a favorite food of deer.

Sideroads to Crowley Lake and Hilton Creek. Crowley reservoir is renowned for its trophy-size fish, which thrive on the lake's plentiful and rich food supply. It is fished heavily; opening weekend may attract 10,000 anglers. Mid-season, fishing regulations change. After August first, minimum size is 18 inches, bag limit is two fish. Three species of trout inhabit Crowley—rainbow, brown and Lahontan cutthroat—as well as Sacramento perch. Owens suckers and tui chubs, both non-game native fish, also live in the lake. Hilton Creek, in the opposite direction, has some of the largest, loveliest aspen trees anywhere along the highway. Richard Hilton, a blacksmith by trade, owned a ranch in Round Valley and in summer operated a milk ranch in Long Valley, in the meadows near Hilton Creek. He supplied butter to the mining camps, beginning in the 1870s. Mrs. Hilton, a midwife, delivered many of the babies in Round Valley.

Scenic viewpoint. This viewpoint, marked by a large parking area, is well worth a long stop. A full-circle panorama includes peaks as far north as June Lake and as far east as Boundary Peak, Nevada's highest peak, on the Nevada-California state line.

Long Valley Caldera. Pastoral Long Valley to the east gives only a few hints of its violent birth 730,000 years ago when molten rock tore through the valley floor in earth-shattering eruptions. Glowing blobs of lava and black clouds of fine ash exploded skyward, some falling back to cover the surrounding area with a thick mantle of light-gray pumice and ash. Downwind drift of the ash reached at least as far as Kansas and Nebraska. The eruption's next phase can be pictured best as an awesome, towering fountain of incandescent lava whose length and width were perhaps measurable in miles. Collapsing out of the fountain's periphery, gigantic glowing avalanches of gas-charged froth roared outward. Probably within moments they shot over the rim of the erupting basin, the *caldera*, producing huge aprons of pumiceous froth. As the layers of froth lost their gases and compacted, the fragments welded together and eventually cooled, to form the gently sloping Volcanic Tableland to the southeast and similar features to the east and in Mono basin to the north. This gray and salmon-colored volcanic rock, Bishop tuff, originally blanketed 600 square miles between Bishop and Mono Lake. Locally the tuff, the mixture of ash and pumice fragments now welded into rock, is up to 600 feet thick. The elliptical basin twenty miles long that you are looking at is the ancient caldera. Laurel and McGee mountains behind you form its south wall, Bald and Glass mountains its north wall and San Joaquin Mountain its west wall; Long Valley lies in its eastern half.

Crowley Lake. Filling the lowest portion of Long Valley is Crowley Lake, the largest reservoir on the Los Angeles Aqueduct. In 1941 the Department of Water and Power (DWP) completed the Long Valley dam across the Owens River, inundating lush meadows that had long been summer pasture for Owens Valley cattle. Crowley gathers the water of the upper Owens River as well as most of the streams flowing into Mono Lake and sends it down the river's natural channel to the aqueduct intake south of Big Pine. The lake was named for Father J. J. Crowley, the Desert Padre, beloved by men of all faiths. Promoting Inyo-Mono as a summer vacation land, he was a major force in helping to re-establish Inyo people's faith in the future—a faith that had dwindled to hopelessness as they watched Owens River water flow away from the ranches into the aqueduct. A monument to Father Crowley stands on Crowley Lake Drive. He was killed in an auto accident in 1940.

White Mountain Peak. Far east of Crowley Lake the White Mountains shape the skyline. How much more appropriate if the mapmakers had retained the Paiute name for the entire range—*Inyo*, dwelling place of a great spirit. Atop the White Mountains grow the oldest of living things, the bristlecone pine. White Mountain Peak, 14,246 feet, is only 248 feet lower than Mount Whitney, the highest peak in the lower 48 states. A local myth that refuses to die is that White Mountain Peak really is higher than Mount Whitney. Supposedly the first surveyors fudged—either on orders or to please someone, the story is a bit vague—and three generations of engineers (highly trained geodesists) have all conspired to lower the height of this one peak. The truth is that the Coast and Geodetic Survey determined the elevation of White Mountain Peak by reciprocal vertical angle in 1950 as 14,246 feet, which su-

Sierra peaks west of Highway 395

persedes a 1913 determination of 14,242 feet. Since modern instruments make it possible to measure more precisely, the most recent measurement of Mount Whitney, 14,494.164 feet—by first-order leveling in 1940—also varies a few feet from previous ones.

To the west, below flat-topped McGee Mountain, a 700-foot-high pile of gravel and rock curves out of McGee canyon. This boulder-strewn ridge, a *glacial moraine*, consists of rock debris that was carried down-canyon by a glacier and that eventually melted out from the edges of the ice. Farther left, up on the Sierra slope, a high, stubby moraine blocks the mouth of Hilton Creek canyon. This "dump moraine" marks the snout of the Hilton Creek glacier; at the lip of its hanging valley the glacier dumped its load of debris onto the steep mountain slope. Well-preserved moraines, some of them over a mile long, stand hundreds of feet high at the mouth of almost every canyon between Sherwin Summit and Sonora Pass.

US 395. Continuing north, the highway passes close to the Sierra's sheer east face. Its colorful, striped rocks—red, rust, purple-brown, blue-gray, white—were formed hundreds of millions of years ago (during Paleozoic time) from sediments deposited in a shallow sea then extending across California and several other western states. The walls of deep-slashed McGee canyon expose the colors and folds of this ancient layered rock in elegant fashion. Along McGee Creek, among the cottonwood and willow, you may discover a tree that is rare in this region—the copper birch, named for its shining, copper-colored bark. Landmarks are named for the McGee brothers—Alney, John and Bart—pioneer cattlemen who had their headquarters near McGee Creek. Alney later worked as foreman for T. B. Rickey, a prominent land baron who in the 1890s owned most of Long Valley and grazed several thousand head of cattle.

Sideroad to McGee Creek canyon. This road winds steeply up the canyon's large moraine, then levels off and follows the creek to a campground and pack station. Trails lead to the lakes and streams of upper McGee canyon and over McGee Pass to the headwaters of Fish Creek. About a mile and a half up the road, if you begin watching and if there are afternoon shadows to help you, you may recognize an extraordinary fault scarp that cuts across the moraine. (See photo section "Fire!") Movements along the fault zone at the base of the mountains formed this striking 50-foot break. A line of green aspen trees accentuates the base of the scarp.

US 395. On the slope west of the highway is the site of the McGee Mountain ski area, where in the 1930s the Eastern Sierra Ski Club of Bishop built a rope tow, the first tow of any size in the region. Eleven miles north of Sherwin Summit, the highway swings left, abruptly revealing one of the most spectacular views along 395—hulking Mammoth Mountain and the jagged peaks of the Ritter Range.

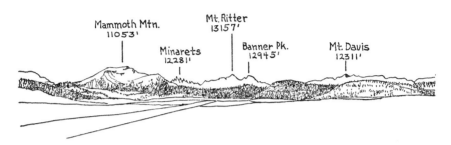

Mammoth Mountain and peaks of the Ritter Range

Sideroad to Whitmore Hot Springs, Owens River, Benton Crossing, Benton. This is the first of several roads leading east, which take you into a desert world that is totally unlike the mountain world to the west—a world of plants and animals and colors that is fascinating and beautiful in its own very different, special way. The road passes Whitmore Hot Springs, natural pools that were a favorite bathing place for as long as anyone can remember. The springs, now enclosed, supply the water for a public plunge. The water averages over 80°F; nearby springs vary in temperature from barely warm to very hot. In a region such as this, where there have been abundant and recent volcanic eruptions, hot springs are to be expected. Generally they represent the last activity of subsiding volcanic forces. Most of the water discharged probably originates as rain that percolates to depths where it subsequently becomes heated. Pressure, caused by the heat, forces the water through fissures to the surface.

About three miles from the highway junction, the road passes near the shallow Alkali Lakes, part of the network of resting ponds on the Pacific Flyway, the north-south route flown by migrating ducks and geese. It is another three miles to Benton Crossing on the Owens River. The original crossing of the old Benton-Mammoth City wagon road is several miles south of the present one and is now covered by Crowley Lake. The river, called "Wakopee" by the Paiutes, was named by Captain John Frémont for Richard (Dick) Owens, one of the leaders of Frémont's 1845-46 expedition. Owens River drains the Sierra Nevada's eastern watershed all the way from Deadman Summit near June Lake to Owens Lake near Olancha. Since rainfall on the

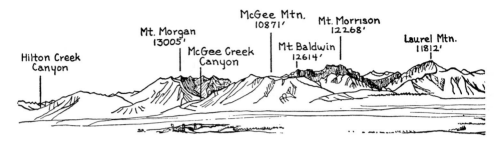

Sierra peaks, seen from Benton Crossing.

western watershed is much greater, the comparable portion of the western Sierra slope is drained by *four* major rivers.

From Benton Crossing, the view west to the Sierra skyline—all the way from the canyon of Hilton Creek north to Mount Dana—is superb, with Mount Morrison particularly impressive. Directly northeast of the crossing is a high ridge of volcanic rocks, Glass Mountain Ridge. Beyond Benton Crossing a graded road, part of it paved, follows the shore of Crowley Lake south. The road then winds through the sagebrush and pinyon pines of Watterson and Wildrose canyons, retracing the general route of the wagon road built in 1878 from the supply center of Benton to Mammoth City. About thirty miles after leaving US 395, the road joins State Highway 120 coming from Mono Lake. For an interesting loop trip, turn left and return by 120—passing Adobe Valley, Mono Mills, the Mono Craters and rejoining 395 a little south of Lee Vining. See below, "Highway 120 East."

Benton. If you turn right, it is but a short detour to Benton, known at one time as a wide-open, shooting, mining town. It also vied with the other early settlements of Aurora, Bridgeport, Bodie, and Monoville for the honor of being selected the county seat. For almost twenty years the town throve on the production of the famous Blind Springs Mining District, located on the hill of the same name just east of Benton. From 1864, when it was organized, until 1881, the district's mines produced close to $4 million worth of silver. In 1883 the narrow-gauge Carson and Colorado Railroad was completed from Mound House, Nevada (near Carson City), south to Keeler at Owens Lake. Benton Station, a few miles to the east, was the nearest train stop and shipping point. Several buildings dating from Benton's early days still stand—the slaughter house, Mrs. J. Lynch's Benton Hotel, and the thick-walled, metal-shuttered Wells Fargo office. Benton may have been named for the prominent Senator T. H. Benton of Missouri, who favored metallic currency and who was also Frémont's father-in-law.

US 395. Northward along 395 there are fine views westward of Mammoth Mountain and of the sheer cliffs of Convict canyon. The highest, light-col-

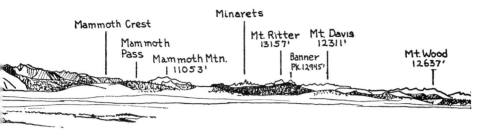

Mammoth Crest · Mammoth Pass · Mammoth Mtn. 11053' · Minarets · Mt. Ritter 13157' · Mt. Davis 12311' · Banner Pk.12945' · Mt. Wood 12637'

ored peak directly left is Mount Morrison. In the dark ridges in front of it, a very important geological find was made in 1953 when small fossils called graptolites were discovered. They proved to be nearly 500 million years old, making these dark rocks among the oldest known anywhere in the Sierra.

Sideroad to Convict Lake. After a gentle ascent of one mile, the road climbs steeply up the moraine. A true wild-west story is behind the naming of these landmarks. In September, 1871, twenty-nine desperadoes broke out of the state penitentiary in Carson City, Nevada, setting off one of the greatest manhunts in California-Nevada history. One group of six—murderers, train-robbers, horse thieves—headed south. On the way, they brutally murdered a young mail rider from Aurora, mistaking him for a former prison guard they intended to kill in revenge for shooting two former convicts. Posses from Aurora and Benton took up the chase, sighting the convicts near Monte Diablo Cañon, now known as Convict canyon. The posses stayed all night at the McGee place and next morning cornered the criminals in Convict canyon. A fierce fight ensued during which Robert Morrison, a Benton merchant and Wells Fargo agent, was killed and the convicts escaped. Three of them were captured several days later near Round Valley. En route to the Carson penitentiary, two were lynched north of Bishop.

The lake's setting is majestic. Mount Morrison, named for Robert Morrison, rises precipitously from the canyon's south side, and Laurel Mountain, with its red, brown, white, and rust-colored cliffs, from the opposite side. Numerous flowers, including many-colored penstemon, white thistle poppies and the brilliant yellow blazing star, grow along the shore of the lake. A trail follows Convict Creek upstream.

Sideroad to Hot Creek State Fish Hatchery and Hot Creek. Visitors are welcome and employees are happy to answer questions at the fish hatchery, an interesting sidetrip of only one mile. Trout of various sizes are segregated into separate pools, including fingerlings 3–5 inches long, catchables 7–9 inches long, and large breeding stock. Close to a million fish from this hatchery are planted annually in eastern Sierra waters; another 1.5 million are planted by air in back country lakes. In addition, the hatchery produces

25

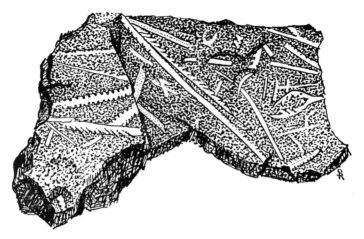

Fossil graptolites from Mount Morrison. Actual size.

around 20 million eggs from its excellent breeding stock and transports them to other hatcheries for rearing. The successful operation at Hot Creek is due largely to the warm springs that supply 56°–58° water year-round, an ideal temperature for fish rearing. The fish grow continually, about one inch per month, without a dormant period in winter.

A graded gravel road continues east, crossing sagebrush flats and meadows and then following the bank of Hot Creek. Small parking places on the left indicate trails leading to the creek. About three miles from 395, a large parking area and sign mark the Hot Creek Geologic Site. Hot Creek rises in the complex of warm springs issuing from beneath the basalt lava table bordering the fish hatchery. Mammoth Creek is tributary to Hot Creek. Along a two-mile segment of Hot Creek here, hot springs, warm springs and *fumaroles* (gas vents), abound. Hot springs come and go unpredictably along Hot Creek. In late August 1973 two new geysers erupted, tearing holes ten feet in diameter in the bank downstream from the bathing pool and gushing scalding water, mud, and pebbles three to six feet high for months. In mid-December small hot springs and geysers erupted from some other new vents upstream. Two years later they had dwindled to small hot pools. In May 1980 other new pools developed and old pools became more active. At low water you can see the springs bubbling up several inches above the creek's surface. Similar hot-water activity in the past, which chemically altered the rocks, is responsible for the creek's colorful banks.

Hot Creek is the source of most of the unusual chemical compounds used by the multi-billion dollar chemical industry at Searles Dry Lake. Since the springs came to life about 300 thousand years ago, they have been pouring their mineral-rich waters into the Owens River. During the Ice Age, when there was more rainfall than today, the Owens River filled Owens Lake, which overflowed into Indian Wells Valley; it, in turn, spilled over into Searles Lake basin, east of Ridgecrest. There the minerals concentrated, resulting in the salts and brines used by the companies to produce a variety of saline products such as borax, potash and soda ash.

Hot pools are extremely dangerous—to dogs and children, who don't know any better, and to adults who should know. Unstable edges and water temperatures close to boiling have led to gruesome, fatal accidents. Whenever you are in sight of hot pools, keep your children close and your dogs on leash *at all times*.

Sideroad to Laurel Creek and Sherwin Creek. The Sherwin Creek Road branches left (W) from the highway, winding through the meadows and sagebrush flats of Laurel Creek. The sagebrush-covered, thousand-foot-high mass at the mouth of the first canyon is a very large, well-preserved glacial moraine, loose material deposited along the margin of an advancing glacier thousands of years ago. Its arc-shaped form stands out clearly, since this moraine is free of trees and since Laurel Creek has washed away relatively little of it. From behind the moraine it is also possible to see the many small concentric ridges, nestled one inside the other, that mark the glacier's fluctuating retreats and advances.

Climbing the moraine is a rough jeep road, built by tungsten interests in 1955 to their claim high on the slope of Bloody Mountain, at an altitude of 11,200 feet. Many people wonder why this mining road was permitted, for when it was built Laurel Creek canyon was included within the High Sierra Wilderness Area; supposedly, motorized vehicles are prohibited in wilderness. The prominent road scar on the canyon's slope is visible miles away; the road itself has destroyed all wilderness quality the canyon once had. The explanation of this paradox lies in the law governing mining on National Forest land, explained in the Trails chapter. See "Agnew Meadows to Shadow Lake."

Some buildings of the Summers family ranch still stand in the aspen near Laurel Creek. Charlie Summers was a pioneer cattleman who settled here around 1900, grazing his cattle in these mountain meadows during summer and driving them to Owens Valley for the winter. On Sherwin Creek, Jim Sherwin operated a shingle mill during Mammoth's mining boom. Continuing on, the road crosses several lava ridges, passes the Sherwin Creek Campground and then joins the Old Mammoth Road (see below).

US 395. The highway continues across rolling brushland. Scattered in the brush are hummocks of the chunky black lava, *basalt*, a lava flow 200–300 thousand years old that erupted from an obscure source northwest of Mammoth Lakes village. It is a common rock type throughout the region; it erupted from different sources at many different times. The meadows

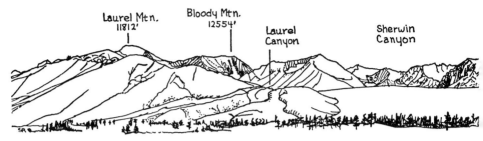

Approach to the Mammoth Lakes basin.

bordering Mammoth Creek in June usually are covered with western blue flag, or mountain iris. Just beyond the creek crossing, on the hill to the right, is a whitish clay deposit. Prospect pits have been dug in this *kaolinite*, a mineral used as a paint filler and in making fine china.

Mammoth Lakes Roads

State Highway 203 to Mammoth Lakes. This highway leads west over low hills of lava to the town of Mammoth Lakes (7800 feet) and its all-year resorts. The name Mammoth came from Mammoth City, a short-lived mining camp during 1878–79, which in turn was named for the Mammoth Mine. It has been known as Mammoth ever since, but when the post office was established "Lakes" was added to the name, to avoid confusion with another Mammoth in northern California.

The first large building on the right is the Mammoth Visitor Center and Ranger Station. The Forest Service has a varied year-round program that includes evening programs and self-guiding nature trails. Stop in for information on these events, on the weather, on campgrounds, on the summer shuttle bus, and on road and trail conditions; also for maps, wilderness permits and trail guides. Beyond the visitor center, on the left (S), you will find the Old Mammoth Road, which leads to the site of Mammoth City.

Hwy 203, continued, to the Ski Area, Minaret Summit, Devils Postpile, Reds Meadow. The trip to Reds Meadow is truly spectacular. The views are immense. And since the slope below Minaret Summit is alive with springs and small streams, wildflowers and birds are everywhere. Inquire at the Ranger Station about self-guiding nature trails at Minaret Vista, Sotcher Lake and among the wildflowers at Agnew Meadow. During the busiest summer months, travel down the narrow road from Minaret Summit to Reds Meadow is limited to overnight campers. A shuttle bus serves all other visitors; inquire at the ranger station. The shuttle bus will let you off at any of the locations listed below.

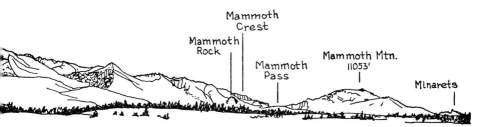

A mile and a half beyond the Visitor Center, 203 turns right (N). The road winds through a magnificent Jeffrey pine forest, passing hills which are some of the volcanic domes described in the geology section. A side road leads to the locally famous rift known as the Earthquake Fault. Near the parking area exhibits explain the origin of the crack, and a self-guiding nature trail takes one down into the bottom of the crack. This long crack, although the best-known, is only one of many fractures in the volcanic rock covering the area north of Mammoth Mountain. It is really not a "fault" at all, for a fault—as the term is used by geologists—is generally defined as a crack along which the rock on one side *moved*, in a different direction from the rock on the other side. The Earthquake Fault shows no such movement; it simply opened. Examine the crack carefully. Wouldn't the sides fit together perfectly if the crack were closed again? The crack, however, is aligned with faults to the north along which movement did occur, suggesting that the crack opened in response to the same stress that caused movement there. Since large red fir grow from its sides, this crack must be at least hundreds of years old, and possibly thousands. In the days before refrigerators were common, Mammoth residents used to come to the Earthquake Fault in summer for the snow that lingered in its shaded depths. They used it for making ice cream and cooling their food.

The paved road continues through the lodgepole pine-red fir forest to Mammoth Mountain's north slope, one of the finest skiing areas in California. Early snows drift over the mountain into the shade on its north side, often providing enough snow to ski on in early November. The high elevation and the lack of exposure to winter sun keep ice formation at a minimum, the snow remaining packed and each new storm adding a few inches or a few feet of powder to the surface. Skiing often continues to Memorial Day weekend, some years even into July. During summer one of the lifts runs every day to the top of Mammoth Mountain, providing a novel sightseeing trip and spectacular panoramic views in all directions.

Minaret Summit. Beyond the ski lift, the road winds among mountain hemlock and then tops Minaret Summit, a low point on the Sierra Nevada crest. Here the crest divides the waters flowing east into the Owens River from those flowing west into the San Joaquin River and eventually into San Francisco Bay. At the summit, turn right to the observation point and self-guiding nature trail. Here at Minaret Vista is one of the grandest alpine views anywhere—magnificent Sierra peaks stretching for more than thirty-five miles, from Mount Lyell in Yosemite Park south to Kaiser Crest above Huntington Lake. In the deep canyon below winds the Middle Fork of the San Joaquin River, its headwaters at Thousand Island Lake below Banner Peak.

Most of the high country to the west is National Forest wilderness, accessible to the rider, hiker and fisherman by a network of good trails, its wildness

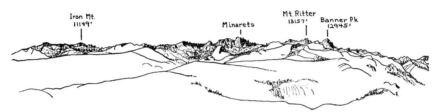

The Ritter Range

and primitive beauty protected against roads and commercial development. This is the home of the famous John Muir Trail, named for the man who first wrote about the Sierra and lobbied to keep it wild. It is a true wilderness trail, the only one in America where one can hike more than 200 miles in the same direction without crossing a road or passing a settlement of any kind. It travels the grandest portion of the High Sierra, shunning the easy passes and the canyon bottoms in favor of the sweeping views and rugged spaciousness of the alpine country. Here the Muir Trail comes over Donohue Pass (11,056 feet), which you can see to the north, contours high among the passes and high lakes of the Ritter Range, drops down briefly to cross the San Joaquin River at Reds Meadow and then immediately swings back up to the high country, near Purple and Virginia lakes.

Above the river, notice the canyon's smooth, almost bare walls. Their rounded form resulted from the pressure and scouring of the huge glaciers that once flowed down these canyons. Small glaciers of a more recent "Little Ice Age" remain on the cool northern slopes of most of the Ritter Range peaks. The entire Ritter Range is an exceptionally rugged divide, partly because glaciers on both the east and west sides carved great steep-sided, theater-shaped basins, *cirques*, into it, leaving a narrow sawlike crest. The range is jagged because its peaks and pinnacles were never sculptured into round, smooth ridges by overriding glaciers. Instead, these peaks stood well above the surface of the ice, where the rock-shattering effects of freezing and thawing were most intense. Rainwater seeps into the cracks and expands as it freezes, wedging the cracks a little farther open with each new freeze, until finally the loosened rock tumbles onto the glacier below. Thus these rugged frost-riven spires stand in marked contrast to the rounded ridges below them.

Agnew Meadows. The first road over Minaret Summit was built in the late 1920s by the Minaret Mines Company. The mine operated through two winters, completely dependent on dog teams for supplies and mail from Mammoth. Descending through a forest of towering red fir trees, the road skirts the edge of Agnew Meadow, named for Theodore (Tom) Agnew, a miner who in 1877 settled here in the North Fork District, a mining district that proved to be more hope than reality. Agnew worked part time as a guide for the U.S. Army troops administering Yosemite Park (there was no National Park Service until 1916), which at one time included much of the Ritter Range and the Devils Postpile. Remains of what may have been Agnew's cabin were found near one of the meadows. To reach Agnew Meadows campgrounds and pack station, take the road that forks to the right; from its end, trails lead to the high country of Shadow, Garnet and Thousand Island lakes.

The main road continues on down the canyon, passing Starkweather Lake, named for a prospector called by some "the human gopher," who had claims on the slopes above during the 1920s. The road then crosses a grassy expanse known as Pumice Flat. A layer of light-weight pumice blankets much of this region—try floating a piece of this frothy volcanic rock on water. Belding ground squirrels, also known as "picket-pins" for their characteristic stance, are common on the flat; early morning is a good time to see them. Here the road nears the meandering San Joaquin River, named about 1805 for Saint Joaquim by Gabriel Moraga, a Spaniard exploring what we now call the San Joaquin Valley, far to the west. A spur road branches to the right half a mile to Minaret Creek campground, opposite Minaret Falls, which slither and cascade down over massive glacier-polished granite. They are exceptionally beautiful in early summer.

Devils Postpile National Monument. The next spur road on the right leads to the Postpile and ends at the Postpile Ranger Station and campground. To reach the main feature of the monument, take the wide trail leading across the meadow, a ten-minute walk.

Devils Postpile is an unusual formation of tall columns of basalt, other well-known examples of columnar basalt being the Palisades of the Hudson and the Giant's Causeway in Ireland. The molten basalt flowed southward from a vent near Upper Soda Springs Campground, pouring into the Middle Fork valley and filling it from one side to the other to a minimum depth of 400 feet, from Pumice Flat south to the Postpile. As the lava cooled and solidified it shrank, developing cracks that radiated out from centers spaced 1 to 2.5 feet apart. The cracks grew until they joined one another, and they also grew downward—the result being the four-, five-, six- and seven-sided columns of the Postpile. The enormous glacier that later moved down the Middle Fork valley quarried away most of the columns, leaving small remnants on both sides of the valley. The Devils Postpile is the largest of these remnants; you can find others at several places along the river. The mosaic-like top of the Postpile, easily reached by a short trail, still shows some of the scratches and the high polish made by the slow-moving, tremendously heavy ice mass, though during the thousands of years since the glaciers melted, much of the polished surface has weathered away. Frost action, the prying effect of freezing water that collects in the cracks, continues today—as it has for many years—to destroy the Postpile columns slowly, pushing them outward until they fall and shatter into the huge blocks of broken "posts" lying in a jumble at the base. The Postpile is the starting point for numerous trails into the Ritter Range; trails also follow the river upstream and downstream.

Reds Meadow. Back on the road to Reds Meadow, after one-half mile there is a short spur on the left leading to Sotcher Lake. This small lake is famous for the mass of yellow pond lilies, usually in full bloom in late July, that cover the surface of the water near its outlet. Beyond the lake the road passes the first of the meadows known as Reds Meadow, named after Red Sotcher (or Satcher)—a large red-bearded man who came here in 1879 herding sheep. It is said that Sotcher began raising vegetables when he found that they grew well in the meadows and that there was a great demand for fresh produce in the bustling camps near the Mammoth mines. In the 1920s Emma McLeod, wife of Ranger Malcolm McLeod, found turnip plants in the meadows, possibly originally planted by Sotcher. True or not, the story also goes that Sotcher was a cattle and horse thief, stealing animals on one side of the Sierra and selling them on the other.

The mining boom at Mammoth also led to the construction of a trans-Sierra toll trail, which passed through Reds Meadow. It was known as the Mammoth Trail or the French Trail, after J. S. French who built it. It led from Fresno Flats (Oakhurst) on the Sierra's west slope over Mammoth Pass to Mammoth City, fifty-four miles in all. The trip took two days or more. Stock being driven to the Mammoth markets and pack trains carrying all kinds of supplies made this a busy trail during Mammoth City's boom days.

A left turn leads to Reds Meadow Campground and a public bath house that provides water from a natural hot spring. Reds Meadow is fed by numerous springs, some of them warm, flowing from the hill behind and also from the meadow itself. East of the bath house is an unusual log cabin; its logs are set vertical rather than horizontal. It was constructed by McLeod, District Ranger from 1921 to 1929, from lodgepole pine cut nearby. It is for him that McLeod Lake on Mammoth Pass is named. Above the campground is a large meadow (not grazed) famous for its profusion of wildflowers from early July through August; most conspicuous are the tall blue larkspur or delphinium, Queen Anne's lace, evening primrose, old-man's-beard and tiger lilies. Mountain meadows are fragile; they can be destroyed quickly by trampling. Enjoy the flowers from the edge of the meadow and leave them for others to enjoy the rest of the summer.

Rainbow Falls. The road ends about a half mile farther at the pack station, store and resort. Before you reach the pack station, a road to the right leads to the parking area at the beginning of the Rainbow Falls trail, a gentle hike of little more than a mile. The famous mountaineer Walter Starr Jr. considered Rainbow Falls to be "the most beautiful in the Sierra outside of Yosemite." Here the water of the San Joaquin's Middle Fork pours over a resistant ledge of lava. Photographers who wish to catch the rainbow at Rainbow Falls should plan to be there by noon, when the rainbow is particularly colorful across the mist that sometimes rises two-thirds the height of the falls. Use caution nearing the edge of the cliff, for loose pumice makes footing precarious. A walkway descends to the base of the falls.

Lake Mary Road to the lakes basin. A mile and a half west of the Ranger Station, where Highway 203 turns north toward the ski area, the Lake Mary Road heads west to the lakes basin south of Mammoth Mountain. Near the post office, the forest is mostly Jeffrey pine—large trees with light reddish brown trunks and long needles—but as the road gains altitude, you will notice that white fir intermix with the Jeffrey. Still higher, above Twin Lakes, the forest is predominantly lodgepole pine and red fir. Such changes indicate the colder climate and the higher rainfall of the higher elevations. After you emerge from the short tunnel that goes under the ski run, watch for a wide shoulder left of the road where you can park and orient yourself to the Mammoth country. To the west are the rough lava cliffs of Mammoth Mountain's east slope; beyond, Mammoth Crest dominates the skyline with its year-round snow fields. To the south, behind brush-covered Panorama Dome, is Red (or Gold) Mountain—focus of an exciting, though brief, mining boom, 1878-80. Below, Mammoth Falls plunges over a ledge of lava. Eastward, in the distant valley, lies Crowley Lake; beyond it, on the horizon, the White Mountains stretch farther than you can see. The road ahead is cut along a glacial moraine, a mass of debris ranging in size from particles of fine clay to large angular boulders. It continues climbing until it levels off to cross the outlet of Twin Lakes. At their far end, Twin Falls tumbles down three hundred feet into the upper lake. These are the first of the Mammoth Lakes—a group of thirteen lakes, none of which is named "Mammoth Lake." The Forest Chapel, where outdoor Sunday services are held in summer, is at the base of the lava cliffs. Beyond the bridge a road forks right, leading to a store, lodge and campgrounds.

From time to time Twin Lakes is plagued with aquatic weeds, which clog the lakes' surface until boating and fishing are barely possible. These plants are not native to Twin. In the early 1930s some Bishop sportsmen, hoping to enhance trout food conditions, introduced scuds (freshwater shrimp) and snails. They collected the plants containing these organisms at Hot Creek and dumped them—weeds, scuds and all—into Twin Lakes. The weeds have thrived and persisted, despite all attempts to get rid of them.

As it climbs on, Lake Mary Road passes the historic Willard Studio, now an art gallery. This was the summer studio of Stephen Willard from 1924 until his death in 1966; we are privileged to publish his photographs.

Old Mammoth Road turnoff. See below.

Mammoth Mountain. At the Old Mammoth Road turnoff, there is a good view of the bald, pumice-covered summit of Mammoth Mountain and of its lava cliffs. This imposing edifice anchors the southern end of a north-south chain of young volcanoes that extends to Mono Craters. Born about 200,000 years ago, it spewed out lava and fragments during ten or more major eruptions, the last one 50,000 years ago. Although at a distance its profile is that of a typical, symmetrical volcanic dome, at closer range its surface is markedly irregular. This is due partly to sculpturing by water and ice and partly to the eruption of lava flows that were too small and viscous to spread out, cooling instead as stubby, steep-sided blobs on the volcano's flanks.

Lake Mary. Among the lodgepole pine to the right of the road as it continues uphill, were the scattered cabins of Pine City, a mining camp contemporary with Mammoth City. A sideroad turns left to the inlet of Lake Mary, where there is a store, resort and a narrow road leading to Cold Water Campground and the site of the historic Mammoth Consolidated Gold Mine (see below). Near this junction with Lake Mary Road an arrastra once stood, a crude mill for crushing ore. In contrast to stamp mills, which were expensive, arrastras could be built by one man with practically no capital and were often powered by burros that walked around and around, pulling heavy stones over pieces of ore to pulverize them. A waterwheel once ran this arrastra; its ditch can still be traced through the trees.

The Lake Mary Road then tops a rise near Lake Mary, the largest of the Mammoth Lakes, nearly a mile long. Perhaps it was named after Mary Calvert of Pine City and Lake George after her husband. However, a Calvert descendant stated emphatically that Lake Mary was not named for her grandmother, but that both Lake Mary and Mamie were named for Bodie dance-hall girls. She says that George carried mail from Bodie to Pine City on skis but she does not believe that her grandparents lived in the Mammoth camps. Other stories from the mining days tell of a raft that took passengers to a dancing platform built on the far side of Lake Mary; others say dancing was on a barge, pushed up and down the lake by long poles. The 13 August 1879 *Mammoth City Herald* advertised Jerry McCarthy's new dancing pavilion on the lake, where on Sundays there would be "music, dancing, picnicking under the trees, flirting, real love making and we don't know what all."

The thumb of gray rock towering above Lake Mary is Crystal Crag, a *cleaver*

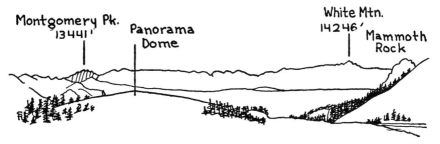

Montgomery Pk.
13441'

Panorama
Dome

White Mtn.
14246'

Mammoth
Rock

The White Mountains

or *island* of resistant granitic rock around which flowed the two arms of a glacier. It is a remnant of a once high ridge separating the drainages of Crystal and T J lakes. Glacial quarrying steepened the sides of the ridge, finally cutting through and destroying it, except for Crystal Crag itself, which apparently was more resistant. Close to its base is a small pond jokingly called "Mammoth Lake." Since visitors long have asked, "Where is Mammoth Lake?" this tiny pond was christened in answer to their question.

Lake George. A road branching left crosses the outlet of Lake Mary, a favorite place for enjoying sunsets and the view of Duck Pass, then winds up the hill to Lake George, where there are more campgrounds and the beginning of the Mammoth Crest trail. Lake George (9008 feet) is the highest of the Mammoth group accessible by car. On the far side of the lake, where several small streams enter, there are small meadows lush with many kinds of wildflowers. Above them rises Crystal Crag; from Crystal Lake at its base tumbles Crystal Falls. A striking variation in vegetation is noticeable around Lake George. On the warmer, drier, south-facing brush slope below the resort grow several stocky Jeffrey pine, while on the cool shaded slope across the lake, mountain hemlock grow down to the water's edge.

Mamie and Horseshoe lakes. The highway continues along the Rim, a bench of volcanic rock in which glaciers carved the basins of Mary, Mamie, and Horseshoe lakes. Lake Mamie (8898 feet), sometimes incorrectly spelled "Mayme," is believed to be named for Mamie Clarke, a beloved superintendent of schools in Bishop. Beyond, to the right, is a large parking area with sweeping views eastward, particularly enjoyable in the evening. The road ends at Horseshoe Lake, ten miles from US 395. Horseshoe is the only lake in the Mammoth group with wide sandy shores; it is ideally suited to swimming. (Swimming is prohibited in all the other lakes, for they supply drinking water). Much of the "sand" is really pumice, so abundant in this region. Horseshoe's water level varies considerably with the season and the year. Although it has no outlet, undoubtedly the lake loses its water through underground drainage into the porous volcanic rock in which it lies. From the end of the road, trails lead over Mammoth Pass, following the route of the historic toll trail that served the Mammoth mines.

Old Mammoth Road to the site of Mammoth City, Mill City and Old Mammoth. About half a mile above the Twin Lakes bridge, the Old Mammoth Road branches left. This turnoff marks the upper end of Mammoth City. In this gulch during 1878–79 sprouted a mining camp of perhaps a thousand people, who had come from everywhere to seek wealth and fame at the Mammoth mines, supposedly "the largest bonanza outside of Virginia City." According to the *Mammoth City Herald* of 3 January 1880, Mammoth City had five general merchandise stores, three hotels, twelve saloons, two breweries, three livery stables, five restaurants and boarding houses, two billiard halls and two newspapers. (Lest the number of establishments give the impression of a permanent city, let it be remembered that a ten-foot-square tent or shack plus a barrel of whiskey and a few glasses were all that was needed to make a "saloon.") As in most boom camps, supplies were scarce and brought big prices. Jim Sherwin carried in eighty pounds of potatoes on his back and sold them for a dollar a pound.

The Mammoth Mining Company. The Mammoth Mining Company, which incorporated in June of 1878 and began construction the very next month, was the center of all this excitement. Into the steep slope of Mineral Hill (now known as Red or Gold Mountain), south of the road, the company drove four tunnels. Their dumps are still clearly visible. The portal of the lowest tunnel is easily reached by crossing the creek. Though its opening has collapsed, there is much to explore—the large dump, big timbers, bits of machinery, rusted tram cars. The next highest tunnel reportedly produced the richest ore. To process the ore a 20-stamp mill was erected half a mile down the slope and, to provide water-power, a dam was constructed on Twin Lakes and a flume built from Twin Lakes' outlet. An elevated tramway carried the ore cars to the mill. According to Chalfant, one day when the tracks were icy the train went out of control and the brakeman was badly injured. After that, a mule was used to control the cars. One stormy day, a wind roaring down the canyon blew the poor beast off the track. Thereafter whenever a fierce wind threatened, the mule just lay down on the tracks until the blast subsided.

Mammoth City. Only two large log buildings are recognizable; both have collapsed under years of winter snow. Among old-timers there is a difference of opinion on whether these two buildings date from the boom days of 1878, or whether they were built about twenty years later when Dr. Guy Doyle of Bishop reopened the mines long enough to lose some money on them. Square nails are often a clue in dating old buildings, for round nails were not widely used until after 1890. Since all of these structures contain square nails or square nail-holes, it is likely that they are pre-1890 and the only remains of Mammoth City. They were no doubt used by later miners, trappers and sheepherders, who added the round nails that are there also. North of the road, you can still find stone foundations of the miners' cabins, dug into the hillside and now overgrown with a hundred years of brush. Many structures burned in the town's fire in November 1880; others were salvaged for their wood.

Two years after incorporation, the company mill suddenly shut down, never to run again. There are tantalizing questions about the mining company that may never be resolved. How much did it produce? Was it nothing but a stock scheme from the very beginning? Was a significant amount of ore stolen, either by the miners or by the foreman and his cronies? Or was the mine just never profitable, swallowing up more dollars than it ever produced? While it was touted as a gold mine, what little information we have on the quality of the ore seems to show that it contained as much silver as gold. It seems quite possible that the mine was unprofitable because it produced not enough gold but too much high-cost silver, which brought far less per ounce than gold. Whatever the case, the company was unable to pay on its loans or its bills, and stockholders were not willing to pour more money into the project. Company stock, worth up to $20 a share in the spring of 1879, was worthless the next year. In 1881 the property was sold at a sheriff's sale. The Mammoth Company was said to have spent almost $300,000; one estimate of Mammoth's output, as reported in the Eighth Annual Report of the State Mineralogist, 1888, is $200,000. Deep snow—it is said that twenty-eight feet fell during December—hastened the departure of people even before the mill closed. The *Mammoth City Times* reported the exodus whimsically, saying, "Twenty pairs of snowshoes, each with a man on top, left this morning."

The Doyle Mill. Fifteen years later Judge Robert Doyle of Chicago invested some money in the Mammoth mines, sight unseen. His son, a young doctor, came west in 1895 and stayed, fascinated with mining. Young Dr. Guy Doyle invested more money and built a 10-stamp mill close to the mouth of the lower tunnel, a cyanide plant and a tramway. Across the road a sturdy frame building served as the assay office. But the mines did not pay for him either, and the property changed hands. An avalanche later demolished the Doyle mill. Some of its remains—large timbers and a stone foundation—still rest under the willows along the creek. Others have continued to explore and work the Mammoth and other claims on Red Mountain intermittently and on a small scale. There is no doubt that there is gold, but the ore discovered so far is a mixture of minerals that is difficult and expensive to mill. Who knows—perhaps "the largest bonanza outside of Virginia City" is there still, waiting to be discovered.

Down the Old Mammoth Road, from the edge of the first sharp curve, if you look carefully you can spot what looks like a wide ditch blasted through the rock. This is a segment of the roofed tramway, built so the ore trains could supply the mill despite deep snow. Above juts a prominent white crag, Mammoth Rock, known in the mining days as Monumental Rock. It is not a volcano as is popularly believed, but an erosional form, composed of marble (metamorphosed limestone) and fine-grained sandstone. A blue-gray limestone near the base contains small white disks ¼ to ¼ inch in diameter. These are fossil *crinoids*, ancient relatives of the sea urchin (see sketch in Trails chapter, "Convict Creek"). Hot springs, once active here, have decomposed the surrounding rocks into the white clay that is abundant at the base of Mammoth Rock. A faint sulfur smell can still be detected, and a careful search will reveal a little native sulfur that was deposited near the old vents. Farther down the road, in the trees to the right, is the grave of Mary Townsend, who died in November 1881, thirty-four years old. Since the ground was covered with deep snow when she died, she could not be buried until the next spring. The original picket fence around the grave has been replaced by a more sturdy one. The story goes that this young woman dreamed of someday having a house with a picket fence. Her grieving husband then gave her the only picket fence he could—around her grave.

Mill City. To see the big flywheel, which is about all that is left of the Mammoth Company's old mill, park near the grave marker and look for a trail across the road. It is a short, easy walk to the mill site. Mill City was headquarters of the mining company and not much more. Stone foundations mark the outline of the mill buildings. A Knight wheel, turned by water from the Twin Lakes' flume, drove the twenty stamps that crushed the ore. The next year, twenty more stamps were added and a steam engine, but it is believed that the mill closed before the engine was ever used. Some of the machinery was sold and taken to Bodie; over the years the rest was taken for scrap. The mill was burned purposely in 1929 because it was considered a fire hazard.

Down the road you will pass the Valentine Eastern Sierra Reserve. In 1972 Carol Valentine and the Valentine Foundation donated these 136 acres to the University of California; U.C. Santa Barbara administers the reserve. Edward Robinson Valentine (Robinsons Department Stores) and associates had owned the property since 1915, using it as a rustic location for hunting and fishing and entertaining their business friends. Though surrounded by developments, the reserve itself is wild and undisturbed, an ideal site for teaching and research. The reserve is open to the public once a year, usually in late July.

Historic waterwheel. The road continues down to the low hills and meadows known in the early days as Mineral Park, site of a sawmill that supplied lumber to the mines and to the surrounding area. After the road passes a fire station and curves left, watch on your left for a small reddish building with a six-foot water wheel. This is the historic water wheel that powered the stamp mill you just visited. Locally, people refer to it as a Pelton wheel. However, a wheel of this particular design is a Knight wheel. Water from the flume was forced through a nozzle, hitting the cups of the wheel under high pressure. Belts and axles transferred the power to the big flywheel and, in turn, to the mill's machinery. This small wheel was at the center of each chapter of Mammoth's early history—first running the Mammoth mill, later the Doyle mill, and finally, after being sledded down to this location, making electricity for Mammoth's first resort, the Wildasinn Hotel in the early 1900s.

Old Mammoth. C. F. Wildasinn of Round Valley picked up parcels of land for taxes (and perhaps homesteaded) until he owned much land in Old Mammoth. He grazed cattle and ran a sawmill and small hotel during the summer. Near the Knight wheel stood the Summers' hotel, built in 1918, a garage, a dairy, a bakery and a store—complete with barber chair, butcher shop, post office, and pot-belly stove—that served as the community center. Only an occasional trapper or a lone caretaker stayed through the winter, until in 1928 freight and passenger service by dog sled was inaugurated. Until they were disbanded during World War II, the dog teams—mostly Greenland malamutes weighing up to one hundred and forty pounds—supplied color as well as winter communication and transportation for this snow-bound country. A few hardy souls began living at Mammoth year-round, and a few skiers (including Europeans, since at that time few Americans had ever seen a ski), came to enjoy the snow. Besides carrying passengers at twenty dollars a head and freight at ten cents a pound from Sherwin Hill to Mammoth, the dog teams carried mail, snow surveyors, workmen to repair power breaks, hauled ice, and made a number of emergency runs such as rescuing people from stalled cars and racing the sick to a doctor. In 1937, when Highway 203 was completed, business moved to better locations on the new road, and this meadow area has since been known as Old Mammoth. The Old Mammoth Road continues on to rejoin Highway 203.

The Mammoth Museum. About 3 miles from the site of Mammoth City, the Sherwin Creek Road branches off right (S) from the Old Mammoth Road. To find the museum, turn left off the Sherwin Creek Road onto a dirt road almost immediately. The museum is housed in a log cabin built about 1930 by Emmett Hayden, well known for his maps of the area. Mining and skiing exhibits and photographs of yesterdays will make your todays at Mammoth far more interesting.

Sideroad to the Mammoth Consolidated Gold Mine historic site. From Lake Mary Road, take the sideroad to the store at the inlet of Lake Mary. There a one-way road heads south through Cold Water Campground. At the far end (E) of a large parking area, you will find a bridge and the trail to the Mammoth Consolidated Mine, dedicated as a historic site in 1989. A. G. Mahan and his son, Arch, formed a company and constructed this mining camp in 1927. A self-guiding trail takes you through the camp, among the buildings and remains of the mill and compressor plant, providing a good picture of how miners lived in the 1920s and how the mill processed the ore. The bunkhouses accommodated up to fourteen workers. Though only fifty years separated the Mammoth Consolidated from the older Mammoth Mining Company, their operations were dramatically different. Here gasoline and diesel motors did much of the work instead of mules and a water wheel. Bank failures and the depression contributed to the mine's closing in 1933. Others leased it and worked it off and on, until in the 1980s the Mahan family decided to preserve the site by donating the buildings and equipment to the town of Mammoth Lakes.

US 395 Mammoth Lakes to Conway Summit.

Sideroad to Casa Diablo. From the Mammoth Lakes junction, a short spur leads north to Casa Diablo, a hot spring long enjoyed by whites and Paiutes alike. The *Mammoth City Times* in 1879 described its wonders in a lyrical article. Steaming pools, a small lake fringed with tules, and a stream created an unusual oasis for birds and animals and for a small resort. In cold weather you can still see steam rising from vents, but drilling for geothermal steam in the 1960s dried up the springs. Long Valley, a potential source of geothermal energy, has been a target for exploratory drilling that continues today. Geothermal plants at Casa Diablo are now producing 35 megawatts of power. The large structures you see are air-cooled condensers. A network of pipes continually brings hot water to the plants; other pipes then carry away the water and re-inject it into the ground. Colorful deposits of travertine and kaolinite on the cliffs above indicate intense hot water activity in times past. Both of these materials form around volcanic vents and hot springs, as acid-charged hot water slowly disintegrates the surrounding rock.

An old log cabin still standing here in the 1960s was probably the original way station on the Bodie-Mammoth City stage line. One old-timer said that inside there was little more than a couple of barrels of whiskey and a single glass that was passed from hand to hand.

US 395. The Jeffrey pine forest. Beyond Casa Diablo the highway enters the largest Jeffrey forest in the world, covering about two hundred square miles. Much of it is managed for logging. To prevent damage to the soil and to other plants and to reduce conflicts with summer campers, logging occurs only in winter, after snow covers the ground.

The high crest of the Sierra causes Pacific storms to drop most of their moisture on the western Sierra slope. Here, however, storm clouds blown inland from the Pacific Ocean back up against the crest and then roar through the funnel over the low saddles at Minaret Summit and Mammoth Pass, dumping their load of moisture east of the crest. This additional water is one of the factors that enable this forest of Jeffrey pine to grow on what otherwise would be dry sagebrush-covered hills.

Swarms of caterpillars, millions—it seemed—of large, fluttering moths and denuded Jeffrey made this a strange looking forest during the summer of 1979. Such an outbreak occurs only every 20 or 30 years, but was well known to the Paiutes who prized the *piüga*, the caterpillars, as a food and trade-good. The Pandora moth lays its eggs in the trees' bark or on the needles. When the eggs hatch in late summer the young caterpillars move to the tops of the trees, feed on the new foliage and hibernate in clusters at the base of the needles. The following spring they feed voraciously on the needles, defoliating the ends of the branches. When they are full grown, they climb down the trees, burrow in the soil and are transformed into pupae. In a year the Pandora moth—it has a four-inch wing span—emerges and begins the cycle again. As the trees put forth new needles, bare branches with tufts of new growth at the ends were conspicuous. By the summer of 1981 the outbreak was over and within a few years the trees recovered.

The Mammoth Scenic Loop. This road wanders through a Jeffrey pine forest to connect with Highway 203 a little west of Mammoth Lakes.

Sideroad to the Inyo Craters and their lakes. Drive the Scenic Loop about three miles from 395 and watch for a graded road branching right. It leads to the Inyo Craters parking area. An easy fifteen-minute walk takes you to the craters and to an unusual self-guiding nature trail. These two explosion craters, about 600 years old, represent a relatively mild form of volcanism, which might be thought of as one of the dying volcanic forces' "last gasps." They are a clear indication, however, that a potent source of heat —probably magma—lay at a shallow depth. Ground water coming in contact with hot rock flashed to steam, blowing out all that was above and leaving these funnel-shaped craters. The craters exploded around 1400 A.D., dated by radiocarbon age determinations on fragments of buried wood and by tree-ring counts. No new volcanic material was ejected. Craters are not uncommon in this area, but craters with lakes are rare. (The lakes have no fish.)

Sideroad to Lookout Mountain. Just opposite the Scenic Loop junction, a dirt road branches right from US 395 to an outstanding viewpoint called Lookout Mountain. The road may not be signed and you may find yourself on old logging roads instead. But keep trying; take the left fork at most road forks. You will be rewarded with a superb panoramic view of the Sierra crest to the west and south, the White Mountains on the skyline to the east, and Long Valley and Crowley Lake to the southeast. There are also excellent views of the chain of volcanic domes that stretches from Mammoth Mountain north to the blocky, crown-shaped Mono Craters. The rough-surfaced, treeless obsidian domes in the foreground to the west, are among the youngest in the chain.

Sideroad to Big Springs. Owens River Road on the right leads to Big Springs. Here springs gush into Deadman Creek, a tributary of the Owens

River, increasing the flow of water to such an extent that Big Springs is commonly considered the headwaters of the Owens. You can continue on the road past two ranches that were homesteaded years ago and are now fishing resorts, and connect with the Hot Creek or Benton Crossing roads.

Sideroad to Deadman Creek. Deadman Creek Road branches left to campgrounds on the creek. Beyond the campgrounds, the road is very rough and narrow. It follows the creek for about 3 miles to a dead end. The creek received its name from one of the tales about the Lost Cement Mine. It seems that a newcomer to Monoville in 1861 gave his name as Farnsworth, said he had a rich claim and offered to share it. He disappeared for a time but eventually showed up again with a man named Hume. The two put together a small outfit and headed out. Shortly after, Farnsworth returned to Monoville—hatless, knife cuts in his clothing, and a bullet hole in the top of his boot. He told a harrowing story of being attacked by Indians and of Hume's being killed. Because his story did not seem to hold together, he was held while a searching party with Indian guides went out to find Hume. They tracked him to Farnsworth's camp, on the fork of the Owens River we now call Deadman Creek, and eventually found his head in the water covered with rocks and, nearby, his body covered in the same manner. Farnsworth escaped and was never heard from again. Treasure hunters of today can refer to the book *The Lost Cement Mine* for details. Many believe the lost mine to be near Deadman Creek; others believe it to be a dozen different places.

US 395. Before it swings up over Deadman Summit, the highway passes Crestview, the site of another grim story from the mining days. A small fence around a large Jeffrey pine commemorates a courageous mail carrier who in the fierce winter of 1879 set out from Mammoth to bring the mail from King's Ranch. On his return trip, just half a mile from Deadman Station, he and his mule were overwhelmed by snowdrifts. A rescue party found him after several days, his hands and feet frozen. He died in Mammoth City two months later. To find the tree, at Crestview Maintenance Station look for the power line across the highway; follow the power line road half a mile north.

Sideroad to Bald Mountain Lookout. Just north of Deadman Summit Logging Camp Road leads east to the top of Bald Mountain, a marvelous viewpoint from which to see almost all the country described in this guidebook. It is a particularly beautiful drive in the early evening. On the way, there is a worthwhile side trip to the Indiana Summit Natural Area, a virgin Jeffrey pine woodland where no grazing or logging has been permitted. The contrast with the rest of the forest is striking—here the grass grows tall and the forest is a natural park with no stumps or slash. To heighten the contrast, you will also drive through forest land that was clear-cut to supply lumber for early communities. Visitors are welcome to visit the fire lookout on the summit. If road signs are not maintained you may have a problem reaching Bald Mountain, for logging roads criss-cross the forest. Obtain a map and ask about road conditions at the nearest ranger station. The road is safe for passenger cars as long as you stay in the road tracks and *stay out of the soft pumice*.

Sideroad to an obsidian dome. Opposite Logging Camp Road, Glass Flow Road branches left to an obsidian (volcanic glass) dome. The road forks left about one-half mile from the highway and goes directly to the base of a large, three-hundred-foot-high dome of solid obsidian. Obsidian is often pure black, or it may be sprinkled with tiny white crystals as it is here, suggesting the name "snowflake obsidian." The streaks of bubbly gray material—obsidian also, but more frothy—show the contorted flow lines of the molten material as it welled up. Obsidian forms when thick viscous lava reaches the earth's surface and then cools rapidly, giving the various minerals in the lava no time to crystallize.

US 395. As the highway crosses a pumice flat beyond Deadman Summit, another obsidian dome, Wilson Butte, is straight ahead. But its rock texture is quite different from the dome described just above. Examine some of the broken blocks at its base. Their texture reminds one of a fine-grained sponge—not as dense as obsidian nor as frothy as pumice. This dome, one of the most recent, erupted about 1300 years ago. Past Wilson Butte a road turns left, leading to Hartley Springs. To the right of the highway there is a conspicuous circular, steep-sided explosion pit similar to the Inyo Craters. On its far side is a large V-shaped gully, formed when water had to be pumped out of the Mono Craters tunnel during construction. This was the discharge point for the water piped from one of the shafts.

Sideroad to the Devils Punchbowl. A narrow road, Pumice Mine Road, turns off to the right to another large explosion pit. Stay in the road tracks, for it is easy to get stuck in the loose pumice. Several signs indicate the road leading up to the lip of the punchbowl. This crater may be considered to have reached a slightly more advanced stage than the explosion pit described just above, for the formation of explosion craters often follows this sequence: first, explosions that produce funnel-shaped craters—like the ones holding the Inyo Crater lakes; second, the rise of a stiff, more-or-less solid obsidian dome from the floor of the pit, as at Panum Crater near Mono Lake; and third, the continued rise of the dome until it may spill over the side in a short chunky flow or completely overwhelm its crater. The punchbowl appears to be a volcano that shut down early in stage two, judging from the junior-size dome in its center.

US 395. Pumice. Everyone familiar with the country between Mammoth Lakes and Mono Lake eventually comes to realize how many square miles are covered with pumice and then begins to wonder where so much pumice

Mt. Ritter 13157'

Banner Pk.
12945'

Carson Pk.
10909'

Mt. Davis
12311'

Reversed Pk.
9473'

Sierra peaks near June Lake Junction

came from. Yet the amount of pumice is relatively small, compared to the outpourings of lava that lie hundreds of feet thick under the pumice and built high mountains—Mono Craters, Glass Mountain Ridge, San Joaquin Mountain, Mammoth Mountain, and dozens of smaller ridges and hills. Pumice is another form of rhyolite lava—a gas-charged, once-molten froth that here was hurled out explosively from a row of vents aligned northward from Mammoth Mountain to the Mono Craters. The youngest pumice that blankets the Mammoth area probably exploded from vents now buried by the domes at Deadman and Glass creeks, between 1400 and 1500 A.D.

June Lake Loop Road. This road branches left to the June Lake basin—where there are campgrounds, resorts, stores, boat landings and a pack station—and rejoins US 395 north of Grant Lake. Stop at the Oh Ridge overlook for grand views of the basin. The wide, sandy beach at the east end of June Lake offers some of the best swimming in the area. Carson Peak (10,909 feet), named after Roy Carson, is the huge, massive mountain rising beyond June Lake. To the north of the lake is Reversed Peak, named for the creek that rises in June Lake and flows toward the mountains—an unusual situation, for streams usually flow *away* from mountains. Following the shore of June Lake (7616 feet), the road cuts through a rocky outcrop on which is balanced a huge granitic boulder, over thirty feet in diameter and estimated to weigh ninety tons, which was left on its perch by a melting glacier. The road then leads through the community of June Lake and past Gull Lake, named for the gulls that fly over from their nesting area on Mono Lake to fish. On the left are the lifts and tows of the June Mountain Ski Area. The five-month ski season usually begins at Thanksgiving. As the road winds through the small valley of Fern Creek with its many large aspen trees, in May and June there are splendid views of Rush Creek Falls cascading down twelve hundred feet over the glacier-smoothed rock. Left of the falls are the sheer cliffs of Carson Peak.

At the base of Rush Creek falls whose water most of the year is diverted into penstocks, is a powerhouse (now owned by Southern California Edison) built in 1916 by the California Electric Power Company. The company,

44

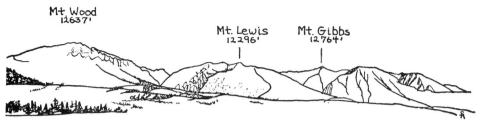

Mt. Wood 12637'

Mt. Lewis 12296'

Mt. Gibbs 12764'

which built most of the early eastern Sierra powerhouses, was organized in the early 1900s. It delivered its first power in 1905, from a plant on Bishop Creek to the prosperous Nevada mining towns of Goldfield and Tonopah, over a 113-mile-long transmission line (then the longest in the world) across the White Mountains. The water for the Rush Creek powerhouse is stored in three reservoirs above the falls. Dams were constructed at Agnew and Gem lakes and at Rush Meadows.

Silver Lake. Carson's Camp, a fishing camp started by Roy and Nancy Carson in 1916 at the northern end of Silver Lake, was the first resort in the June Lake basin. The exceptional fishing attracted Pasadena businessmen, Hollywood stars and other notables such as ex-president Herbert Hoover. The lakes are still famous for their monster fish. In 1985 a 19-pound, 12-ounce, 36-inch-long brown trout was taken from Grant Lake and a 9-pound, 4-ounce, 32-inch rainbow from Gull Lake.

A parking area between Silver Lake and the pack station marks the trailhead for the back country. It is big, high, open country, less peopled than some canyons, with many lakes and many small streams. The stretch of Rush Creek connecting Silver Lake to Grant Lake is a lovely bit of stream-meadow landscape. From the aspen- and willow-lined banks of the creek, there are fine views back toward Carson Peak. It is always changing and always beautiful—from early June, when the wild roses and iris bloom, to late autumn when the aspen turn yellow to reddish orange and burnished pink. In connection with its work on the Mono Craters tunnel, the Los Angeles Department of Water and Power built the Grant Lake reservoir. It inundated formerly extensive meadows and Jeffrey pine and aspen groves, and now reaches up into the canyon of Rush Creek. Grant Lake collects the diverted water of Lee Vining, Walker, and Parker creeks in addition to Rush Creek water; it acts as the control point for shunting Mono Basin water through the tunnel into the Owens River and the aqueduct system.

US 395. Just beyond June Lake junction there is a glimpse of some Ritter Range peaks to the southwest. The landscape in the foreground combines two quite different geological features—glacial moraines and volcanic cinders. Most of the red cinder used locally on driveways comes from this area.

Mono Pass, Mount Gibbs and Mount Dana

Left of the highway there is a splendid example of a long moraine—the low brush-covered ridge, sprinkled with boulders and a few trees, extending from the June Lake basin toward Mono Lake for over a mile. The highway winds down a canyon cut through Bishop tuff, the same pinkish rock you first encountered on Sherwin Grade. A short walk east takes you to the Aeolian Buttes where the winds have sand-blasted the tuff into grotesque rosy tan sculptures. (Turn off onto West Portal Road, two miles north of June Lake junction.) An evening walk here is something special.

Left of the highway on the skyline are the summits of Mount Gibbs and Dana, the latter named by the Whitney Survey after Professor Dana of Yale, the foremost American geologist of his time. The Whitney Survey was organized in 1860 when the legislature appointed Josiah Whitney, of Harvard, state geologist and directed him to make a geological survey of the state. Since much of California had never been mapped, members of the Survey were privileged to name many Sierra peaks, some for obvious reasons such as Red Slate Mountain and the Minarets (for their resemblance to the slender spires of a mosque). Several peaks were named after members of the Survey—Whitney, Brewer, Gabb, Gardiner, Hoffmann and Clarence King. Other peaks were named for prominent men of the time, both Americans and Europeans—California Senator John Conness (who helped establish Yosemite), the eminent English geologist Sir Charles Lyell, and the famous German geographer Karl Ritter.

Mono Pass, Bloody Canyon. The broad saddle left of Mount Gibbs is historic Mono Pass; below it is Bloody Canyon, whose perils were described graphically by William H. Brewer, leader of the Whitney Survey party that travelled it in 1863. In a letter to his family, Brewer wrote: "...a terrible trail. You would all pronounce it utterly inaccessible to horses, yet pack trains come down, but the bones of several horses or mules and the stench of another told that all had not passed safely....The horses were so cut by sharp rocks that they named it 'Bloody Canyon'...and it is appropriate—part of the way the rocks in the trail are literally sprinkled with blood from the animals." Over Mono Pass there had long been a trail, worn by the Paiutes of Mono Lake and the Miwoks of Yosemite over centuries as they crossed the Sierra to trade with each other.

The first white men to cross Mono Pass that we know of were soldiers under Lt. Tredwell Moore, who in June 1852 left Fort Miller in Mariposa County for Yosemite Valley to punish the Miwoks who reportedly killed three prospectors. Moore captured and shot six Miwok men; the rest fled east to hide among their friends, the Paiutes of Mono Lake. Moore never caught up with them, but in chasing them over the Sierra crest and exploring around Mono Lake, Moore and his men picked up pieces of gold ore, which led others to prospect the Mono basin. Later prospectors and pack trains, swarming to the gold strikes at Mono Diggings and Aurora, followed the general route of this ancient Indian trail which came to be known as the Mono Trail.

The Mono Craters. To the right of the highway, the odd flat-topped forms of the steep-sided Mono Craters cut the skyline. This unusual chain of obsidian domes and stubby obsidian flows rises about 2400 feet above Pumice Valley. Yet they excite much less comment than is due them, dwarfed as they are by neighboring Sierra peaks that tower three and four thousand feet higher. Unlike the fluid lava of the well-known Hawaiian volcanoes, which flows down-slope in fiery streams, the lava that built the Mono Craters was very viscous, almost solid, when it reached the surface. Some of it rose as gigantic columns of solid, but much-fractured obsidian, building dome-shaped mountains such as the three high domes at the center of the Mono Craters chain. Some of it rose as not-quite-solid obsidian and spilled over as the stubby steep-faced flows that you can see both north and south of the central domes. Much of the pumice in the area came from explosions associated with the rise of the domes. On the leeward (east) side of the craters, pumice is twenty feet thick; and wind-blown pumice drifted east at least as far as the Nevada boundary, thirty miles away. On the windward (west) side, pumice is seldom more than five feet thick. Eruptions that built the Mono Craters spanned about 35,000 years, although most are younger than 10,000 years.

The Mono Craters are usually depicted on maps as a single feature, which is geologically misleading. They are really the northern end of a north-south alignment of domes and craters that extends from Mammoth Mountain 30 miles northward to Negit Island in Mono Lake. The island contains a stubby lava flow that is younger than any rock or event dated thus far in the 30-mile chain. Geologic detective work has discovered that a 220-year-old shoreline of Mono Lake, preserved on both sides of the flow, cannot be found on the flow itself, indicating that the flow is younger. The volcanic fires in the eastern Sierra have been quiet for many years, with hot springs and steam vents the only surviving traces of activity.

Highway 120 East, Sideroad to Panum Crater, Mono Lake Tufa State Reserve, Mono Mills and Benton. On hot summer days, plan this trip so most of it can be enjoyed during the cool hours of the morning or early evening. About three miles from the junction a graded road branches left to Panum Crater (unfortunately called North Crater on the Mono Craters topographic map). Panum, an Indian word meaning *lake*, was given its name by I. C. Russell, a geologist whose classic report on the Mono Basin was published in 1889. Panum is a classic example in miniature of the eruptive processes that built Mono Craters. The last two phases of its eruption are clearly visible. The next to last phase was a moderately explosive eruption of pumice and small fragments of volcanic glass that apparently fountained from the vent in the center of the crater. Much of the debris fell back to form the circular parapet that is so conspicuous. During the last phase, several extrusions of stiff, quickly-chilled obsidian essentially plugged its own vent, as the energy of the eruptive system subsided. The contrast between the gently sloping, pale gray circular rim and the dark, jagged plug (or dome) in its center is striking. The Panum story actually includes two early, larger, and more violent episodes, but subsequent explosions destroyed most evidence of their occurrence, leaving only obscure remnants. Continuing east, as Highway 120 nears the base of the Mono Craters there are many opportunities to see the steep-fronted craters close up—their rough, blocky obsidian flows contrasting with their smooth, steep pumice slopes.

Tufa Reserve. About 5 miles from the junction, a dirt road on the left leads to South Tufa parking area near the shore of Mono Lake. Exhibits explain the lake's unique features and a trail takes you to the shore and the tufa towers. Inquire when guided walks are given, for some of Mono's wonders are subtle. On your first visit it is much more interesting to go with someone you can ask questions of.

Mono Mills. Farther on, as Highway 120 enters a forest of Jeffrey pine and lodgepole, notice that most of the trees are small—few exceeding 12 inches in diameter, though there are many 3- and 4-foot stumps. Parts of this forest were clear-cut long ago, to supply the tremendous demand of nearby mining camps for wood. Besides all the wood used for cooking and domestic heating, the mills and hoisting works needed enormous amounts to run their steam engines. It is said that Bodie used as much as 45,000 cords in a year. In addition, millions of feet of lumber were needed to construct houses, buildings, mills and flumes, and to shore up tunnels and shafts. Entire hillsides of pinyon pine were cut for fuel; their wood makes a very hot fire. For lumber, the Jeffrey pine were prized most highly. Many sawmills employing hundreds of men kept busy year-round—among them several large sawmills west of Big Meadows (as Bridgeport was then called) that supplied Bodie and Aurora, and a wood ranch in Lee Vining canyon.

A large sign by the highway indicates the site of Mono Mills, a large sawmill that supplied Bodie with wood from 1878 to 1916. It could turn out 80,000 feet of lumber every 10 hours. Behind the sign is the depression of the large millpond and portions of the flume bringing water to it. A boarding house, general store, saloon, bunkhouses and railroad shops clustered nearby. At first, wood for Bodie was barged across the lake and hauled up the steep grade by teams. Later, during Bodie's flush days, the Bodie Railway and Lumber Co. incorporated and built a 31-mile narrow gauge track around the east end of the lake, connecting Mono Mills with Bodie. The Bodie and Benton Railroad (which never went on to Benton) was completed in 1881. Especially powerful locomotives—named the Inyo, Mono, Tybo, and Bodie—were built to haul the lumber trains up the grade to Bodie, a 1900-foot rise in ten miles. Though the tracks were taken for scrap years ago, you can still trace portions of the route.

Adobe Valley. As the road heads east and then south, circling around behind Glass Mountain Ridge, you will discover dramatic canyons cut into the bright red rock. Montgomery and Boundary peaks tower on the White Mountain skyline to the east. When you cross Sagehen Summit, you leave behind the Mono country and drop down to the meadows of Adobe Valley, fed by River Springs. The streams here are the northernmost tributaries of the Owens River. Antelope Mountain and Antelope Spring, names on old maps, attest to the fact that the graceful pronghorn is native to this land. Here in Adobe Valley—or east of Mono Lake in the Bodie Hills, or along Highway 167 or near Hammil Valley—you may be lucky enough to see one. Although they have been protected by law since 1883, poaching, fencing, and livestock grazing decreased their numbers until they disappeared completely from the eastern Sierra in the 1920s. During the 1980s, groups of pronghorn from northern California were released at several sites in northern Inyo and southern Mono counties. It is too soon to tell if they are well established, but the prognosis for their survival is hopeful.

Nearing Benton, you will begin to find scattered juniper trees and pinyon pine. Just beyond Black Lake at the lower end of Adobe Valley, thirty-nine miles after leaving 395, a graded road turns right and loops back to 395, joining it near Convict Lake. (For a description of this road and of Benton, see above "Sideroad to Whitmore Hot Springs...Benton.")

US 395. After the highway crosses Rush Creek, a road sign used to indicate the Mount Diablo Base Line—a line running east and west from Mount Diablo, a prominent peak near Oakland and the starting point for all the surveys in California. Before California became a state, property boundaries, particularly of the old Mexican land grants, were described in vague terms (so many paces toward the large oak tree, etc.). A fixed point on top of Mount Diablo was chosen in 1851 and a meridian line and a base line surveyed from it. Since then, all land has been described in relation to these lines.

Sideroad to Grant Lake. This is the northern portion of the June Lake Loop Road, described in detail above.

US 395. Descendants of the Paiutes who have long made their homes along the shores of Mono Lake live in and near Lee Vining. Before the white man changed their lives, one of their important trading items with the Yosemite Miwoks was obsidian, so plentiful here yet scarce on the other side of the Sierra. The Paiutes also traded baskets. Choice collections of their very beautiful baskets are on display at the Bodie Museum, the Mono County Museum in Bridgeport and at the Eastern California Museum in Independence. Toward the east you have good views of Panum Crater, the low crater that is at the north end of the Mono Craters chain.

Highway 120 West to Mono Lake Ranger Station, Tioga Pass and Yosemite National Park. Twelve miles from US 395, Highway 120 enters Yosemite Park at Tioga Pass (9945 feet), the highest highway pass in the state. It is a spectacular road and a safe one, although frightening to some who are not accustomed to mountain driving. Yosemite Park is one of the scenic wonders of the world. Information on all aspects of the Park are available from rangers at Tioga Pass and at the Tuolumne Meadows Visitor Center, six miles west.

The road follows Lee Vining Creek and then passes the Mono Lake Ranger Station. The informative and artistic exhibits at the ranger station are well worth stopping for. They include displays of the plant communities of Mono Basin, the rocks and the old mining camps. There you will also find maps and wilderness permits, and information on roads and trails.

As you drive up the canyon, if you are very lucky you may see bighorn sheep on the steep slopes above the road. Bighorn have been absent from Lee Vining canyon since about the 1890s. Diseases caught from domestic sheep wiped out many Sierra herds completely. About 300 bighorn remain in the Sierra today; they are listed as "threatened" on the California endangered species list. In an effort to maintain Sierra bighorn, animals have been reintroduced to Lee Vining canyon. At present, the transplanted herd is doing well.

In the vertical walls of upper Lee Vining canyon, there are striking contacts of gray and multi-colored rocks. The tremendous heat and pressure accompanying the intrusion of the gray granitic material twisted, baked and recrystallized the old sedimentary—now metamorphic—rocks. At the top of the grade are Ellery and Tioga lakes, both dammed to store water for the power plant below. A road branches off right to Saddlebag Lake, another large reservoir in this system. On the colorful slopes north of Tioga Lake are a few well-preserved buildings dating from the time of the Tioga Mine and the camp of Bennettville. To develop this mine, eastern investors organized the Great Sierra Consolidated Silver Mining Company in 1881. The company set up the camp, constructed a road from Crocker's Station on the Big Oak Flat Road on the west side of the Sierra, and drove a tunnel eight hundred feet. A sawmill provided lumber. Quantities of charcoal were prepared for the furnace that was to be built to process the ore that never was mined. Three years later, before any ore was worked, the mine closed, never to reopen; later the sheriff sold it for taxes. *Tioga* is an Iroquois name, meaning *where it forks*, applied to some towns and rivers in Pennsylvania and New York. Probably the eastern owners of this mine transferred a name that was familiar to them to their new mine in California, which in turn gave the name to the pass and the lake.

US 395. Lee Vining. A small settlement called Lakeview near Mono Lake changed its name to Lee Vining when the post office was established because there was already a Lakeview Post Office elsewhere. The name commemorates Leroy Vining who, as far as we know, was the first prospector to look for gold in the Mono Basin. When Lt. Moore and his men returned from Mono in 1852 and displayed their ore samples in Mariposa, Leroy Vining, excited by their find, set out to locate their source. Vining and a few companions, coming by Mono Pass and Bloody Canyon with one of Moore's men as guide, were probably the first to prospect the Mono Basin. There is no record of Vining's discovering any gold, though it is known that in 1863 he was operating a sawmill on Lee Vining Creek and delivering lumber to Aurora. There he was accidentally killed by his own revolver. Vining's Gulch, a name on early maps, may have been a humorous name for the immense chasm of Lee Vining canyon, or it may have referred to Vining's "rancho," which early maps show on Lee Vining Creek near the lake.

Lee Vining has several interpretive centers to help you enjoy the wonders of the Mono Basin. On the east side of town, adjacent to Hess Park you will find the Schoolhouse Museum, which focuses on the history of the basin. In town, the Mono Lake Tufa State Reserve office offers information and a schedule of events that includes guided tours. Just north of town, at a spectacular site overlooking the lake, the Forest Service's Mono Basin Visitor Center features outstanding exhibits, films, auto tours, hikes and an interpretive program on the native people, the geology, the plants and the animals of the Mono Basin. In the center of town, the Mono Lake Committee Information Center and Bookstore offers maps, books, nature walks, and canoe trips. There you will find the latest news about the Mono Lake controversy and how catastrophe at Mono—touched on briefly below—can be avoided.

Mono Lake. Near Lee Vining, the highway borders Mono Lake, an alkaline body of water eight miles wide and thirteen miles long. Since it has no outlet, evaporation has concentrated the water's mineral content, making it bitter and almost three times as salty as the ocean. When Ice Age glaciers fed it, Mono Lake was three or four times larger and its water level over six hundred feet higher. Shorelines of that ancient lake show clearly on the Sierra front, hundreds of feet above the present level. You can see them best in late afternoon light, looking west from Highway 167.

Mono Lake's two islands are both volcanic. Geologist I. C. Russell gave both islands Paiute names. *Negit* probably referred to gulls, for they nest on Negit by the thousands (Russell may have been misinformed when he translated it "blue-winged goose.") *Paoha* are "diminutive spirits, having long, wavy hair, that are sometimes seen in the vapor wreathes ascending from hot springs." Black Negit Island is a volcanic cone and lava flow; part of the flow forms the tiny islands to the north. White Paoha Island is formed of young lava flows and older lake sediments that were uplifted by volcanic forces; it has some hot springs and small craters. The story is told that Paoha served as a haven for Chinese laborers, who were building the never-completed Bodie and Benton Railroad, during an anti-Chinese agitation in Bodie. Learning of plans to run them out, the railroad contractors sent messengers on swift horses to the construction camp near Warm Springs, east of Mono Lake. The Chinese were loaded on barges and ferried to the island, returning only after the trouble-makers' enthusiasm (and firewater) had given out. Another story from the mining days relates that gulls' eggs were collected and sold in the camps; with hens' eggs selling in Aurora for up to $1.50 a dozen in 1863, they found a ready market.

From the Yokut Indians, western neighbors of the Paiutes, come the names *Mono* and *Monache*—names the Paiutes themselves never used. They come from a Yokut word meaning *flies*. To the Yokuts, the people at Owens and Mono lakes were the *fly people*, after the alkali-fly pupae that were a food staple and an important trade good. The harmless, non-biting alkali flies inhabit the shore and the shallows; the larvae hatch under water. The Paiutes at Mono Lake called them *koo-cha-vee* or *kut-sa-vi*. They scooped them from the shallows and also gathered quantities from the heaps that drifted to shore. Brewer, mentioned before, said the dried pupae resembled yellow grains of rice and made a fine soup, "oily, very nutritious, and not unpleasant to the taste."

The conspicuous knobby white *tufa towers* scattered about the shore are deposits of calcium carbonate. These limy deposits, clustered around freshwater springs that bubble up from the lake bottom, formed under water and are exposed only because the water level has dropped. A chemical reaction between the calcium in the fresh spring water and carbonates in the mineral-rich lake water causes calcium carbonate to precipitate. Tiny plants, calcareous algae, may facilitate this process and account for the tufa's texture.

Mono Lake's web of life. To a casual observer, Mono Lake may seem barren—no trees, little grass, no fish. Yet Mono's waters abound with life. If you look closely you will see that its waters teem with brine shrimp (*Artemia* *monica*) and its shores with alkali flies (*Ephydra hians*); both shrimp and fly feed on microscopic algae. Both provide critical food for at least 900,000 waterbirds that stop in late summer and fall to rest and feed and molt their worn feathers, as they migrate south along the eastern Sierra flyway. Up to 750,000 eared grebes at one time rest on the lake in October. Up to 80,000 dainty Wilson's phalaropes rest on the lake in late July, up to 65,000 red-necked phalaropes in August. Other birds nest in the fresh-water marshes around the lake, and the conspicuous California gulls fly inland to nest on the islands from April through July. Before water diversions increased the water's salinity and dried up the extensive freshwater marshes that used to border the lake, conditions ducks cannot tolerate, a million migrating ducks and geese used to feed and rest at Mono. Today fewer than fifteen thousand ducks stop at the lake.

Mono Lake's rapidly declining level and the increasing salinity of its waters are a potential catastrophe to its web of life—algae, shrimps, flies and birds. Its shoreline indicates how far the water has receded since its historic high of 6428 feet in 1919. This white band is widening rapidly. Between 1919 and 1940, owing to natural causes, the lake dropped ten feet. Between 1940 and 1982, with much of its inflow diverted into the Los Angeles Aqueduct, the lake's level dropped forty-five feet. At its lowest level, during January of 1982, the lake stood at 6372, four feet below the critical level of 6376, the level at which coyotes can wade to Negit Island.

There is no longer any question about what will happen if the lake continues to drop a foot or two per year. In 1979 the low lake level allowed coyotes to invade the gull colony on Negit Island, completely disrupting all 34,000 nesting gulls. Not a chick fledged on Negit that summer; previous years had seen up to 17,000 chicks fledged. In 1991 the lake's lower level again allowed coyotes to walk to Negit, again causing the gulls to abandon their nests. If the lake continues to drop and the small islets that some gulls nest on also cease to be islands, gulls will have no place to nest at Mono.

Potential catastrophe. We now have a handle on a critical question—whether a shrunken Mono Lake would continue to be a haven and a source of abundant food on the eastern Sierra flyway. The answer to that question depends on the ability of two small creatures—shrimp and fly—to survive in increasingly saline water. The answers are grim: it wouldn't and they couldn't.

As the lake level falls and its water becomes more concentrated, its increasing salinity adversely affects every form of life in and on the lake. Trouble begins with the blue-green algae, upon which all life in the lake ultimately depends. Increasing salinity inhibits the ability of the blue-green algae to fix nitrogen, the essential ingredient in the food chain. With less nitrogen for other algae, with less algae for the flies and shrimp, with fewer flies and shrimp, nesting gulls and migrating grebes would find less and less food at Mono. The more serious question is whether the birds could migrate successfully if this major resting place deteriorated. Most other lakes along the eastern Sierra flyway are already decimated. DWP dried up Owens Lake years ago; the Carson and Humboldt sinks south of Reno have had all their water diverted for irrigation; and Honey Lake north of Reno has shrunk, due to diversions. Grim projections are spelled out in two recent studies, one in 1987 by the National Academy of Sciences and funded by the U.S. Congress, the other in 1988 by the University of California's Water Resources Center and funded by the California legislature. If the lake were continuing to fall a foot or two a year, as it has since diversions began, total catastrophe would be only 20 to 30 years away. At 6352, alkali flies and brine shrimp would be unable to reproduce. In addition, as the lake level has fallen below 6377, Mono Basin has been subject to ever more severe and more frequent dust storms as winds kick up alkali dust from the increasing expanse of exposed lake shore, similar to the alkali dust from dry Owens Lake that now plagues Owens Valley residents. Measuring devices installed in the late 1980s have recorded a number of dust storms that exceed federal air quality standards.

But catastrophe at Mono is not inevitable. Court-ordered minimum flows for the lake's four tributary streams already have slowed its decline. To learn more about these problems and about what you can do to help, stop in at the Mono Lake Committee's Information Center and Bookstore in the center of Lee Vining.

US 395. Three miles north of Lee Vining, on the left, are two historic buildings that were moved here around 1900 from two of the old mining camps—a store from nearby Lundy and a saloon from Bodie. The saloon was used for the same purpose here until 1914 when Mono County went dry. A small stream used to gush out from under it; this was no accident. Water ran under the saloon's north side, near the bar, so that the beer could be let down through a trap-door and kept cool. A mile farther on, beside the road, a plaque commemorates the grave of Adeline Carson Stilts, said to be the favorite child of the famous mountain man, Kit Carson. She came to the Mono Diggings with her husband about 1858 and died the following year, at age 21.

Sideroad to Mono Lake County Park. Cemetery Road takes you to a large, peaceful, shaded picnic area at the county park. A long boardwalk—lengthened as the lake level continues to drop—enables you to walk across the wet meadows among the tufa towers toward the shore. You may find red-winged blackbirds, killdeer and snipe near the small streams.

Sideroad to Lundy Lake. This is a scenic drive any time of year, but in late September or October when the aspen turn brilliant gold, it is unequaled. Above the road is the flume (the wood-stave line built in 1910 has been replaced with pipe) that carries water from Lundy Lake to the Mill

Creek power plant. About three miles from the junction the road forks—the left fork going down to the dam at the outlet of Lundy Lake and leading to the May Lundy Mine road, the right fork going to a resort at the west end of the lake and to the beginning of the Lundy Falls trail.

William O. Lundy started a sawmill in this canyon in 1876, or possibly earlier, selling lumber to Bodie. In August of 1879 prospectors discovered gold quartz on the south wall of Lundy Canyon and on the slopes above Lake Canyon; the next month they formed Homer District. Among those who located claims were William Wasson, L. L. Homer and O. J. Lundy. The May Lundy Company's mine, named after Lundy's daughter, was situated high on a steep slope in Lake Canyon; its lower tunnel was over 11,000 feet in altitude. Homer District produced about a million dollars from its discovery until 1888, most of that amount from the May Lundy's operations between 1880 and 1884. Two towns supplied the mines. Wasson, two miles upstream from the lake, supplied the miners in Lundy Canyon. Lundy, at the upper end of the lake, supplied the May Lundy Mine. A toll road that you can hike today led from Lundy to a mining camp and stamp mill in Lake Canyon. Toll rates, as published in 1881: a wagon and two animals, $1.50; saddle animals, 50¢; loose stock, 10¢. A pack trail was built from Lake Canyon over the high ridge to Bennettville and the Tioga Mine, so the miners there could get supplies from Lundy. It was impossible, however, to transport pipe and machinery, such as boilers, by pack train. Eight tons of heavy equipment for the Tioga Mine were shipped from San Francisco to Bodie, by train and freight-wagon. It then took two months and the heroic efforts of twelve men and two mules to sled the equipment over the snow from Lundy to Bennettville. See History chapter.

Highway 167 to Bodie State Historic Park, the "pole-line" road. This highway leading east fifty-five miles to Hawthorne, Nevada, is an important auxiliary road for Mono Basin residents when winter snows temporarily block US 395 to the north. A power line stretched from the Lundy Lake generating station to the Navy's base at Hawthorne. Although the poles were removed in 1987, locals will always think of it as the *pole-line road*. If you look west from the pole-line road in late afternoon light, the shorelines of ancient Lake Russell, the large lake that occupied this basin during glacial times, show clearly on the Sierra slope, hundreds of feet above the present lake surface.

Seven miles from US 395, a graded road climbs Cottonwood Canyon to Bodie, one of the best preserved ghost towns in California; in fact, it is one big outdoor museum. No attempt will be made here to condense Bodie's colorful history into a few paragraphs. The park is open every day of the year; however, in winter the roads are often blocked with snow. Since loop trips are always more interesting and since this approach is steep, an easier route to Bodie continues north on US 395, turns off to the right about six miles north of Conway Summit and then loops back to 395 by this Cottonwood Canyon road.

Bodie was Mono County's largest mineral producer by far. No superlatives were too great for Bodie's boom years. It claimed the wildest street, the wickedest men, the worst climate, and the best water. Beyond Bodie a road leads northeast, down a canyon to the ghost town of Aurora, Nevada, another famous boom town. Inquire at Bodie whether this road is open, for flash floods and washouts frequently make it impassable.

US 395. Conway Summit. Past the Hawthorne junction, Highway 395 skirts the edge of an extensive meadow belonging to the family of John Andrew Conway, who settled here in 1880 and for whom Conway Summit is named. Nearing Conway Summit (8138'), stop at the parking area on the highway shoulder for the stupendous panoramic view south over much of the country described in this guidebook—Mono Lake and Mono Craters in the foreground, the White Mountains on the skyline to the southeast, and the Sierra Nevada as far south as Bloody Mountain.

Once you have traveled the roads described in this chapter, you will have a beginning, nodding acquaintance with the magnificent Mammoth Lakes Sierra. Then the fun really begins. There are back roads to explore and trails to hike and then no telling how many old, neglected roads and trails to discover on your own. It might just take a lifetime!

Mountain stream   *Bev Steveson*

Jeffrey pine bark   *Gerhard Schumacher*

Mountain hemlock cone   *T J Johnston*

Melting snowbank   *Sierra Club photo*

Mosaic!

Pumice from the craters, sand washed
down by the streams, gravel dumped by the
glaciers—this is the raw material that sup-
ports all life here today. On the few inches
of topsoil that have evolved depend all the
living things—sagebrush, grass, trees, insects, deer, nutcrackers—in wondrous ways
depending on each other. Upon them all,
we too depend.

Rabbit and chipmunk tracks   *Bev Steveson*

Rabbit tracks in dust   *Bev Steveson*

Thistle poppy   *Bev Steveson*

Willow 6-20 feet tall   *Bev Steveson*

Corn lily, Queen Anne's lace   *Bev Steveson*

Alpine willow 1 1/4 inches tall   *Bev Steveson*

Cow parsnip   *Bev Steveson*

Evening primrose   *Bev Steveson*

Swamp whiteheads 2-5 ft. tall   *Bev Steveson*

Pyrola   *Bev Steveson*

Golden-mantled ground squirrels   *Bev Steveson*

Sage grouse courtship display   *Bev Steveson*

Coyote   *Bev Steveson*   *Marmot*   *David J. Dunaway*

Trails

Rugged and majestic, the Sierra Nevada is also friendly, welcoming, and lavish with her beauty. Long summers of little rain provide a hiker's paradise along a narrow strip that straddles her crest. Fondly known as the High Sierra, this strip of blue lakes and shining rock begins at an elevation somewhere around 9000 feet—wherever it is that the trees thin and the views begin. Wild and rugged though it is, this magnificent mountain wilderness is readily accessible. Dozens of roads wind far up the canyons, and from the road ends good trails lead on over the passes.

The John Muir Trail, the Pacific Crest Trail

Shunning the valleys and the easy routes, the famous John Muir Trail winds among the loftiest peaks and passes of the High Sierra, from Tuolumne Meadows to Mount Whitney. It is the longest mountain wilderness trail in the country, touching no towns nor paved roads along its two hundred miles. The Pacific Crest Trail, when completed, will reach 2600 miles from the Mexican to the Canadian border, generally following the mountain ranges of the Pacific states. In the central Sierra, the Pacific Crest Trail and the Muir Trail follow the same route most of the way. One exception is the stretch between Thousand Island Lake and Reds Meadow.

Wilderness permits

A wilderness permit is required to hike overnight on many mountain trails in the High Sierra. Permits are free and are available at the ranger stations listed in the front of the book as well as at seasonal entrance stations. Inquire about reservations and limitations as far in advance as possible, lest you arrive at the road end packed and ready to take off, only to find the day's quota is full. Within the broad policy of accommodating as many people as possible without destroying the very wilderness qualities they come for, back country rules vary from place to place. That policy may include: a reservation system; limits on the size of groups and length of stay; daily quotas; where wood is scarce, prohibitions on wood fires (stoves required); where forage is scarce, limits on grazing; where meadows and lakeshores are hard packed from trampling, closure to all camping and grazing until plants return.

Trail maps

Wilderness maps. The best trail maps for this area are the wilderness maps published by the US Forest Service. Each one covers a large area, over a thousand square miles, so you need carry only one map, instead of five or six quadrangle maps. They are inexpensive, so you can cut them up and use smaller pieces if you prefer. They include detailed wilderness information and travel tips, all are in color, and all show the John Muir and Pacific Crest trails. These are topographic maps; if you don't know how to read them, find someone to show you. Contour intervals of 80 feet accurately depict altitude and relief. Scale: one inch = one mile. Available at ranger stations.

John Muir Wilderness. Two sheets (4 sides), 36 x 48, 1993. From Cottonwood Canyon near Lone Pine north to Mammoth Pass. Includes the high country adjacent to the Inyo and Sierra National Forests in Sequoia and Kings Canyon National Parks. A marvelous map, updated in 1993.

Ansel Adams Wilderness. 32 x 48, 1987. From Duck Pass and Mammoth Pass north to Tioga Pass, and the adjacent high country in the Sierra National Forest and Yosemite National Park. Includes Mammoth Lakes, June Lake, Reds Meadow and the Ritter Range.

Hoover Wilderness. 36 x 40, 1987. The Toiyabe National Forest, from its southern boundary near Mono Lake north to Sonora Pass. Includes the adjacent high country in northern Yosemite Park and in the Emigrant Wilderness.

USGS Topographic Maps, *the 15 minute series.* US Geological Survey. Scale: 1 inch = 1 mile. Contour intervals, 80 feet. Each map covers 15 minutes of longitude and 15 minutes of latitude, an area roughly 14 miles by 17 miles. Even though some road and trail information on these maps is out of date, the topography is not. These are the standard maps hikers have used for many years. Unfortunately, these 15-minute maps are being phased out as the newer 7.5-minute maps replace them. If you prefer the old maps, as many people do, because they cover four times the area of the new maps, you can still find many of them in eastern Sierra sporting goods and bookstores. See also, below, The Map Center.

The 7.5 minute series. US Geological Survey. Scale: 1 inch = 2000 feet. Contour intervals, 20 or 40 feet. Each map covers 7.5 minutes of longitude and 7.5 minutes of latitude, an area roughly 7 miles by 8.5 miles or 60 square miles. To really confuse matters, some of the maps use metric measurements; others use US measurements (feet and miles). Since each map covers one-fourth the area of a 15-minute map, they show altitude and relief in much greater detail. However, because these maps cover such a small area, even on a short hike you may need to carry three or four of them, which is a bother. The USGS totographic maps are the official maps upon which all other maps are based. Maps in this new series are now available for the eastern Sierra.

USGS maps are available at many eastern Sierra bookstores, sporting goods stores and ranger stations. Write for the free *California Index to Topographic and Other Map Coverage* and *California Catalog of Topographic and other Published Maps* (you need both the index and the catalog to determine which maps are in print). Send also for the free Map Symbol Sheet, which explains all the symbols used on topo maps. Purchase by mail (prepaid orders only) from: USGS Map Sales, Box 25286, Denver, CO 80225. Over-the-counter map sales in California at the Earth Science Information Center, Building Three, 345 Middlefield Road, Menlo Park.

The Map Center, 2440 Bancroft Way, Berkeley, CA 94704. Stocks all the USGS topographic maps for California. The Map Center says it will continue to reprint the most popular USGS 15-minute maps, with roads and trails updated. Also maps of foreign countries, street atlases, geologic maps, National Park and Forest Service maps. Write for a catalog.

High altitude adjustment

The higher the mountain, the less oxygen in the air. In that simple fact lies the cause for many a misery—headache, nausea, shortness of breath, rapid pulse, irritability, insomnia, lack of appetite. Lack of oxygen—particularly insufficient oxygen to the brain, which is especially sensitive to lack of oxygen—and the low barometric pressure cause these symptoms of high altitude illness. Some people feel the altitude at 5000 feet. Almost everyone who lives near sea level feels it at eastern Sierra road ends that are 8000 and 9000 feet high. Age and strength have little to do with it. Athletic teen-agers are sometimes hit the hardest.

Most altitude illness is mild and will resolve on its own with rest and fluids. Aspirin may help. Be aware, however, that there are serious and even life-threatening forms of high altitude illness. High altitude pulmonary edema—*HAPE*, excess fluid in the lungs—and high altitude cerebral edema—*HACE*, excess fluid in the brain—require immediate descent to low elevation and oxygen. Symptoms of HAPE may include cough, severe shortness of breath and tiredness far out of proportion to the activity engaged in. Symptoms of HACE may include confusion and poor coordination in addition to a headache. Get to lower altitude if possible and get medical care immediately, as victims will not get better on their own.

Dr. Carolyn Tiernan, an eastern Sierra physician experienced in treating high altitude illness, offers these suggestions to ease the adjustment to higher elevations and to avoid serious illness. Start your trip to the eastern Sierra healthy and rested. Avoid alcohol and sedating medications. Spend a night at a half-way elevation and take relatively easy hikes for the first day or two. Drink plenty of fluids and eat high-energy foods. Listen to your body. When it has adjusted to the altitude it will tell you that you are ready for longer hikes and higher elevations. Pushing yourself and your children is the worst you can do, for above 10,000 feet reactions usually become only more severe.

For otherwise healthy people who have chronic problems adjusting to altitude, medications are available that are successful in preventing high altitude illness. Consult a physician knowledgeable in mountain medicine.

Defenses against chilling

Generally hospitable and good-natured, the Sierra Nevada can be unexpectedly harsh and brutal. If you approach her with humility, she will reward you with safe journeys and days of happiness. But if you fail to accord her the respect due one of the world's great mountain ranges—if you fail to prepare for her black moods, her bitter weather, her high altitudes—she is unforgiving. You may pay with your life, as did four of the five climbers on Mount Ritter, one Memorial Day weekend. As did the two boys, in separate parties, who died one Labor Day weekend less than ten miles from road ends, when an unexpected storm soaked their clothes and their sleeping bags.

Hypothermia is the medical term for a cooler than normal body temperature, at which bodily functions such as coordination and thinking are affected. Hypothermia occurs when the body loses heat faster than it can produce it. A drop of just a few degrees in body temperature can cause physical collapse or even death. The body loses heat faster if there is a wind chill or if it is wet. If your clothing is wet and a cold, strong wind begins to blow, you are in deadly peril. The defenses against chilling are proven: ample down or wool clothing and water*proof*, not water repellent, jacket or poncho. Remember that wool and some of the new synthetic outdoor-clothing materials (such as pile, polypropylene, Capilene, Polarplus and Synchilla) will keep you warm even when they are wet. Remember too that a chilled per-son must be warmed immediately. If you are caught unprepared, there is no time to lose in getting down and out of the mountains. Second best, find a warm, dry shelter under a boulder.

Giardia: What happened to our water?

Some of us fondly remember the days when, tired and hot from hiking a steep, dry mountain slope, we dipped our cups into a clear, icy stream for a drink. Nothing ever tasted better. A little creature called Giardia has changed all of that. No stream or lake, no matter how high or remote, can be considered free nowadays from this misery-causing protozoan.

Giardia causes an unpleasant gastrointestinal illness; water must be treated to avoid it. Each method of treating water—filtering, boiling and chemical treatment—has its advantages and disadvantages. The filter pumps sold in mountaineering stores have their ardent supporters. The water is quickly hand pumped through a filter and you can drink it immediately. Their disadvantages are their weight (not much) and their cost. Boiling on a stove takes time and involves weight also; and in some areas wood fires are prohibited. Suggested boiling times range from 5 to 15 minutes; the higher the altitude, the more time. Then you must wait for the water to cool. The third method, chemical treatment, uses iodine or tetraglycinehydroperiodide, which are available in mountaineering stores. Usually the water must stand 30 to 60 minutes before it is drinkable; even then it may have an after-taste. The chemicals are less effective at colder temperatures. After considering all these complications, day-hikers may decide that it is simpler to carry their water with them.

Some other trail notes

Trail distances are one-way, unless noted otherwise. To help you choose which trails you will enjoy the most, trails are classified as follows:

easy hike	less than 500-foot gain in altitude
moderate hike	600- to 1500-foot gain
strenuous hike	over 1600-foot gain

Mileage and the altitude are also factored in this equation, but in the mountains elevation gains determine how long and how rough the trip will be, far more than do miles traveled. Fortunately, in the Mammoth Lakes Sierra there is something for everyone. Trails range from very easy to very strenuous and altitudes range from lower to higher. Remember that in this high, dry eastern Sierra your body craves fluids and your skin needs protection from the sun.

We describe all the regularly maintained trails in the area and we purposely do not describe (and hope no one else will) the dozens of abandoned trails that can still be followed—game trails, horse trails, fishermen's trails, sheep trails, and undoubtedly some mining trails that are more than a hundred years old. They are all yours for discovering.

Mountain-wise

Happiness in the mountains is keeping warm, dry, and safe. The wise mountaineer—

- *Doesn't succumb to the myth* that "it never rains in the Sierra in summer." He is prepared for rain, hail and snow. Yes, even in August!
- *Carries these essentials* always: drinking water, flashlight, matches, whistle, extra food, map, dark glasses, sun screen.
- *Always tells someone where he is going* and when he expects to return.
- *Avoids risky stream crossings* and steep snow slopes if possible, making detours instead. If fording a stream is necessary, he wades across with boots *on* (dry socks in pack). Boots dry after a few minutes of walking.

A special happiness lies in being aware of all the other creatures—plant, animal and human—that share the mountains. The thoughtful mountaineer—

- *Gives stock the right of way*, moving several yards off the trail, standing still and talking quietly so that the animals will see and hear him. Appreciating the precarious balance of heavy-laden, short-tied mules, he guards against spooking them by *not* waving his arms and not letting his poncho flap in the wind. He parks his gear well off stock trails, lest a mule take a notion to kick it to pieces. Why? Well—although mules are among the most patient and faithful of animals, they are also sometimes quite beyond understanding.
- *Refrains from cutting across switchbacks* lest he start gullies.
- *Buries body wastes* in a shallow hole at least 100 yards from water; burns or carries out toilet paper.
- *Leaves the least possible evidence that he has passed*. He carries out all that he carries in. He walks *around* meadows instead of trampling the grass and flowers. He steps *over* small plants lest he break off stems that have taken several years to reach stubby lengths, so brief are alpine summers. Most important, he does all these things without being odiously virtuous about it. He is almost a paragon, but there are more and more like him. This is a good thing, because there are lots of people camping in the wilderness. His kind take up less room.

Rock Creek

Rock Creek flows down a huge glacial canyon, which was scooped out of typical gray Sierra granite. However, most of the canyons described in this guidebook are *atypical*, not in granite. The road up Rock Creek canyon goes higher than any other in the area, ending at 10,300 feet above sea-level, 350 feet higher than Tioga Pass. Since the trailheads are almost at treeline, you can reach the high country with less climbing than from any other starting point. Little Lakes Valley and the East Fork of Rock Creek both have miles of streams and ponds, and wildflowers all summer long. Almost flat, they are ideal for early season hikes to adjust to the altitude, and for families with small children. The canyon contains more than forty lakes; a few miles over Morgan and Mono passes, there are many more.

Rock Creek Gorge (6880') to Paradise Camp.

Paradise Camp (4960'), moderate hike, about 8 miles.
Trailhead. Junction of US 395 and Lower Rock Creek Road (old 395), a mile south of Toms Place. Look in the brush on the east side of Lower Rock Creek Road and you will find a gentle trail, partly overgrown, leading down to the creek.

This is a hike like no other you have ever made. Rock Creek has cut a strange, 500-foot gorge into the pink and tan rocks of the Bishop tuff, exposing the marvelously varied colors and textures in its vertical walls. A trail follows the creek through the gorge for about eight miles. The most scenic hike (the gorge is deeper) and also the easiest (it's all downhill if you can arrange a car shuttle) begins at the second bridge across Rock Creek, not quite 3 miles down the road from the junction with 395.

Rock Creek Lake (9682') to Kenneth, Francis and Tamarack Lakes.

Kenneth Lake (10,350'), moderate hike, 2 miles.
Francis Lake (10,880'), moderate hike, 3 miles.
Tamarack Lakes (11,580'), strenuous hike, 5 miles.
Trailhead. East side of Rock Creek Lake.

The East Fork of Rock Creek lies in a wide, flat-bottomed valley with ponds and meadows and a most amazing forest of whitebark pine—miles of whitebark growing in granite sand, with sagebrush between. If you ever wondered about the name *whitebark*, look at the upper part of the trunks and at young trees' bark. Wheeler Crest, the massive granite ridge whose sheer east face is so impressive from Highway 395 north of Bishop, bounds this parklike basin on the east.

The trail goes up a brushy slope for half a mile, then levels out as it follows an old logging road. A trail turns off right (S) from the logging road and winds through the forest to the large meadow surrounding Kenneth Lake. Gentian are abundant in late August and September. At Kenneth, a side trail branches off to Francis Lake, which lies in a small canyon on the north slope of Mount Morgan. The main trail crosses a low rise to Dorothy Lake and to the stream coming from Tamarack Lakes, following its gentle little valley for about a mile and a half, until it is blocked by abrupt cliffs. The trail swings to the right (W) and switchbacks up to the high basin of Tamarack Lakes 800 feet above.

At the outlet of Tamarack Lakes, there is a noticeable change in the color of the cliffs—light gray to the left (N), dark brown to the right (S). Both are igneous rocks, but they differ in mineral composition and in age, the dark rock being older. Easterners may wonder about the name of these lakes, for their "tamarack" is the eastern larch tree, which is not native to California. In parts of the west, the name *tamarack* somehow became attached to the lodgepole pine. Tamarack Lakes are poorly named, however, for there are no trees of any kind in their high basin.

Mosquito Flat (10,300') to Little Lakes Valley and Morgan Pass.

Long Lake (10,543'), easy hike, 2 miles.
Morgan Pass (11,104'), moderate hike, 3.5 miles.
Trailhead. The end of Rock Creek Road.

Little Lakes Valley is a very special alpine garden—with gentle walks, wildflowers in profusion throughout the summer, low willows, short grasses, many small streams, dozens of lakes and ponds, all encircled by ridges towering two and three thousand feet above and dominated by snowy Bear Creek Spire. In late August the grasses turn golden and the meadows purple with gentian. Trails lead to some of the lakes, but the country is so open and flat that you can easily walk almost anywhere cross-country and discover many more. The trail follows the old road of the Pine Creek Tungsten Mine, abandoned after a more direct road was built to the mine from Round Valley. The famous Pine Creek Mine was for a time the largest tungsten producer in the country. The road is almost level until the short, gradual climb over Morgan Pass. Lower Morgan Lake is about a mile beyond the pass.

Mosquito Flat (10,300') to Mono Pass, Mount Starr and Trail Lakes.

Mono Pass (12,000'), strenuous hike, 3.5 miles.
Mount Starr (12,870'), strenuous hike, 4 miles.
Trail Lakes (11,240'), strenuous hike, 5 miles.
Trailhead. The end of Rock Creek Road.

Mono Pass is the gateway to the extensive High Sierra wilderness that incudes Pioneer and Hopkins basins and the four Recesses west of the crest. (If you expected Mono Pass to be somewhere else, it is, for there are two Mono Passes. The one referred to in historical writings, famous as an Indian trail across the Sierra, is 40 miles northeast, just south of Tioga Pass.)

Start early up this trail and aim to be off the shadeless, relentless switchbacks and over the pass before noon-day heat. On the way there are fine views of Little Lakes Valley and its imposing eastern wall topped by Mount Morgan (13,748'). Just over the pass are the still waters of Summit Lake and, farther down, the Trail Lakes. The 1983 John Muir Wilderness map seems to indicate that Mono Pass is 12,643 feet high; it isn't. For an incredible view, scramble up another 900 feet to the summit of Mount Starr, half a mile northeast. No other 12,900-foot Sierra peak is so easy to climb: 3.5 miles of excellent trail, little rough hiking, and an elevation gain of only 2600 feet. The half-mile to the summit is very steep, but not exposed; only the last 300 yards require rock-hopping. Sheltered in the summit rocks grows the fragrant, bright blue, sturdy sky pilot (*Polemonium*), an alpine flower occurring only on the highest ridges. The view from the peak is full-circle—you may feel you are seeing the whole world. The White Mountains lie to the east, the broad-topped Mono Craters to the north, and the dark gray peaks of Mount Ritter and Banner to the northwest. Nearby are seven stately peaks over 13,000 feet high—Mount Mills, Abbot, Dade, Gabb, Hilgard, Red Slate and Bear Creek Spire; a dozen others are only slightly lower. In the distance, seemingly infinite numbers of ridges and peaks blend into the horizon.

Rock Creek Road (9840') to Hilton Lake Four.

Davis Lake (9801'), moderate hike, 5 miles.
Lake 4 (10,400'), moderate hike, 5 miles.
Trailhead. Toward the upper end of Rock Creek Road, half a mile beyond Rock Creek Lakes Resort, look for trailhead parking on the right (W).

This is the easiest, most pleasant route to the Hilton Creek Lakes, for it starts high, is shaded much of the way, rises only 500 feet to cross the Hilton Creek-Rock Creek divide, and then drops down to meet the Hilton Creek trail. At this junction, one trail goes right to the largest of the Hilton lakes, Lake 2 and Davis Lake, both of them forested. Davis Lake's pale yellow beaches, sprinkled with bits of rust and black, are granite sand. The other trail goes left to the upper lakes, numbered from 3 to 10, a peaceful region of clear waters, whitebark pine and close-in, towering peaks. A good trail leads to Lakes 3 and 4. To reach Lake 5 from Lake 4, boulder-hop up the ridge to the southeast. Beyond, there isn't much of a trail; to reach the smaller, higher lakes follow the streams. At the higher altitudes, the whitebark become more shrub-like until finally, on the unstable talus slopes, they are unable to grow at all. Lake 10, quiet and remote at the end of the canyon, lies just below Mount Huntington.

Hilton Creek Canyon

The ten Hilton Lakes are strung along Hilton Creek on the floor of a high glacial canyon gouged into Sierra granite. Above the canyon walls, which stand 12,000 feet and higher, a dozen peaks tower another thousand feet higher. Hilton and neighboring McGee and Rock Creek canyons have outstanding displays of golden aspen in fall.

The route along Hilton Creek is hot and dusty. It climbs 1600 feet up the brush-covered moraine and then climbs another thousand feet to reach Davis Lake. The trail is little used and is no longer maintained. The most pleasant route to the Hilton Lakes begins from a trailhead in Rock Creek canyon (see above).

McGee and Convict Canyons

Don't be fooled by the drab sagebrush entrances to these two canyons. They give little clue to the dramatic scenery up-canyon. There precipitous canyon walls reveal extraordinary exposures of wildly contorted and highly-colored rock layers. Red-purple, rich brown, bright rust, blue-gray and whitish rock-layers—standing on end, upturned, overturned or swinging off at crazy angles to bend and plunge beneath other layers. Into these layers Convict and McGee creeks and their glaciers have cut narrow gashes three thousand feet deep, exposing their long, tortured history of repeated tilting, folding and squeezing. Yet this seemingly chaotic striping and banding is, in reality, an orderly sequence of rock layers that, although badly mangled, forms a remarkable section 50,000 feet thick of sediments accumulated in ancient seas between 400 and 125 million years ago. Trails up these canyons are steep, the scenery magnificent—east-side Sierra sculpture at its most colorful.

McGee Creek (8100') to Round Lake, Big McGee Lake.

Round Lake (9950'), strenuous hike, 4.5 miles.
Big McGee Lake (10,480'), strenuous hike, 6.5 miles.
Trailhead. Park at the end of McGee Creek Road, a mile above the pack station.

During high water it is very dangerous to ford McGee Creek on foot. Inquire whether it is safe to cross and postpone your hike until it is. On hot August days, start on this trip early, for there is little shade for about three miles, until the road enters the lodgepole forest. Besides, the canyon walls are especially colorful in the early morning light. Near the trailhead watch for the rare copper birch, named for its copper-colored bark. About a mile beyond you may discover another uncommon tree, the limber pine, with silver bark on its upper trunk, long branches curving upward, and a 3-10-inch cone. In the eastern Sierra, this tree usually grows well above 9000 feet; but here in the canyon bottom a few trees have found the right environment.

The trail follows the creek up the canyon, first to Round Lake and then to Big McGee Lake, which is walled in by Mount Crocker (SE) and Red and White Mountain (SW). From Big McGee, the trail ascends steeply to cross McGee Pass (11,900'), on its way to the high, wild back-country of Upper Fish Creek. A magical garden of bright blue *Polemonium* grows just below McGee Pass, on its west slope.

McGee Creek (8100') to Grass and Steelhead Lakes.

Grass Lake (9800') strenuous hike, 4.5 miles.
Steelhead Lake (10,400'), strenuous hike, 6 miles.
Trailhead. Same as above.

Proceed as described above for about 4 miles. A trail branches to the left (E) and climbs steeply up the canyon's east wall to Grass Lake, which is surrounded by a fine high-mountain meadow. It is a steep climb to Steelhead

Lake above, which lies in a large cirque almost at treeline. Its setting affords a spectacular view across the canyon of the red and gray rocks of Mount Baldwin ridge to the west. The color difference results from complicated folding of iron-stained quartz-rich rocks and gray marble.

McGee Creek (8100') to Meadow, Golden and Crocker Lakes.

Meadow Lake (10,160'), strenuous hike, 5 miles.
Golden Lake (10,400'), strenuous hike, 6 miles.
Crocker Lake (10,900'), strenuous hike, 6.5 miles.
Trailhead. Same as above.

Follow the trail up McGee Creek as described above to Round Lake. About a half mile farther, look for the turnoff left (E) to Meadow, Golden and Crocker lakes. Cross McGee Creek, then follow the meadow downstream about a hundred yards, past a mass of granite boulders, to the mid-point of the meadow. From there the trail proceeds up a forested slope. Just beyond its junction with a connecting trail to Grass Lake, if the trail seems lost in a small meadow, go along the upper side of the meadow toward the sound of a noisy stream. Cross it and follow the trail to clear, shallow Meadow Lake. Beyond Meadow Lake, the trail is not always easy to find. Follow the meadow around to its upper end, cross the stream coming from a small waterfall visible above, and follow its right bank to the waterfall; at its head lies Golden Lake. You can reach Crocker Lake by scrambling up the boulder slope at the inlet of Golden Lake (no trail) and following the stream to its source, just below the peak of Mount Crocker (to the left, SE). Mount Crocker and the three peaks near it (but not visible from this basin) were named after the "Big Four" of Central Pacific Railroad fame: Charles Crocker, Mark Hopkins, Collis Huntington and Leland Stanford.

Road End (7620') to the Inlet of Convict Lake (7580').

Easy hike, less than 1 mile.
Complete circle around the lake, easy hike, over two miles.
Trailhead. At Convict Lake, take the paved road that forks left. The trail begins at the road end.

The trail circling Convict Lake occasionally dips down to the water's edge, passing through willow, aspen, cottonwood, copper birch, and a few limber pine. In July watch for a brilliant yellow flower several inches across with five broad petals—the blazing star, which opens in the evening and closes the following afternoon. A small gravel beach at the inlet, where Convict Creek cascades into the lake, is a favorite picnic spot.

Convict Lake (7580') to Lakes Mildred, Dorothy and Genevieve.

Lake Mildred (9760'), strenuous hike, 4.5 miles.
Lake Dorothy (10,250'), strenuous hike, 5.5 miles.
Lake Genevieve (10,000'), strenuous hike, 6.5 miles.
Trailhead. About 2 miles up the Convict Lake Road, before you catch sight of the lake, look for the parking area on the right.

The stream crossing 3 miles up the trail, where a tributary from Lake Genevieve cascades down to join Convict Creek, can be very dangerous. Before you start this hike, inquire whether the creek is safe to cross. There is no bridge; it washed out and will not be rebuilt. If the waters are high, postpone your trip until late summer.

The trail climbs over a small brush-covered moraine that gives you a fine view of the canyon. It drops to the lake, rounds the north shore and follows the creek upstream. In the stream bed and along the trail just below Lake Mildred, look for black platy rocks within which are circular light-gray or white structures the size of an 8-penny nailhead. These are disks from the stems of fossil *crinoids* (sea lilies), animals which lived in the shallow ocean covering this region 300 million years ago. Stacks of these small hard disks, held together by soft tissue, made up the stems.

Mildred—part marsh, part lake—lies at the low end of a broad U-shaped valley carved by ancient glaciers. After the last glacier melted away, the bottom of the trough filled with water; ancient Mildred Lake may have been larger than Dorothy today. With streams carrying in gravel and mud over thousands of years, most of the bottom of the trough has become meadow and marsh. Mildred, slowly filling with sediments, is on its way to becoming a meadow.

A 500-foot climb takes you on to mile-long, deep blue Lake Dorothy, rimmed with whitebark pine along its east shore. From the far end of Dorothy, a quarter-mile, 400-foot climb brings you to Bighorn Lake, another quarter-mile to Lake Wit-so-nah-pah, and a quarter-mile up its creek to Constance Lake, at the very base of Red Slate Mountain. From the outlet of Dorothy, the trail swings over a low pass and drops down to Lake Genevieve.

From the pass, looking back toward the south, you can appreciate the form and scale of the glacial canyon above Mildred Lake. The creek, gently meandering through its broad meadows, contrasts with the sheer canyon walls and emphasizes its trough-shape. Gray marble and rusty red, iron-stained rocks account for the striking colors in the ridge across the canyon. The dark red rocks of Bloody Mountain and Laurel Peak dominate the basin of Lake Genevieve. Edith Lake is a ten-minute walk up the creek from the west side of Genevieve. From Genevieve, a trail heads northwest and drops down into Laurel canyon—a grand loop trip if you can arrange a car shuttle.

Mammoth Lakes

Unlike most eastern Sierra canyons, which are short narrow gashes cut into the steep mountain front, the Mammoth basin is a broad opening into the eastern slope, with a two-mile-long lakes basin in its upper reaches. The great hulk of Mammoth Mountain, its red-purple cliffs rising sheer above

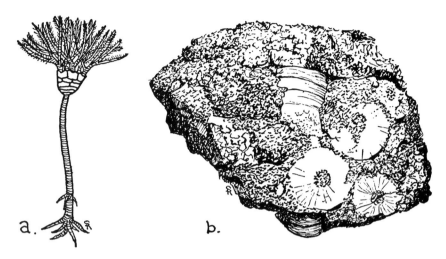

a. A living crinoid, less than life size. b. Fossil crinoid stems, actual size.

Twin Lakes, borders the lakes basin on the north. Mammoth Crest borders it on the west and south, the whitish granite of its cliffs standing prominently above Horseshoe Lake. Many of the trails here are less steep, the hikes less strenuous than in other canyons. Lakes, streams, and quiet meadows nestle below Mammoth Crest and Mammoth Mountain. Trails lead to lakes within the basin itself as well as leading out of the basin over Duck Pass, Mammoth Crest, and Mammoth Pass. From many high points there are grand views west toward the Ritter Range. Crystal Crag and Mammoth Rock are distinctive and dramatic landmarks.

Laurel Canyon (9770') to Lake Genevieve (10,150').

Strenuous hike, about 3 miles.

Trailhead. From Old Mammoth Road, drive east on Sherwin Creek Road for 4 miles. A very rough jeep road that gets rougher every year climbs the Laurel Canyon moraine and continues up the canyon. The trail starts just east of Laurel Lakes. If you don't have 4-wheel drive and start hiking at the bottom of the moraine, add four miles and 2000 feet of climbing to the figures above. And start before sunup; it's a long, hot grind.

Magnificent views, precipitous canyons, and multi-colored mountains make this hike spectacular every step of the way. In fall glittering yellow aspen in the meadows behind the moraine add even more color. The trail switchbacks up to the saddle between Laurel and Bloody mountains, passes through a strange bowl-shaped basin and climbs the ridge to its east. Shrublike whitebark pine manage to cling to the exposed ridges, but few manage to grow more than a few feet high. Wind-driven ice particles shear them off as neatly as any hedge-trimmer. Once you have reached the top of the ridge

(10,800'), find a soft rock and take time to immerse yourself in the glorious views. (See sketches in Roadsides chapter.) Eastward a broad view encompasses Long Valley and all the highest peaks of the White Mountains. Most dramatic of all are the airplane-like views straight down to Convict Lake more than 3000 feet below.

From this viewpoint, if you squint your eyes, it is not difficult to imagine a great white tongue of ice lying where Convict Lake is now. The curving arc-shape of the canyon's huge moraine clearly outlines the size and shape of the vanished glacier's snout. From another great viewpoint, on the small ridge southeast of Lake Genevieve, looking up-canyon you can easily picture the upper glacier—heading in the broad cirque below Red Slate Mountain and filling the U-shaped canyon behind Lake Mildred with ice more than a thousand feet thick. The precipitous walls of the scooped-out canyon also expose the long, tortured history of the ancient rock layers—a history of tilting, folding and squeezing. The striking rusty red and gray colors near Mount Baldwin come from layers of gray marble and iron-stained metasediments. Lake Genevieve is encircled by the dark red slopes of Bloody and Laurel mountains. On the far side of Genevieve, the Convict Creek trail comes in from Lake Dorothy. It is twice as far to hike out by this trail and you'll have to arrange a car shuttle at Convict Lake, but the loop makes a superb day. See above, "Convict Lake to Lake Genevieve."

Sherwin Creek (7760') to Sherwin Lakes and Valentine Lake.

Sherwin Lakes (8620'), moderate hike, 2 miles.
Valentine Lake (9650'), strenuous hike, about 5 miles.
Trailhead. From Old Mammoth Road drive 1.3 miles on the Sherwin Creek Road, turn right (S) and drive to a parking area.

The five Sherwin Lakes lie close together behind the steep-fronted glacial moraine that blocks the mouth of Sherwin Creek canyon. The form of the moraine is obscured by the forest of tall pine and fir, but aerial photos reveal that its arc-shape is much less well defined than that of the conspicuous, treeless moraine next to it, at the mouth of Laurel canyon. The composition of the canyons' rocks accounts for the striking difference between the two moraines. Laurel's gravelly moraine comes from its canyon's dark, thin-bedded metamorphic bedrock, which consists of abundant platy minerals that disintegrate readily into gravelly rubble. For some reason, trees do not find it to their liking. In sharp contrast, Sherwin's moraine comes from its canyon's whitish, massive granite, which fractures into enormous blocks that trees find quite to their liking.

The trail leads through manzanita-covered slopes and then in long, easy zigzags climbs the 800-foot moraine and goes to the two upper lakes. The boulders and the dense forest make for rough going if you want to reach their shores. To find the three smaller, lower lakes, head downstream from the upper lakes. Birds are abundant in this forest. You are likely to see nutcrackers, chickadees, wood pewees, robins, flycatchers, woodpeckers and you might hear grouse *whomping*.

Walled in on three sides by austere, 2000-foot-high granite cliffs and rimmed with boulders, Valentine Lake lies at the very end of Sherwin Creek canyon. This deep, rockbound lake is named for W. L. Valentine, one of the original owners of Valentine Camp, an exclusive club-camp in Old Mammoth. To reach the lake, continue on the trail as it winds through a park-like grove of extraordinarily beautiful western juniper trees. Sheltered from the fierce winds that twist and dwarf many junipers, here they grow tall, straight and symmetrical. As the trail follows the creek upstream, the canyon narrows. A few more zigzags near the waterfall below the lake's outlet (watch for dippers) bring you to the shore of Valentine Lake.

Another trail, from the boys' camp 1.5 miles farther down Sherwin Creek Road, also leads to Valentine Lake. You can make a loop trip by arranging a car shuttle.

Twin Lakes (8540') to Mammoth Falls (8400').

Easy hike, one-quarter mile.
Trailhead. East side of Lake Mary Road, about 50 yards above the bridge at Twin Lakes outlet.

From the placid lakes basin, Mammoth Creek tumbles suddenly out of Lake Mamie to fall 250 feet into Twin Lakes. Racing from the outlet of Twin, it leaps over lava cliffs to form a second fall, before cascading down its gorge into the forest below. This walk—through a streamside woods of aspen and pine to a viewpoint of this lower fall—is particularly dramatic in early summer when the creek is high and also in October when the aspen are golden.

A jumble of hiking trails and fishermen's trails may confuse the route to the falls. About 180 yards down the trail from the road, take a left fork that crosses a large ditch. This is the flume that carried water from Twin Lakes to turn the waterwheel of the Mammoth Mining Company's mill during the 1870s. The flume was built as an open ditch, but it became obvious the first winter that it had to be covered to prevent its being choked with snow. From the flume the trail winds down through the forest, a spur path turning left to Mammoth Falls.

Twin Lakes (8540') to Panorama Dome.

Panorama Dome (8892'), easy hike, one-half mile.
Trailhead. About 400 yards above the bridge at Twin Lakes outlet, on the east side of the highway.

The dome provides sweeping views in all directions—west to Mammoth Crest and east across Long Valley to the White Mountains—views that are especially lovely at sunset. From June to August, rose-pink paintbrush, scarlet gilia, pussypaws and other dry-hillside flowers bloom among the sagebrush. You may notice many old 2- to 4-foot stumps throughout this forest—some rotted and toppled over, but many still standing, weathered to silver gray and only half decayed at their base. Here in the eastern Sierra, with its arid summers and long, deep-freeze winters, decay proceeds at a very slow pace. You may also discover some four-foot lengths of cordwood, split and neatly stacked, but never hauled to the boiler before the mill closed. All of these probably date from Mammoth's mining days of 1878. The top of the dome is one of the best places to view the old Mammoth Mine's four levels of dumps and portals, across on the steep slope of Red Mountain (Mineral Hill). See Roadsides chapter.

Leaving the highway, the trail plunges into a forest of majestic red fir. The trail swings up to the top of Panorama Dome, passing a large snowbank on the shaded northeast slope that often lingers into August. Cold-adapted whitebark pine border the trail on this slope, in contrast to the Jeffrey pine that thrive on the sunnier, warmer west and south slopes.

Twin Lakes (8540') to the Bottomless Pit.

Bottomless Pit (9300'), moderate hike, three-quarter mile.
Trailhead. Cross the auto bridge to the campground on the far side of upper Twin Lakes. Follow the one-way road leading toward the mountain in a gradual left hand curve. About 200 yards from the bridge turn sharp left, walk toward the base of the steep slope, and look for the trail.

After leaving Twin Lakes Campground, the trail winds upward gradually through a forest of tall red firs and "creeping" aspen, bent from the weight of winter snows. It then switchbacks across the sunny, brush-covered base of Mammoth Mountain to the top of the lava cliffs, where the trail levels out. Use caution in approaching the edge, for loose pumice makes it unstable. At the end of this bench is a large opening, the Bottomless Pit, and at its bottom a natural lava arch—both probably formed by erosion and weathering. If you panic at heights, it is best not to continue farther for the trail on to Seven Lakes Point is narrow with sheer dropoffs. Beyond the Point, the trail swings around to the mountain's east slope and winds steeply upward another 1700 feet to Mammoth Mountain's broad, treeless summit. At the top, if you feel let down to find people on mountain bikes and riding the gondola, just remember that you had many more hours of glorious, immense and unparalleled views.

Mammoth Rock (8480') to Sherwin Creek Road (7840').

Easy hike, 2.5 miles one way.
Trailhead. Drive up the Lake Mary Road, turn left onto Old Mammoth Road. The trail begins at the third hairpin turn from the top.

You may feel as if you are in a low-flying airplane on this trail, as you start near Mammoth Rock and contour gradually down the side of the hill with views to the east and north all the way. The trail starts in the trees and ends in sagebrush and manzanita. If you do not have a car parked near Sherwin Creek Road, it is an additional .7 of a mile to Old Mammoth Road.

The Mammoth Lakes basin.

1-Twin Lakes	*5-Barney Lake*	*10-Lake George*
2-Lake Mary	*6-Barrett Lake*	*11-Horseshoe Lake*
3-Arrowhead Lake	*7-T. J. Lake*	*12-McLeod Lake*
4-Skelton Lake	*8-Crystal Lake*	*13-Mammoth Crest*
	9-Lake Mamie	

Cold Water Canyon (9050') to Arrowhead, Skelton and Barney Lakes, Duck Pass, Duck Lake and Purple Lake.

Arrowhead Lake (9660'), easy hike, 1.3 miles.
Barney Lake (10,200'), moderate hike, 2.5 miles.
Duck Lake (10,427'), strenuous hike, 5 miles.
Purple Lake (9900'), strenuous hike, 8 miles.
Trailhead. From the inlet of Lake Mary, drive to the end of the Cold Water Campground road. At the southern edge of the parking area, a large sign marks the beginning of the trail.

Cold Water canyon. Between the red-gold slopes of Red Mountain and the crags and late-lying snow fields of Mammoth Crest lies Cold Water canyon. The crest, curving around to the southeast, also forms the canyon's headwall.

Two streams carry the canyon's waters to Lake Mary—Mammoth Creek drains the string of lakes resting on the canyon floor; Cold Water Creek, fed by springs and snow fields, drains an alpine basin below Mammoth Crest. Small meadows are scattered along the streams. Lodgepole pine forests the lower slopes, hemlock and whitebark pine replace them on the colder, higher slopes. Three trails explore Cold Water canyon. The Duck Pass trail follows Mammoth Creek along the canyon floor, crosses the canyon's headwall at Duck Pass. The Heart Lake trail climbs the canyon's east wall a short distance up Red Mountain. The Sky Meadows trail follows Cold Water Creek to its headwaters below the great Blue Crag at the southern end of Mammoth Crest.

The Duck Pass trail is probably the busiest in the lakes basin, attracting fishermen and hikers out for the day as well as backpackers and pack trains heading for the high country. It is popular because the road end is high and Duck Pass at 10,790 feet is "low," as Sierra passes go. Beyond the first set of dusty zigzags, after the trail levels off, a short side trail drops down to Arrowhead Lake, which is partly obscured by the trees.

The trail continues another half-mile to Skelton Lake, named for the "Skelton boys," early prospectors who had a 3-stamp mill below the lake. From Skelton the trail climbs over several low ridges, worn round and smooth by glacier movement, and through mountain meadows to Barney Lake, which rests in a glacier-scoured basin as do all the lakes in this canyon. Barney is noted for its unusual jade-green color, possibly caused by algae in its waters. From Barney Lake the trail climbs steeply to Duck Pass (10,790'). In July clumps of alpine columbine—creamy white with tints of pink, blue, or yellow—bloom among the rocks. Alpine buttercups bloom at the edges of melting snowbanks that lie late in the shadows. As the trail crosses Duck Pass, you may glimpse a small lake across the canyon. This is Pika Lake, named after the *pika*, a small rabbitlike animal that is abundant among the large boulders surrounding the lake. As the trail rounds a bend, the full expanse of Duck Lake comes in view, stubby whitebark pine in the foreground, the Silver Divide and Sharkstooth Peak in the distance across Cascade Valley. Duck Lake's intense, deep blue color, appropriately compared to that of Crater Lake, is unusual among Sierra lakes. So deep and clear are its waters that the light from the sun is absorbed, except for the deep blue portion of the spectrum, which is reflected back. The setting of Duck Lake is typical of above-treeline country—barren, rough, lonely, with a wild beauty all its own. There are two stories about the lake's name, one claiming that at certain times the letters DUK are spelled in snow in the dark rocks of the Duck Lake-Purple Lake divide across the lake. The other claims that one fall a group of ducks landing on the lake to rest for the night were found next morning frozen in the newly formed ice.

From the outlet of Duck Lake the trail drops down to join the John Muir Trail, then rounds a granite slope and heads for Purple Lake. Many-hued rocks reflect into its water, giving it a purple tint at certain times of day. These are some of the ancient metamorphic rocks discussed in the geology chapter.

Cold Water Canyon (9050') to Heart Lake (9590').

Easy hike, about 1 mile.
Trailhead: From the inlet of Lake Mary, drive to the end of the Cold Water Campground road. From the eastern edge of the parking area, take the trail to the Mammoth Consolidated Mine exhibit and look for the Heart Lake trail heading uphill.

During June and July, this is a walk of wildflowers. Acres of grasses and wet-meadow flowers such as corn lilies are watered by Mammoth Creek. On the brush-covered slope above, forget-me-nots grow thirty inches high, next to small star-shaped scarlet red gilia and bright yellow mule ears with their two-foot-long woolly leaves. Hummingbirds frequent this colorful garden. Any time of year, however, this short hike offers a superlative view of the lakes basin and of the Ritter Range looming up behind Mammoth Pass. The first part of the trail follows an old mining road. From the upper part of the road there are magnificent views of the Mammoth basin. To the left is the entire expanse of Mammoth Crest, in the foreground is Lake Mary. In the distance, over Mammoth Pass, are Mount Ritter and Banner Peak; to the right, Mammoth Mountain. The road dwindles to a trail that contours along the mountainside to Heart Lake, pocketed on the steep slope of Red Mountain and named for its perfect heart shape.

Cold Water Canyon (9050') to Emerald Lake and Sky Meadows.

Emerald Lake (9440'), easy hike, three-quarter mile.
Sky Meadows (9700'), moderate hike, 2 miles.
Trailhead. See above. The trail begins at the southwest edge of the parking area near Cold Water Creek.

Alpine wildflowers (completely different from the dry-hillside flowers along the Heart Lake trail on the slope opposite), icy streams, and a tranquil forest of hemlock—all in an alpine setting at the base of the great Blue Crag and Mammoth Crest—the Sky Meadows trail is one of the best. The main trail climbs upward through a high-mountain mixed forest. To its right, a more scenic footpath follows Cold Water Creek upstream almost all the way to the lake. Along the stream you may see a kingfisher flying or a dark gray bird, the dipper, bobbing up and down on the rocks in the cascades. Along the cool stream, wildflowers grow tall and lush—delicate saxifrage, lupine two feet high, tiger lilies and monkshood three feet high.

Emerald is a deep green lake nestled in trees, the sheer cliffs of Mammoth Crest looming behind it. Many rare and lovely mountain flowers bloom during late July and August in the meadows at the lake's inlet. Near the inlet the trail forks. The left fork climbs the hill and a dim trail eventually leads to Skelton Lake. The right fork crosses a small creek and then follows the bank of a larger creek a short distance to Gentian Meadow, a very small meadow at the juncture of two small streams. In late summer, after the snows that lie late in this north-facing glen have melted, this is a choice spot to see alpine flowers—alpine shooting stars just after the snow is gone, red heather and bog laurel in late July, and in late August thousands of blue gentian.

From the meadow, the trail veers right up over a low ridge. Though the trail is less distinct from here on, if you are watchful you will find it. The trail continues upward past the cascades of Cold Water Creek to Sky Meadows, an open area of short grass that lies at the base of the great Blue Crag, the local name for the massive peak above Sky Meadows. The meadows and the surrounding rocky slopes are one of the few truly alpine areas in the Mammoth basin. Snow fields that linger into August, ample water all summer, fertile stable soil, and protection from winds make this protected hollow an ideal habitat for many plants rarely found elsewhere. (In early sum-

mer carry insect repellent; mosquitoes as well as flowers thrive in dampness.) From early August until the snow flies, this is a flower garden in
miniature, for—typically alpine—the flowers are tiny. In August elephant
head and purplish-red paintbrush cover the ground, in September blue and
white gentian. On the rocky slopes above, the first to bloom are the Sierra
primrose, followed by white columbine and stonecrop.

Lake George (9008') to Barrett Lake and T. J. Lake.

Barrett Lake (9210'), easy hike, one-quarter mile.
T. J. Lake (9260'), easy hike, one-half mile.
Trailhead. The outlet of Lake George.

After crossing the outlet of Lake George, follow the lakeshore about a hundred yards until you see a trail branching left, uphill. Follow it through a
fine stand of mountain hemlock to Barrett Lake, named for early forester
Lou Barrett. The trail to T. J. goes along the west shore of Barrett a short
distance and then over a small ridge to the lake. T. J. are the initials of Tom
Jones, one of the first supervisors of the Inyo National Forest. Through red
heather and Labrador tea, a footpath follows the east shore of T. J. Lake to
its upper end, where wildflowers are abundant during the summer. Sure-
footed hikers may prefer to make a loop trip from the outlet of T. J. to Lake
George by taking the footpath along the creek's cascades. Along the shore
of Lake George there are a number of springs that are ringed with beautiful
flower displays in mid-summer.

Lake George (9008') to Crystal Lake, Mammoth Crest, Deer Lakes.

Crystal Lake (9640'), moderate hike, 1.5 miles.
Mammoth Crest (10,640'), strenuous hike, 3 miles.
Deer Lakes (10,660'), strenuous hike, 6 miles.
Trailhead. Park at Lake George. The trail begins on the north side of the paved road.

Spectacular views every step of the way are yours on this trip to Mammoth
Crest. From the ridge separating Lake George and Horseshoe Lake, the
trail zigzags up through fine stands of mountain hemlock. There are striking
views down into the blue depths of Lake George and across the canyon to
Red Mountain. The trail to Crystal Lake, which lies in a glacial cirque at
the base of Crystal Crag, branches off to the left.

To reach Mammoth Crest continue on the main trail, each switchback
bringing wider views in all directions. The rock underfoot suddenly
changes from whitish granite to deep-red volcanic cinder whose eroded
outcrops partly outline an old crater. On the crest a quarter-mile south of
the southernmost cinders, lies a patch of lava older than the cinders. Similar lava (3.1 million years old) on Red Mountain to the east suggests that
the land surface in between sloped gently and that the two widely separated patches are remnants of a once-continuous flow. Since that eruption
Mammoth and Cold Water creeks, aided by the glaciers, have excavated

the canyon now separating Red Mountain from Mammoth Crest.

The trail forks, the left fork crossing the shallow basin which is a volcanic crater, the right fork climbing a ridge of red cinder, from which there is a magnificent view of the Sierra, from the Silver Divide north to the Ritter Range. From the ridge, circle south around the rim of the basin mentioned above. After the two forks rejoin, the trail heads south along the gently sloping top of Mammoth Crest. Viewed from the crest itself, the contrast between the vertical east-facing cliffs and the gentle west-sloping surface is particularly striking. Such contrasts are not uncommon in the high country. Since the leeward, shady side of a ridge favors the accumulation of snow, during the Ice Age glaciers grew largest there and did their most extensive cutting on the slopes most protected from sun and winds, usually the east and north slopes.

Small clumps of wind-torn, dwarfed whitebark pine and occasional lodgepole grow on the crest. Severe weather and exposure account for their low, spreading growth forms. The wind, nearly always blowing, nips the growing tips of the branches on the windward side, producing these lopsided forms. Branches closest to the ground grow most successfully because they are most protected from the winds' blasts, especially in winter when drifting snow covers them. Many cushion-type alpine plants grow along the crest, such as tiny lupines and sulfur flowers. Watch along the trail for granite slabs with shallow, circular cavities. These are neither streambed potholes nor Indian grinding holes. They are formed by water collecting in small depressions in the rock and dissolving some of the minerals, thus enlarging the depression and allowing more water to collect. The shallow cavity resulting is known as a *weather pit*, and may be one to three feet in diameter though only a few inches deep. They are not uncommon in granitic rock.

From the main trail several short side trails branch to the east, leading to the edge of the crest where there are sensational views down to the Mammoth Lakes. The trail continues along the crest until it descends to Deer Lakes. The lower lake is bordered by alpine meadows where you will find dwarf willows only three or four inches high, flaunting catkins almost as large as those of their 10-foot brothers.

Unfortunately many maps show a trail from Deer Lakes to the John Muir Trail. This is a serious error. The trail has not been maintained for more than twenty years and is no longer recognizable.

Horseshoe Lake (8950') to McLeod Lake, Mammoth Pass, Reds Meadow.

McLeod Lake (9250'), easy hike, one-half mile.
Mammoth Pass (9290'), easy hike, 1 mile.
Reds Meadow (7600'), moderate hike if one-way, 4 miles.
Trailhead. Western edge of the Horseshoe Lake parking area.

This trail follows the general route of the historic Fresno Flats Toll Trail, an historic route from the west. Pack trains from Fresno Flats (Oakhurst) brought passengers and supplies to the miners at the Mammoth Mines. Today this portion of the old trail is little used, for most people prefer to drive to Reds Meadow. However, it is a pleasant, leisurely trip through a virgin forest of huge red fir trees, downhill all the way from Mammoth Pass, if you ride the shuttle bus back.

The first part of this trail is steep, sunny and in deep pumice, but there is shade here and there from the lodgepole and mountain hemlock. Between Horseshoe and Mammoth Pass, trails are confusing, for there are old trails, new trails, horse trails, foot paths and pipelines. However, most lead to McLeod Lake, which is where you want to go for an important junction. The lake is named for an early forest ranger of Reds Meadow, Malcolm McLeod; the spelling McCloud and McCleod are both incorrect. Its pumice beach is inviting, but since the lake provides drinking water for resorts and campgrounds, bathing is not permitted.

Just beyond the outlet of McLeod Lake, the Mammoth Pass trail branches to the right, leading through a lodgepole pine forest to the broad saddle between Mammoth Mountain and Mammoth Crest known as Mammoth Pass. From the pass, the trail swings downhill. Nearing Reds Meadow, trails can again be confusing. If you're in doubt where you are, generally take right forks and you will come out near Reds Meadow Campground.

Horseshoe Lake (8950') to Crater Meadows and the Red Cones.

Crater Meadows (8800'), moderate hike, 3.5 miles.
Trailhead. Western edge of the Horseshoe Lake parking area.

Go to the outlet of McLeod Lake as described above. At the lake take the trail which follows along its north shore, Mammoth Crest's granitic cliffs rising almost vertically across the lake. The trail swings left and contours along the slope through a forest of huge, stately red fir. Depending which branch of the trail you may have taken (trails are just too complicated to explain; see a map) you will find yourself in either upper or lower Crater Meadow, incredible flower gardens all summer long. Here Crater Creek rises from springs. To the right are two perfectly shaped cinder cones. (For detail about the cones, see "Reds Meadow to Crater Meadows...." below.)

Minaret Summit Ridge (9240') north along the Sierra Crest.

Easy hike, 1–2 miles, or as far as you want to go.
San Joaquin Mountain (11,600'), strenuous hike, about 7 miles.
Trailhead. At Minaret Summit, turn right and park at the vista point.

One sublime view follows another every step of the way north along the Sierra crest. Yes, this is the Sierra crest, even though the snow-plastered Ritter Range opposite is 1500 feet higher and far more imposing. The crest divides the waters flowing east into the Owens River from those flowing west to the Pacific. A panoramic view of Sierra peaks stretches more than 35 miles, from pyramid-shaped Mount Lyell on the northwest skyline to Kaiser Crest far to the southwest. Eastward, beyond the bulky, odd-shaped volcanic domes and flows, views extend to the White Mountains on the Nevada border, fifty miles away. Below is the full length of the Middle Fork canyon, from its headwall at Agnew Pass south to its junction with Fish Creek, where the river turns abruptly west. Most dramatic of all, across the deep canyon are close-up views of the jagged Minarets, Mount Ritter and Banner.

Besides the grand views, this is one of the easier hikes. A great way to start this trip is to first walk the self-guiding Minaret Vista Discovery Trail, a short loop that will acquaint you with some of the plant and animal creatures that live here. It begins near the vista point, where you can also identify the peaks you will be looking at the rest of the day.

Leave the vista point, walk north, and you are on your way, to walk as far as you please. You can join the jeep road that trends generally north along the crest for 2 miles to Hill 10,255, just south of Deadman Pass. As you gain altitude, to the southeast you can see Mammoth, Bloody, and Red Slate Mountains; to the north, San Joaquin Mountain. From mid-July to early August, the pumice covering the ridge is carpeted with small purple lupine, yellow buckwheat, tiny magenta mimulus and many other dwarf flowers. Mountain bluebirds and raucous Clark's nutcrackers are common; you may sight a Sierra hare or a golden eagle. Several large snowbanks last until late July. Clumps of whitebark pine make fine shelters for picnic lunches. Cold winds often sweep over the ridge; be sure to carry a wind jacket, along with some drinking water.

Ahead, the crest trends northwest toward Two Teats; San Joaquin Mountain, although higher, is hidden behind. Beyond Deadman Pass the climb steepens. Staying high on the crest, however, despite the ups and downs, is easier than contouring around, for the slopes are rubbly unstable pumice.

Middle Fork of the San Joaquin River

Born of the snow fields flanking Banner Peak, the Middle Fork of the San Joaquin tumbles out of Thousand Island Lake to begin its run through the broad, flat-bottomed canyon that lies between the Ritter Range and the Sierra Crest. Gathering the waters of both slopes—from the springs below San Joaquin Mountain and Mammoth Crest, from the streams draining the alpine lake basins below Mount Ritter, the Minarets and Iron Mountain—it flows gently south for fifteen miles until it abruptly turns right and disappears into the deep gorge it has cut through the western Sierra slope. Well-watered meadows of wildflowers are scattered along the canyon's length, while open pine and fir forests cover its lower slopes. Crowning the canyon walls on the west and dwarfing the lower, rounded Sierra crest opposite, the dark, lofty Ritter Range peaks tower 5500 feet above the canyon floor.

Within this magnificent canyon, there is an extraordinary concentration of superbly scenic trails: the John Muir, the High Trail, the Shadow and Minaret Creek trails, and the trails along Mammoth Crest and on Minaret Summit ridge. On trails leading from Reds Meadow or the Postpile, you may notice scars from the 8000-acre Rainbow Fire of 1992 (named after Rainbow Falls). Only heroic efforts by more than a thousand fire fighters kept the fire from spreading westward to the ski area and the town of Mammoth. Notice how quickly plants are erasing the scars; two months after the fire, some plants were already sprouting new growth.

Reds Meadow (7600') to Crater Meadow and the Red Cones (8800').

Moderate hike, 3 miles.
Trailhead. Parking area near the end of the Reds Meadow road.

This is the old route of the John Muir Trail. You may still find it so marked on some maps. The trail climbs gradually but steadily through a virgin red fir forest. Some of the trees are more than fifteen feet around. Compared to some forests, this is a "messy" one—many splintered snags still standing and dead limbs littering the ground. Firs are more subject to rot than the pines; hence they break in many pieces, in contrast to the pines which usually fall as a unit, roots and all. This broken wood, along with decaying leaves, needles, cones, and grass, is not wasted; it will become an important part of the new soil now forming and will provide nourishment for future generations of trees.

At Crater Meadow, to the right of the trail, is the first of the Red Cones, excellent examples of small volcanic cinder cones. They are symmetrical, have small craters near their summits, and are composed of reddish brown porous lava cinders that were blown out of a now inactive vent. A rubbly lava flow extends west down the slope and appears to have been extruded from near the base of the cones. Crater Meadow is an extensive flower garden all summer long. The slope east of Reds Meadow seems to be a huge sponge, a natural underground reservoir for rain and melting snow water. Even in late summer there is abundant water for dozens of springs, streams and small meadows.

At Upper Crater Meadow, you will meet the John Muir Trail/Pacific Crest Trail coming from Reds Meadow on a different route. If you make a loop trip by returning on this route, you can meet the shuttle bus at the Rainbow Falls trailhead or you can hike farther and cross the bridge over the San Joaquin at the Devils Postpile.

Some editions of the topographic map show the Muir Trail following Deer Creek to Deer Lakes. This is a serious error. The Muir Trail *crosses* Deer Creek and heads for Purple Lake.

Reds Meadow (7600') to Crater Creek, Fish Creek, Island Crossing.

Crater Creek Crossing (6800'), moderate hike, 3 miles.
Island Crossing (6320'), strenuous hike, 8 miles.
Trailhead. The Rainbow Falls Trailhead parking area, near the end of the Reds Meadow road.

This is the only trail in the area that is *down* all the way going, and *up* all the way coming back—always a discouraging situation, made even more so by the very dusty pumice trail and the mid-summer heat at these relatively low altitudes. The trail passes the Rainbow Falls turnoff, and meets Crater Creek at the bottom of a cool ravine lush with ferns, alders and large aspens. The portion of the trail from here to the creek's crossing deserves to be enjoyed leisurely. Left of the trail, Crater Creek slides over clean slabs of granite. From the top of a small ridge just to the right of the trail are good views of the Middle Fork canyon, which here is composed of massive granitic walls and ridges, all rounded and smoothed by the tremendous glaciers that once filled it. This area is unlike any other described in this book; it is more like the Yosemite high country.

Beyond Crater Creek, carry a snake-bite kit, for rattlesnakes are not uncommon. Watch for them particularly near wet or damp places. Be duly but not *un*duly cautious; they are far less dangerous than freeway traffic.

The trail crosses several small streams, then climbs up out of the trees; here, before it swings left (E) into Fish Valley, it passes some outstanding viewpoints a few yards to the right (W) of the trail. The deep gash of Fish Valley comes in from the left, the broad canyon of the Middle Fork from the right; beyond their junction is the impassable gorge through which the Middle Fork of the San Joaquin flows west. From the rim of Fish Valley, the trail drops down steeply to Fish Creek and then follows it upstream into Cascade Valley. Beyond the first crossing at Fish Creek Hot Springs is a camp known as "Iva Bell Camp." It is named after Iva Bell Clark, whose parents had packed in to the springs to relieve Mr. Clark's arthritis. Iva Bell was born unexpectedly in July 1936, greatly surprising both parents. Neither suspected that a child was the cause of Mrs. Clark's "tumor." Ten days later, mother and child were packed out safely to Reds Meadow.

Devils Postpile (7559') to King Creek and Fern Lake.

King Creek (7607'), moderate hike, 2.5 miles.
Fern Lake (8800'), strenuous hike, 7 miles.
Summit Meadow (9020'), strenuous hike, 7 miles.
Trailhead. Parking area, Devils Postpile National Monument.

We know of a horse that always balked when started on this trail! She knew what was coming—ankle-deep pumice all the way and little shade beyond King Creek. Be sure to start before sun-up—or roast on the way. Take the path crossing the meadow south of the parking area, turn right and cross the bridge over the San Joaquin River. A quarter-mile beyond, the trail to Summit Meadow branches left. It climbs a granite hump (8000'), then drops down to the wide clear stream of King Creek. The grind up the south side of Snow Canyon begins just beyond the creek. This is a part of the old Fresno Flats Trail, (also known as the French Trail, after the man who built it) one of the oldest trails crossing the Sierra. First built as a toll trail to serve the Mammoth Mines in the late 1870s, it was later used by prospectors, stockmen and sheepherders. The present trail follows much the same route as the old one, connecting Reds Meadow with Clover Meadow, a road end on the Sierra's west slope twenty miles away by trail.

About 6 miles from the Devils Postpile there is a trail junction. The trail straight ahead goes to Fern Lake, climbing a bit and crossing two marshy springs. Fern Lake is a small alpine lake encircled by steep cliffs and a timbered flat bench. The trail to the left goes to Summit Meadow, an expanse of green at the very top of a broad ridge, that comes as a pleasant surprise. Until 1963 the trail was used as a sheep trail. In early summer, sheep from the western foothills were driven across the North Fork of the San Joaquin River at Sheep Crossing, up to 77 Corral and then to Summit Meadow. In earlier years the sheep went on to Reds and Agnew Meadows for summer pasture. However, grazing has been curtailed until now there is none at all this side of the North Fork. Conflicts between sheep and wildlife and recreation, as well as damage to meadows and young trees account for this change. Unfortunately 77 Corral, named for the dry summer of 1877 when it was one of the places where feed was available, has lost its historic name. On the maps today it is "Corral Meadow."

Devils Postpile (7559') to Beck Cabin, Superior Lake, Beck Lakes.

Beck Cabin (9100'), strenuous hike, 6 miles.
Superior Lake (9370'), strenuous hike, 7 miles.
Beck Lakes (9840'), strenuous hike, 8 miles.
Trailhead. Parking area, Devils Postpile National Monument.

Five miles of walking through loose pumice is the price of enjoying the rugged high-country near Iron Mountain and the many lakes and streams of the King Creek drainage. Start early, before the sun comes over Mammoth Crest, for the pumice trail is far more pleasant in the cool of the morning than later when the sun beats down through the sparse forest.

Follow the path through the meadow south of the parking area, turn right at the trail junction and cross the bridge over the San Joaquin River. Proceed along the Minaret Lake trail. Just before reaching Minaret Creek, the trail to Beck Lakes branches left. It climbs steadily to almost 9500 feet, drops down a bit, then rounds a corner where the whole King Creek basin suddenly comes into view. Iron Mountain, dominating the steep ridge circling the basin, was named for a weathered iron-ore outcrop. Subsequent diamond drilling showed that the quantity of high-grade ore is small. A half-mile farther stands a log cabin built many years ago by prospector John Beck. The trail to Superior Lake branches off to the right (W) near the cabin and follows a stream all the way to Beck Lakes. Above Superior the trail is less distinct, though it is ducked (marked with cairns) most of the way. You need to scramble a bit to reach the upper end of the first lake; from there it is an easy walk to the higher lake.

From Beck Cabin it is possible to loop back to the Postpile by taking the little used trail that heads south. Near Fern Lake it connects with the well-defined trail leading to the Postpile. This is a very strenuous trip, about a twenty-mile loop if you make the side trip to Beck Lakes, and should be attempted only by experienced travelers with a good map. The trail is rocky and has not been maintained for many years. It is further confused by fishermen's trails, some branching off left into Snow Canyon, some right to the high lakes.

Devils Postpile (7559') to Holcomb Lake and Ashley Lake.

Holcomb Lake (9500'), strenuous hike, 9 miles.
Ashley Lake (9600'), strenuous hike, 9 miles.
Trailhead. Parking area, Devils Postpile National Monument.

Go to Beck Cabin as described in the preceding trail. Do not turn right (W) to Beck Lakes, but stay on the main trail for about another half-mile. Then turn right, cross King Creek, and follow it upstream. The stream's right fork goes to Holcomb Lake, its left to Ashley. Both lakes are in barren but spectacular country, Ashley being just below the glacier of Iron Mountain.

Devils Postpile (7559') to Soda Springs and Minaret Falls (7650').

Easy hike, 1 mile.
Trailhead. Parking area, Devils Postpile National Monument.

Take the wide path through the meadow, turn right at the trail junction and cross the bridge over the San Joaquin River. Just beyond the bridge, a few steps off the trail, several soda springs bubble forth from a gravel bar in the river. (If you can't find the springs, they may be hidden by high water.) Such springs are not uncommon in areas of recent volcanic activity. Molten magma, cooling far below the earth's surface, may give off gases for thousands of years. Carbon dioxide, often one of the last to be given off, may be absorbed by spring water, thus producing the carbonated water of a soda spring.

From Soda Springs proceed along the west side of the large meadow on a well-defined trail. (This is the Pacific Crest Trail, heading for Agnew Meadows.) It leads generally upstream along the west bank of the river, then swings left through the forest to the base of Minaret Falls. In June and July this foaming cascade may be more than a hundred feet wide. In late summer, the falls are reduced to several streams, flowers growing abundantly among the rocks between them. The falls were created during the Ice Age by glaciers. As the enormous Middle Fork glacier scoured out its canyon, the smaller tributary glacier in Minaret Canyon cut its valley at a slower rate. As a result, when the glaciers melted away, the mouth of Minaret Creek's valley was several hundred feet above the main canyon. Such a valley is called a "hanging valley."

Devils Postpile (7559') to Johnston Lake and Minaret Lake.

Johnston Lake (8100'), moderate hike, 2 miles.
Minaret Mine (10,000'), strenuous hike, 8 miles.
Minaret Lake (9800') strenuous hike, 8 miles.
Trailhead. Parking area, Devils Postpile National Monument.

Take the path across the meadow south of the parking area, turn right and cross the bridge over the San Joaquin River. Proceed through deep pumice along the well-marked Minaret Lake trail to Minaret Creek, Johnston Lake and Johnston Meadow—lush with varied wildflowers, including the rare giant shooting star. Above Johnston Lake, named for a promoter of the old Minaret Mine, much of the present trail follows the old mining road—recognizable by its width and by the young lodgepole (4–8 feet high) that have sprouted up in the roadbed since the mine closed in 1930. Several miles above Johnston Lake, the trail leaves dense forest and follows the rushing, noisy cascade of Minaret Creek a short way.

To reach the Minaret Mine, worked 1928–30, watch for the mining road turning off to the right and follow it to the mine. In winter, the dozen men working at the mine were completely dependent on the Mammoth dog teams for supplies, mail and transportation. Though the 20-mile trip usually took two days, on one emergency run to rescue a badly burned miner, a team made it from Old Mammoth to the mine in the record time of four and a half hours.

Nearing the dramatic spires of the Minarets, beyond the mine junction, the trail passes through a forest of unusually large mountain hemlock and lodgepole pine and climbs on up to deep, clear Minaret Lake, cupped in a rock basin at the very base of Clyde Minaret. Alpine wildflowers abound above the lake, where the ground is saturated with melting snow water. From the far (NW) shore of Minaret Lake, a faint, steep trail (the last pitch requires a little rock climbing) ascends to Cecile or Upper Iceberg Lake (10,300').

Devils Postpile to Trinity, Castle, Vivian and Rosalie Lakes.

Strenuous hikes. Hikers wanting to reach these lakes are advised to start at Agnew Meadows rather than the Postpile, in order to avoid 3.5 miles of uphill hiking in deep pumice above the Postpile. See below, "Agnew Meadows to Rosalie and Vivian Lakes."

Devils Postpile (7559') to Lake Olaine (8080').

Easy hike, 5 miles one way.
Trailhead. Parking area, Devils Postpile National Monument. Or pick up the trail at the bridge at Upper Soda Springs Campground; from there it is 3 miles to Lake Olaine.

Before the John Muir Trail from the Postpile to Shadow Creek was routed by Vivian and Rosalie lakes, it followed the San Joaquin River and is so marked on old maps. Cross to the river's west bank at the Postpile and there pick up the Pacific Crest Trail and head north. Above Upper Soda Springs Campground, the trail follows the river closely, which here flows quietly in its deep canyon past meadows and gravel beaches and through small rock gorges. At Lake Olaine, named for Charles Olaine who prospected here around 1910, there are bright yellow pond lilies. As an alternative to hiking the river trail back to the Postpile, take the trail to Agnew Meadows that branches east about half a mile below Lake Olaine and there catch the shuttle bus.

Sotcher Lake Nature Trail (7680').

Easy hike, 1.3 mile loop.
Trailhead. Sotcher Lake parking area, off the Reds Meadow Road.

This nature trail is a marvelous introduction to the variety and the wonders of the Middle Fork canyon.

Agnew Meadows (8335') to Shadow Lake, Lake Ediza, and Iceberg Lake.

Shadow Lake (8750'), moderate hike, 3 miles.
Lake Ediza (9300'), strenuous hike, 6 miles.
Iceberg Lake (9800'), strenuous hike, 7 miles.
Trailhead. From the pack station go north to the second large parking area. You'll find the trail skirting the south side of the meadow.

Shadow Lake is considered by many one of the jewels of the Sierra, particularly because of its setting below the peaks of the Ritter Range. A favorite spot for photographers is the outlet of the lake, across the stream from the trail, where the view west is especially striking.

From Agnew Meadows, the trail drops 400 feet to the San Joaquin River, then remains almost level to the river crossing. Along the way it passes Lake Olaine, where you may find brilliant yellow pond lilies and where you may hear the low *whoomp* of grouse in early summer. From the bridge crossing the Middle Fork, the trail zigzags up a hot, dry slope. Watch for the old wind-battered juniper trees along the way, their bark shining red-golden in the early morning sun, and notice the fine view back toward Mammoth Mountain. Just below Shadow Lake there is a good viewpoint to see Shadow Creek's roaring falls.

From the upper end of Shadow Lake, the trail follows Shadow Creek to Lake Ediza, often the base camp site for mountain climbers who come to scale the peaks of the Minarets. If you wander cross-country up the ridges, you may wonder about the trenches and cores and foundations that you come across. As far as we know, David Nidever was the first to locate claims in this canyon, in the early 1900s. He built a log cabin at Cabin Lake and another about half a mile below Lake Ediza.

This cabin was headquarters in 1956 for extensive mining exploration by the Climax Molybdenum Company. Though all the heavy equipment necessary for diamond drilling was brought in, there is no road scar destroying the wild beauty of Shadow Creek as there is in Laurel Canyon. Both of these canyons were classified as wilderness by the Forest Service because of their natural beauty and their outstanding wilderness quality. To preserve their primitive character, commercial development and roads are prohibited. Yet by law any miner with a legitimate claim has the legal right to build a road on National Forest land, even if it is a Wilderness Area. Often the claim proves to be of little value and all is abandoned—lumber, pipes and empty oil drums left strewn on the slopes, the landscape bearing the scar for fifty years or more. Yet at Shadow Creek, where deposits proved to be non-commercial, the process of exploration destroyed none of the canyon's wildness. The supplies for the large operation were taken in by helicopter and mule, and neither miner nor wilderness was the loser.

To reach Iceberg Lake, named for the ice sometimes still floating on its surface in late summer, walk around the east side of Lake Ediza and take the first path to the left that goes uphill. This is one of the best places to see alpine plants; the meadows support a cover of dwarf, brilliantly colored alpine flowers. Across the lake and below the Minarets are some small glaciers. Though these may look like snowfields, they are masses of glacial ice—dirty gray on top, bluish within—moving slowly downward and cracking open into crevasses where they flow over cliffs. Upper Iceberg Lake (also called Cecile) lies 500 feet above. A dim path crosses the steep talus slope above Iceberg Lake and then follows up the stream dropping out of Upper Iceberg.

Agnew Meadows (8335') to Rosalie Lake and Devils Postpile.

Rosalie Lake (9350'), strenuous hike, 5.5 miles.
Gladys Lake (9600'),strenuous hike, 6 miles.
Devils Postpile (7559'), strenuous hike, 12 miles one way.
Trailhead. Same as for previous trail and proceed to Shadow Lake.

Rosalie, Gladys, Vivian, Lois, Emily, Castle and a number of ponds and smaller lakes are in a little world of their own high on the broad shoulder of Volcanic Ridge, named for the old recrystallized volcanic rocks composing it. Rounded rock slopes or dense forest completely encircle the lakes; to the west they are walled in by somber cliffs.

At the inlet of Shadow Lake, cross the creek and follow the John Muir Trail as it switchbacks up the steep, densely forested north-facing slope above.

From the grass-rimmed lakes of the Trinity group, a side trail leads to Castle Lake, about half a mile up a steep 700-foot slope. The Muir Trail zigzags down to Minaret Creek in the canyon below. The two slopes of Volcanic Ridge support different kinds of trees—hemlocks and western white pine on the shaded Shadow Creek side, red fir on the sunny Minaret Creek side and lodgepole on both. The trail crosses Minaret Creek over a large log and continues on to the Postpile, where you can pick up the shuttle bus.

Agnew Meadows (8335') to Thousand Island Lake (9834').

Strenuous hike, 9 miles.

Thousand Island Lake, with its small tree-studded islands, lies in a broad rock basin dominated by massive Banner Peak. Bare rock ridges, rounded and worn low by ancient masses of grinding, moving ice, enclose the lake. Scratches on the rock are so well preserved that it is easy to trace the direction of the glacier's movement. This windswept, harshly beautiful basin is wonderful for cross-country hiking. The rock is hard and smooth, the forest sparse, and small streams and ponds more numerous that you might expect. In the alpine meadows at the lake's inlet, flowers often bloom until late September.

The three routes from Agnew Meadows to Thousand Island Lake are about the same length but differ markedly in scenic beauty. The river trail is the easiest and most gradual, but it provides none of the grand views of the other two. The High Trail offers one striking view after another across the Middle Fork canyon to the lofty Ritter Range peaks. The most strenuous route, which follows the Shadow Creek and then the John Muir trails, traverses the forests and the three magnificent lake basins lying just below Mount Ritter and Banner Peak. For a superlative— though very strenuous—loop trip, start off on the Shadow Creek trail and return by the High Trail.

Trailhead. From the pack station go north to the second large parking area. You'll find the trail skirting the south side of the meadow.

Via the river trail. This section of the river trail could better be called the "canyon trail," for though it is often within sound of the river, seldom is it within sight of it. However, to see its foaming cascades, small waterfalls and gorges, you need make only small detours to the river's banks. From Agnew Meadows, follow the trail down to the bottom of the canyon, where it joins the river trail coming from Reds Meadow. The river trail continues leisurely on, following close to the infant Middle Fork and finally climbing up the slope to meet the High Trail swinging in from Agnew Meadows. Turn left and proceed to the inlet of Thousand Island Lake.

Via the High Trail (the Pacific Crest Trail). Whatever superlatives you have in your vocabulary, the High Trail deserves them all. Views of the glacier-spangled Ritter Range are yours every step of the way. Sensational displays of wildflowers—shoulder-high monkshood, delphinium and tiger lilies—occur along the numerous streams that cross the trail. High on the slopes above, at the contact between a thick layer of porous lava and underlying dense metamorphic rock, rainwater and snowmelt stored in the lava gush forth. Watered by these springs throughout the summer, aspen, willow, grasses and flowers grow luxuriantly, covering hundreds of acres. With feed and water abundant, animal life is also abundant. You may come upon quail, hummingbirds, hawks, deer, nutcrackers and chickadees. From early summer to late fall, the scenery is breathtaking. In early summer, the Ritter peaks sparkle with snow. Mid-summer, the flowers are most extravagant. In fall great splashes of golden aspen brighten the slope of San Joaquin Mountain.

Pick up the trail just north of the pack station. It climbs the slope in long, gradual switchbacks. Just before the trail stops climbing, about 3 miles from Agnew Meadows, as you round a rocky slope and the trees on the left thin out, a viewpoint a few yards off the trail is an essential stop. If you do not wish to make the strenuous hike to Thousand Island, do come at least as far as this spectacular Shadow Lake viewpoint. You can hear the roar of Shadow Creek falls barely a mile away and you can see the length of Shadow Lake, small below the looming summits and blue-white glaciers of the Minarets, Mount Ritter and Banner Peak.

The trail stays high as it contours along the slope, expanses of sagebrush alternating with flower-filled ravines. If you wander west of the trail now and then, you will discover other fine viewpoints. You may also come upon prospect pits and caved-in mine portals; this is one of the slopes that was searched again and again for the Lost Cement Mine. Near Badger Lakes several other trails heading for Thousand Island Lake—one coming up the river, two coming over the divide from Rush Creek—join the High Trail.

Via the Shadow Creek trail, the Muir Trail and Garnet Lake. Go to Shadow Lake. See above, "Agnew Meadows to Shadow Lake...." About a mile above Shadow Lake, turn right and follow the Muir Trail. At the top of the 1300-foot ridge separating Shadow and Garnet lakes, before dropping down to Garnet Lake, leave the trail for a few minutes to climb one of the higher points a few hundred yards off the trail. There are sweeping views not only of the Ritter Range, but also of peaks far to the south. Possibly Garnet Lake was named for the small garnet crystals that are locally abundant. In rocks north of the lake fossil clams were found and dated as having lived 190,000,000 years ago. From the lake, the trail climbs over the 500-foot ridge separating Garnet and Thousand Island lakes.

Agnew Meadows (8335') to Agnew Pass, Clark Lakes and Silver Lake.

Agnew Pass (9900'), strenuous hike, 5.5 miles.
Clark Lakes (9850'), strenuous hike, 6 miles.
Silver Lake (7223'), very strenuous hike, 14 miles total.
Trailhead. Follow the directions given above for the High Trail.

Proceed along the High Trail for about 5 miles, until the trail leading to Agnew Pass forks to the right. A short, steep climb leads to Agnew Pass, Summit Lake, and the meadows around the Clark Lakes. Take the time to go a few yards to the left of the trail for spacious views to the north and west—Gem Lake and the large drainage basin of Rush Creek, with towering Mount Lyell (13,114') at its head. The famous Lyell glacier, second largest in the Sierra, is on the mountain's north slope and hence not visible from here.

The loop trip to Silver Lake is a very strenuous trip. It is downhill all the way from Agnew Pass, which can be harder on the knees than going uphill. (Arrange to have a car waiting for you; there is no shuttle bus at Silver Lake.) The trail to Silver goes from the Clark Lakes to Rush Meadows west of Gem Lake. There you join the main trail following Rush Creek down the canyon. An old trail, very steep and not maintained, also goes to Silver Lake via Spooky Meadow and Agnew Lake.

Agnew Meadows (8335') to Carson Peak and San Joaquin Mountain.

Carson Peak (10,909'), strenuous hike, 7.5 miles.
San Joaquin Mountain (11,600'), strenuous hike, 8.5 miles.
Trailhead. To reach Agnew Pass, follow the directions in the preceding trail. Be sure to carry water and a wind jacket on this trip.

This is the best-defined "trail" to these two mountains. Poor as it is, the others shown on some maps (coming from Yost Lake or Deadman Creek) are much worse, impossible to follow. From Agnew Pass, a good trail climbs southeast about a mile to a high pumice flat, then peters out. Not enough people come to this wind-swept pumice country to keep a trail trampled. From the pumice flat turn left (N) and walk up the gentle slope to Carson Peak, the highest point on a cliff that rises 3500 feet above Silver Lake. To reach San Joaquin Mountain turn right and walk southeast across the pumice flat, then circle around to its gentle, easily-climbed northeast slope. The view is unequalled anywhere in the area. There is a full-circle panorama—west to the Ritter Range, north to Koip and Parker peaks, east across domes, craters, lava cliffs and miles of pumice to the White Mountains, and south to the Silver Divide.

June Lake

Four large lakes, one of them named June, lie in a broad canyon whose general area is known as June Lake. Carson Peak (10,909'), whose sheer cliffs rise south of Silver Lake, dominates the entire canyon. A classic U-shaped glacial canyon, its ridges and peaks rise abruptly two to four thousand feet above the canyon floor; consequently, all trails out of the canyon are steep. Rush Creek, which drops down from an upper valley and empties into Silver Lake, drains an immense basin with fifteen streams and their tributaries, fifteen good-sized lakes and dozens of small ones. After you make the 1300-foot climb to Rush Creek's upper basin and you reach the first lake, Agnew, you can take a deep breath and wander Rush Creek's gentle valley for five miles—unless you decide to hike the side trails to some of the higher lakes. Rush Creek will surprise you with its small meadows, pocketed among rocks and cliffs where you never would expect them.

Fern Creek (7350') to Fern Creek Falls and Fern Lake.

Fern Creek Falls (8080'), moderate hike, 1 mile.
Fern Lake (8900'), strenuous hike, 1.5 miles.
Trailhead. From Gull Lake drive west; 1.3 miles past the June Mountain Ski Area look for a gravel road on the left and park. Walk uphill and at the Tee in the road go right. The trail goes steeply uphill through a grove of large aspen.

Fern Lake rests in a small, steep-sided cirque below the north slope of San Joaquin Mountain and the precipitous east face of Carson Peak. This short but steep hike is a good introduction to the trees of the eastern Sierra. You will encounter nine of the ten trees described in the tree chapter. The trail climbs gradually through a grove of large aspen—brightened by silvery-leaved lupine, scarlet gilia and pennyroyal—and then across a sagebrush slope, the cliffs of Carson Peak rising sheer to the right (SW). The trail to Fern Lake branches off to the right (S) just before reaching the tumbling cascades. This is a very steep trail that parallels the cascading creek about half the distance to the lake. The trail continuing on to Yost Lake is described in the following loop trip beginning at June Lake. June is recommended as the starting point because the ascent is both more shaded and more gradual, and because the trailhead is 300 feet higher than at Fern Creek.

June Lake (7680') to Yost Lake and Fern Creek.

Yost Lake (9100'), moderate hike, 4.5 miles.
Fern Creek (7350'), moderate hike, 7 miles total.
Trailhead. Drive 2.3 miles down the June Lake road from its junction with US 395. Just beyond a narrow place in the road, opposite the Fire House, a small parking area indicates the trailhead. Arrange to be met at Fern Creek (see previous trail). An alternative is to ride the ski lift to June Meadows Chalet and from there hike to Yost meadow.

Flower-filled meadows high on the slope of June Mountain above the lower ski slopes—Yost Meadow the most extravagant of all—may come as a surprise on this trail. Streams from June Mountain and from the east slope of San Joaquin Mountain water many acres of marsh and meadow. Early in July they may be yellow with buttercups, later blue and lavender with wet-meadow flowers such as shooting stars, penstemon and elephant heads. (Carry insect repellent; flowers and mosquitoes both thrive in dampness.)

The trail angles up the slope for about two miles, then follows along the nearly level crest of a moraine. Blue lupine are everywhere. After crossing the ski area, you come to the first of many meadows. It is the largest, almost half a mile long. Sheep are often driven here from Deadman Creek in late summer. Beyond Yost Lake the trail follows Yost Creek downstream to a small meadow. If the trail crossing the meadow and the creek is difficult to follow because of criss-crossing sheep trails, watch for tree blazes. Beyond the falls of Yost Creek there are good views north. Reversed Peak lies directly across the canyon; Mono Craters are to the right (NE); and Mount Wood is the high red peak rising behind Silver Lake. The trail slants down a steep forested slope, crosses Fern Creek Falls, and continues to the road end at Fern Creek.

Silver Lake (7212') to Agnew, Gem, Weber and Waugh Lakes.

Agnew Lake (8508'), moderate hike, 2.5 miles.
Gem Lake (9052'), strenuous hike, 3.5 miles.
Weber Lake (10,000'), strenuous hike, 8.5 miles.
Waugh Lake (9424'), strenuous hike, 7 miles.
Trailhead. The parking area south of the pack station near Silver Lake.

Start early; otherwise the 1300-foot climb to Agnew Lake reservoir can be a hot, tiring pull. The trail crosses the tramway and penstock of the Southern California Edison Company. Buildings, wires and old roads remain from the hydro installations. Where the switchbacks end and the trail heads into the narrow mouth of Rush Creek canyon just below Agnew Lake, notice the rounded, smoothed, striated rock just across the stream—striking evidence of the glaciers and especially well preserved. The trail climbs on up past Agnew Lake to a high point (Hat Ridge, where the wind blows hats off) which offers the first view of Gem Lake and of Mount Lyell (13,114'), the highest peak on the skyline to the right, large snowbanks lying in a cirque just to its left. Gem Lake received its name in the early mining days from Tom Agnew, who called it "Gem-o'-the-Mountains."

About half a mile beyond the Gem Lake dam, the trail goes through a 3-foot-wide trough gouged in solid rock—an outstanding example of a large glacial groove. Many *striations*, parallel scratches, are visible, although the glacial polish has weathered away. The trail from here on is more gradual and stays in deep forest, with only occasional glimpses of Mount Davis and Rodgers Peak to the west. Above Gem Lake the trail continues along an old tractor road which was used for maintenance of the Waugh Lake dam (called by old-timers Rush Meadows Dam). The lake is named for E. J. Waugh, chief construction engineer. Just below the dam, the trail to Weber Lake takes off to the left (S). The main trail follows the north shore of Waugh Lake and intersects the John Muir Trail two miles farther on.

Silver Lake (7212') to Clark Lakes and Thousand Island Lake.

Clark Lakes (9850'), strenuous hike, 8 miles.
Thousand Island Lake (9834'), strenuous hike, about 10 miles.
Trailhead. The parking area south of the pack station near Silver Lake.

Proceed as above to the meadow on the west side of Gem Lake. Here the trail branches south and climbs to the Clark Lakes clustered below Agnew Pass. The trail to Thousand Island Lake follows the west shore of the largest Clark Lake, crosses a gentle saddle west of Agnew Pass and then joins the High Trail coming from Agnew Meadows. See above, "Agnew Meadows to Thousand Island Lake." An alternate trail to the Clark Lakes crosses the outlet of Agnew Lake and zigzags up a very steep abandoned trail to Spooky Meadow.

Silver Lake to Carson Peak and San Joaquin Mountain.

These peaks can be reached via Agnew Pass from either Silver Lake or Agnew Meadows. However, since Agnew Meadows is a thousand feet higher than Silver Lake, it is recommended as the starting point. (See above, "Agnew Meadows to Carson Peak and San Joaquin Mountain.")

Silver Lake (7212') to Alger Lake (10,640').

Very strenuous hike, 9 miles.
Trailhead. Parking area south of the pack station near Silver Lake.

Proceed to the north shore of Gem Lake as described in the trail above, "Silver Lake to Agnew, Gem...." Just after crossing Crest Creek the trail to Alger Lake branches to the right (N). As it switchbacks up the forested slope to Gem Pass, it enters the high country of mountain peaks, snow and alpine lakes, and the home of whitebark pine, nutcrackers, alpine chipmunks and pikas. Looking back, you have impressive views west toward the Ritter Range and south toward San Joaquin Mountain and the imposing lava cliffs surrounding Spooky Meadow. From Gem Pass (10,700') it seems you can see at least a hundred miles east into Nevada. Beyond Gem Pass the trail winds around rocky cliffs of many colors—purple, red, black, rust—and then drops into the Alger Lakes basin, which is encircled by the high peaks of Mount Wood, and Parker, Koip, and Blacktop peaks. Looking north from Alger Lake you can make out where the trail crosses the saddle between Parker and Koip peaks on its way to Dana Meadows.

Silver Lake (7212') to Parker Lake.

Top of ridge (9200'), strenuous hike, 3.5 miles.
Parker Lake (8400'), strenuous hike, 5.5 miles.
Trailhead. Parking area south of the pack station near Silver Lake.

Since much of this route goes through sagebrush, not through a shaded forest, it is more enjoyable during the cooler days of late spring or early autumn. From the broad, gently rolling shoulder of Mount Wood there are gorgeous views east to the Mono Craters and Mono Lake, and back to Silver Lake and all the peaks surrounding it. You can make this a loop trip if you arrange to have a waiting car at the Parker Lake trailhead; total loop mileage would then be 6.5 miles.

From the parking area head diagonally a bit toward the right to the high sagebrush-covered ridge; you will find the trail somewhere among the sagebrush at the base of the slope. The trail climbs steeply from Silver Lake as it angles across the slope, crossing a surprising number of small streams. Wild rose and yellow mule ears brighten the gray ridge in early summer. Sage grouse, quail, or deer may surprise you. The aspen groves farther on serve as sheep camps in August and as hunters' camps in fall. At the top of the ridge, the trail intersects an old road. Turn left and follow the "main" road as it drops off the ridge and comes to a gate. Leave the road and follow the trail as it climbs the moraine and then drops down to intersect the Parker Lake trail. Turn left for the lake, right for the Parker Lake trailhead.

Parker and Walker Lakes

Parker and Walker are located in two small canyons between June Lake and Lee Vining. Both lie in U-shaped glacial canyons cut in richly-colored rocks.

Parker Creek (7950') to Parker Lake (8400').

Easy hike, 2 miles.
Trailhead. From US 395 (at the *northern* junction of Highway 158, the June Lake Loop Road) drive toward Grant Lake for 1.5 miles. Turn right (SW) onto the Parker Lake road. This rough road, though it winds a bit through the sagebrush, heads directly toward the mountains for 2 miles. Low-slung passenger cars may have difficulties.

The trail starts up a typical eastern Sierra brush slope of sagebrush, bitterbrush, bunch grass, mountain mahogany and rabbitbrush. The trail climbs over Parker canyon's brush-covered moraine, an immense pile of loose material pushed down-canyon by an advancing glacier during the close of the last Ice Age. This is the only terminal (front) moraine in the region that remains whole and perfect, just as it was deposited thousands of years ago. Others, as at Grant Lake and Convict Lake, have been cut through and partly washed away by streams. In Parker canyon the stream cut through a lateral (side) moraine, leaving the terminal unchanged. Nearing the lake, the trail enters a forest that contains several huge, magnificent Jeffrey pine.

Walker Lake (7930') to Bloody Canyon, Mono Pass (10,600').

Strenuous hike, 5 miles; or 7 miles from Walker Creek.
Trailhead. There are two approaches to Walker Lake: a short steep trail to the lake's inlet, and a long hot walk from Walker Creek to the lake's outlet. Signs and maps may be confusing; follow these directions precisely. Take the Parker Lake road as described above. Follow it one-half mile until it crosses a wide, graded, relatively straight road. This is the aqueduct road. Turn right (W) and follow the aqueduct road for almost one mile. Turn left (W) and drive two miles up a rough but passable road to its end. From this road end, a rocky trail climbs over the moraine bordering Walker Lake on the south, makes a steep traverse down to the lake, crosses the creek above the inlet, and there joins the Mono Trail.

The Walker Creek approach is at least two miles longer. Drive on the aqueduct road about 2.5 miles. Just beyond Walker Creek, turn left and drive to the locked gate, which marks the boundary of private land. Proceed on foot to the lake (named for a William J. Walker who settled near the lake, not for the famous Joseph R. Walker) and follow its right (N) shore to the beginning of the trail.

This is part of the historic Mono Trail long used by the Paiutes of Mono Lake and the Miwoks of Yosemite to trade with each other. See "Mono Pass, Bloody Canyon" in Roadsides chapter. Rocky switchbacks climb this rugged canyon to Lower Sardine Lake (9840 feet), past cascades and waterfalls. The forest is especially interesting because the orderly progression of tree species from lower to higher altitude, described in the climate chapter, doesn't apply to this narrow, steep canyon. Junipers, mountain mahogany, willow and aspen mingle chaotically with the fir and pine. The usual clues of sun or shade, dampness or dryness, are no help at all. How refreshing! For while it seems to please us humans to explain everything in nature, to put things into neat pigeonholes, here trees—for reasons we can not fathom—are thriving in locations and in combinations that we would least expect. About 600 feet higher is Upper Sardine Lake, and a gradual half-mile beyond is Summit Lake and Mono Pass, at the boundary of Yosemite Park. The old log cabins near the pass remain from the Ella Bloss Mine, a contemporary of the May Lundy and the Mammoth mines. The *Mammoth City Herald* predicted in 1879 that thousands of men soon would be working at the adjoining Golden Crown Mine—a prediction that never came close to being true.

Tioga Pass

Trails near the pass begin only slightly below treeline. All of the trails west of the pass are within Yosemite National Park. You may obtain information on all aspects of the park at the Tuolumne Meadows Visitor Center, about 30 minutes drive from Lee Vining.

Saddlebag Lake (10,087') Loop Trail.

High lake basin (10,400'), easy hike, 1–2 miles.
Helen Lake (10,100') loop, moderate hike, about 5 miles total.
Trailhead. West of Ellery Lake a paved road leads north to the outlet of Saddlebag Lake.

A broad, mile-wide, high-alpine meadow slopes gently beyond Saddlebag Lake—open country that is ideal for leisurely cross-country wandering and for families with small children. Short-stemmed alpine flowers bloom from August into late September. Gentian and paintbrush purple the damp areas; buckwheat and red heather and bunchgrass color the rocky slopes. Scattered, stunted whitebark and lodgepole pine indicate the treeline. Stubby willow clumps cling to the streams. This is the home of marmots and pikas and, if you go higher, rosy finches. Evidence of glaciation is plentiful and well-preserved—the rocks rounded, grooved and highly polished. There are so many lakes that you can probably have one all to yourself. The highest peak on the ridge to the southwest is Mount Conness. Below it is Conness glacier, one of the larger Sierra glaciers; its meltwater forms a waterfall.

A motorboat taxi to the lake's inlet is available. The trail mileage above starts at the *inlet*. If you prefer to walk to the inlet, at the south end of the dam pick up the trail that skirts the lake; add two miles (roundtrip) to the figures above. From the inlet, you may want to just wander. It doesn't matter in which direction, for it is all beautiful. If you wish to go to some of the larger lakes, follow the old mining road that heads northwest to a tungsten prospect at Steelhead Lake. East of Steelhead is a low broad ridge that divides the streams flowing into Saddlebag Lake from those flowing north into Lundy Canyon.

From the northern end of Steelhead Lake you can pick up the trail that makes a loop to Helen Lake, climbs about 300 feet to Lundy Pass and brings you back to Saddlebag. The dark, pointed peak to the south that you see from the pass is Mount Dana (13,053 feet). Many maps indicate a trail going down to Lundy Canyon. It is not maintained and rock slides have obliterated parts of the old trail; it is dangerous.

Lundy Canyon

Of all the canyons, Lundy Canyon has the most beautiful fall coloring. Red-gold and brilliant yellow aspen, their color intensified by the Jeffrey pines' deep green, gleam against Lundy's steep reddish cliffs in late September and early October.

Mill Creek (8050') to Lundy Falls (8560').

Easy hike, 1.5 miles.

Trailhead. From the west end of Lundy Lake the road continues up an old mining road close to 2 miles—maybe. It is rough but passable, at least part of the way. If the road is not passable, walk to its end, where the trail begins. The road passes extensive beaver ponds.

The trail follows the cascades and small falls of Mill Creek through flower-filled meadows to the foot of Lundy falls. To see these five-hundred-foot falls in their glory, make this trip in June or early July. Although many maps show a trail going on to Helen Lake and Lundy Pass, this trail slid out time after time and is no longer maintained. It is dangerous.

Lundy Lake (7800') to Lake Oneida (9680').

Moderately strenuous hike, 3 miles.

Trailhead. About 3.5 miles after leaving US 395, the Lundy Canyon Road forks. Take the left fork, which crosses the stream below the dam, and park near the gate to the old mining road.

Choose a cool day for this trip, enjoyable mostly for its historical interest. The rocky mining road, now abandoned, leads to Lake Canyon and the famous May Lundy Mine. (See History chapter.) As you near the top of the cascades, begin watching for remains of the old mining days—flumes, shacks, pipes, an old waterwheel. Activity centered in a small settlement near Crystal Lake. Here were boarding houses, bunkhouses, cabins and a 20-stamp mill. Though probably all the standing buildings date since 1900 (between 1898 and 1914 the mine was worked intermittently, and in 1937 tailings were re-worked), there are remains of the very early days too. Machinery and stamps of the mill lie in a twisted mass near the largest mine dump; iron-stained tailings rest in the meadow and in Crystal Lake. High up the canyon's west wall are several small dumps and timbers from the tramway. Just beyond the settlement is sparkling Lake Oneida, an old log and rock dam at its outlet. Up and over the cliffs beyond Lake Oneida, eight tons of machinery were hauled by sled to the Tioga Mine during the winter of 1882.

Beyond Conway Summit

North of Conway Summit there are more eastern Sierra canyons to explore, each one different, each with a character all its own. Perhaps these brief descriptions will entice you to get out your maps and find them.

Virginia Lakes. From US 395 at Conway Summit, take the Virginia Lakes Road west. From the end of the road (9750'), eleven lakes are within an hour's hike. From the highest, Frog Lake (10,400'), a good trail leads over a divide to Summit Lake, connecting with the Green Lakes trail.

Green Lakes. From US 395, about 8 miles north of Conway Summit take the Green Lakes Road west. The trail begins at the end of the road (8080'), in a shaded, moist canyon. Near Green Lake the trail forks. One fork goes to West Lake, one climbs Glines Canyon to Virginia Pass, and the left fork (S) goes past a series of lakes and alpine meadows to Summit Lake (10,203'), which is on the northeast boundary of Yosemite National Park. A park trail continues on, following Return Creek and joining the Matterhorn Canyon trail in a beautiful and relatively little-traveled portion of the park.

Twin Lakes near Bridgeport. The commanding Sawtooth Ridge towers 5,000 feet above Bridgeport Valley. Pinnacles and small glaciers crown its summit. Famous among mountaineers for its clean, granite climbs, Sawtooth country has many trails for hikers. From Bridgeport drive west on the Twin Lakes Road. Horse, Cattle, and Robinson creek trails all start near the inlet of Upper Twin Lakes (7096'). Other trails start from Buckeye Campground. To reach it, about 8 miles from Bridgeport, watch for a dirt road heading north. Over the passes these trails drop down into the wild northern portion of Yosemite Park.

Mammoth Mountain   *Bev Steveson*

Fire!

Known in Paiute legend as "the burnt land," the eastern Sierra

between Bishop and Mono Lake has been a center of intense, often explosive volcanic activity the last three million years. The marks of that violence are everywhere—craters, volcanoes, red cinder cones, black glassy obsidian cliffs, acres of pumice, and miles of lava.

Mammoth Mountain is one of the volcanoes. Born about 200,000 years ago, ten or more major eruptions built the mountain up to about the size it is today. Its last eruption occurred around 50,000 years ago.

Boiling springs, Hot Creek   LaMoine R. Fantozzi

Casa Diablo geyser, 1959   Gerhard Schumacher

Obsidian flow (detail, 17 inches wide)   Bev Steveson

Explosion pit, Inyo Craters   Edwin C. Rockwell

Rhyolite domes and stubby flows of the Mono Craters   Robert C. Frampton

Another rhyolite dome, Wilson Butte   Robert C. Frampton

Large as it is, Mammoth Mountain is insignificant compared to the enormous eruptions centered at Long Valley 730,000 years ago. Pumice and dust-size particles called *ash* exploded in such quantities that the skies may have been darkened for months at a time. Shattering explosions hurled out glowing gas-propelled clouds that shot out in all directions and blanketed 600 square miles with as much as 600 feet of fragmental pumice. One hundred and fifty cubic miles of volcanic material was ejected. Ash from these eruptions has been identified as far away as Nebraska.

Steam vents and hot springs tell us that the volcanic fires are not yet spent. Among the most recent explosions, those that ripped out the Inyo Craters have been dated at about 1400 A.D. Only a few years earlier, the pumice that mantles the Mammoth area exploded from a vent south of Deadman Creek.

The Mono Craters are a chain of rhyolite domes and stubby flows. Their flat-topped shapes were determined by the viscous nature of the lava that formed them. When pressures below pushed it upward, instead of flowing, it solidified, piling up on itself in a jumble of blocks that spread sluggishly outward. Wilson Butte was formed in the same way.

Devils Postpile, remnant of a basalt flow   Bev Steveson

Basalt Column   *Ed Cooper*

Glacier-polished columns   *Bev Steveson*

Rainbow Falls dropping over lava cliff Ed Cooper

Devils Postpile is a spectacular remnant of a basalt flow

that erupted about 100,000 years ago in the valley of the Middle Fork of the San Joaquin River. Unlike the almost-solid rhyolite that formed the stubby domes of the Mono Craters, basalt flows freely. It flowed at least three miles, filling the valley to a depth of around 300 feet. As the basalt cooled and shrank, an intersecting network of cracks produced the five- and six-sided columns or "posts." The glaciers that later flowed down the Middle Fork valley quarried away much of the flow. They also planed off and polished the top of the rock-columns, producing an extraordinary parquet-floor effect.

Downstream from the Postpile, Rainbow Falls drops a hundred and forty feet over a cliff of lava. The height of the falls is maintained by an upper layer of massive, resistant lava. Underlying it is a softer layer of platy lava that is easily undercut by the plunging water at the base of the falls.

Abrupt eastern Sierra front formed by repeated faulting,
Sawtooth Ridge above Bridgeport Valley

Bev Steveson

Fifty-foot fault scarp in moraine, McGee Creek   *John S. Shelton*

During this period of volcanic fury, large-scale faulting

occurred along the 400-mile length of the eastern Sierra. Breaking along faults at the base of its eastern slope, the entire Sierra block tilted downward to the west. Its eastern portion lurched upward, while many of the adjacent blocks to the east dropped downwards. This faulting occurred not as one great cataclysm, but probably as hundreds of repeated jerks, of about the same intensity we experience during earthquakes today.

Perhaps the fifty-foot break in the McGee Creek moraine, pictured above, can help us understand the large-scale faulting of the entire eastern slope. Recognizing this break for what it is—a recent, very fresh fault scarp—is a key to understanding much about the eastern Sierra, its origin, its rocks, even its weather. It was formed by movement along a fault; one side moved up relative to the other. Repeated movement, similar to this, along the fault zone that extends the length of the Sierra accounts for the abrupt mountain front characteristic of the eastern Sierra. The steep mountain front above Bridgeport Valley (opposite) and the sheer face of Carson Peak (following page) are colossal examples of ancient, eroded fault scarps.

Sheer face of Carson Peak, an ancient fault scarp

Stephen H. Willard

Probably the Sierra crest is rising today,

and continuing to tilt toward the west. Field evidence and radiometric dating indicate that the Sierra began rising about 50 million years ago. The rate of uplift today is probably around an inch and a half per century. That may not sound like much, but multiply by a million years or two!

Geologic Story

The somber dark gray and reddish brown cliffs encircling Convict Lake were looked at and tramped over by several generations of people without any thought that they might be more important than any other dark rocks nearby. Then, on their very first day of field work in June 1953, USGS geologists discovered tiny fossil *graptolites* in loose slaty rocks above the lake's south shore. They proved to be 500 million years old (Ordovician), dating these rocks as the oldest in the entire Sierra Nevada. These graptolites, whose name is derived from "written on stone" for their resemblance to pencil markings, were free-floating marine organisms that flourished in an ancient sea. (See illus., "Sideroad to Convict Lake," Roadsides chapter.) However, the Convict fossils' fame endured but a brief twenty-seven years, when their age was eclipsed by a find near Big Pine. There, older fossils were dated as 550–570 million years old (Early Cambrian).

The oldest rocks. Much of the story explaining the Sierra's rugged setting can be deciphered from its rocks. Like any other story, this one should start at the beginning, and the geologic beginning in this area is a vast shallow sea. Five hundred million years ago, as part of the Pacific Ocean, it covered much of the West, including what is now eastern California. Salt water covered the region for at least a hundred million years. During that

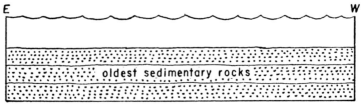

a. The oldest sedimentary rocks (Ordovician) in the Mammoth Lakes area were deposited in the sea about 500 million years ago.

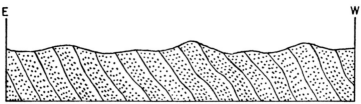

b. 400 million years ago the land rose above the sea. The oldest sedimentary rocks were folded, and were tilted to the west.

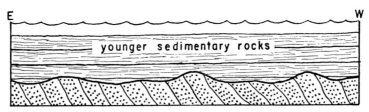

c. Younger sedimentary rocks (Pennsylvanian-Permian) were deposited in the sea about 300 million years ago.

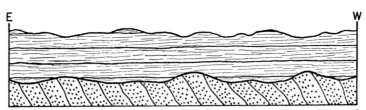

d. About 225 million years ago the land again rose above the sea, and some of the younger sedimentary rocks were stripped off by stream erosion.

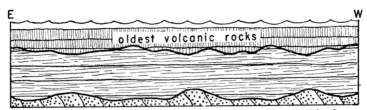

e. The oldest volcanic rocks (Triassic?-Jurassic) were deposited in the sea about 190 million years ago.

Geologic history of Mammoth Lakes region.

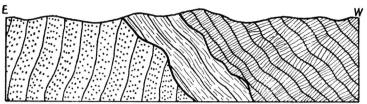

f. About 100 million years ago the land rose above the sea for the third time. The rocks were folded, and again were tilted westward.

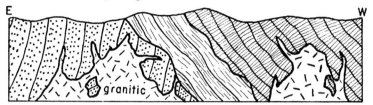

g. After the folding shown in the preceding figure, fluid granitic rock invaded the folded sedimentary and volcanic rocks. Heat given off by the granitic rock metamorphosed the older rocks.

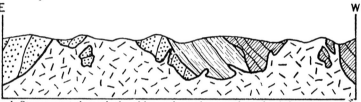

h. Streams cut through the older rocks and exposed much of the now-cooled and crystallized granitic rock, leaving disconnected remnants of the former "roof" as islands in a sea of granitic rock.

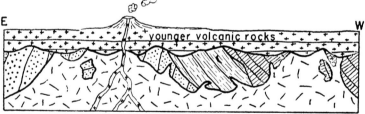

i. About 3.5 million years ago, widespread volcanic eruptions (Pliocene) commenced to blanket the area with lava flows and showers of fragments. Eruptions continued sporadically, the most recent being the explosion that ripped out the Inyo Craters about 1400 A.D.

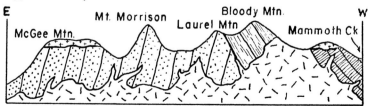

j. Streams and glaciers removed vast amounts of the volcanic rock, leaving only remnants scattered through the mountainous areas. This is a diagrammatic cross-section of the local terrain today, as seen by an observer at Mammoth Lakes looking south.

time mud, silt and sand were deposited on the ocean floor in horizontal layers or beds (diagram *a*, preceding page), finally accumulating to a thickness of more than twelve thousand feet. Today this same process takes place as rivers carry dirt and sand grains to the ocean; ocean currents distribute and winnow them into the layers of mud, silt and sand now accumulating on the ocean floor. The formation of sedimentary beds can be simply illustrated by putting a handful of mixed silt, sand and gravel into a jar of water and shaking it. The sediments will settle out in layers according to the density and size of the particles.

Evidence obtained in the Mammoth Lakes area—also in the Hawthorne-Tonopah area and the Inyo Mountains—indicates that the land then rose above the sea and remained so for a long time. Accompanying this period of uplift, the sediments—now compacted and hardened into mudstone, siltstone and sandstone—were subjected to great stresses that squeezed the layers into folds and tilted them toward the west *(b)*. The land, now standing high above the sea, was vulnerable to erosion. Rain, creeks and rivers wore away the rocks. Water and gravity transported the rock particles from the higher altitudes to the lower and eventually deposited them far away in the ocean. Similarly, the rocks of the Ritter Range are at this moment being slowly worn away and their constituents carried by the San Joaquin River to the ocean through San Francisco Bay. Actually only the finest particles reach the bay, the pebbles and gravels being deposited upstream where the current is not swift enough to carry them farther. The coarse materials eventually break down into smaller and smaller particles until nearly all is finally swept to the sea.

Again the region sank beneath the sea, remaining submerged seventy-five million years. The sea floor was blanketed by new layers of sediments, this time mostly silt, totaling a minimum of six thousand feet *(c)*. *Crinoids*, sea lilies lived in this ocean, their remains constituting a significant part of a thick limestone bed exposed today in Laurel and upper Convict canyons. (See illus., "Convict Lake," Trails chapter.) The remains of *brachiopods*, clamlike contemporaries of the crinoids, also are found in the crinoid-bearing beds and in other rocks deposited during this submergence.

The sea floor was elevated once again, but this time stresses did not develop enough to fold the rocks, and they remained essentially horizontal. Subsequent stream erosion washed away part of the newly formed sedimentary rock *(d)*. Accompanied by widespread volcanic eruptions, the land for the third time again sank beneath the sea. The eruptions persisted intermittently for perhaps ninety million years, depositing layer upon layer of fragmental volcanic material—a mass nearly five miles thick *(e)*. Much of the material erupted as dust or sand-size particles, although some fragments two to six inches across were intermixed, and was deposited directly in the sea. When the land rose again and the sea retreated once more, the volcanic rock layers and all the older sedimentary rocks beneath them were subjected to enormous stresses that squeezed and folded them and again tilted them steeply westward *(f)*.

Granitic intrusions. After the rocks were folded, a great mass of molten granitic material invaded them tens of thousands of feet below the surface, in some places shouldering aside the rocks to make room for itself, in others dissolving its way into the folded rocks by dislodging huge fragments and partially or wholly assimilating them *(g)*. The molten material remained at such great depth that it took a very long time to cool and solidify; laboratory work suggests that it required several million years. The solidified material is called granitic rock or granite, the most common rock of the Sierra. The great heat absorbed by the overlying sedimentary and volcanic rocks was sufficient to cause new minerals to crystallize in them at the expense of their original minerals, locally changing completely the appearance and character of the rocks. This is essentially the process of *metamorphism*; the resulting rocks are called metamorphic rocks. The preceding events (folding, invasion of molten granitic rock, metamorphism of the folded rocks, and cooling of the granitic rock) occurred during an interval of perhaps 100 million years. All during this time, streams and rivers were eroding away the deformed metamorphic rocks until the region finally became an area of low, gently rolling hills, and much of the now-solid granitic rock was exposed at the surface. Remnant patches in a mass of granitic rock were all that remained of the original metamorphic "roof" *(h)*.

After the granitic rock was exposed, widespread volcanic outbursts again occurred, covering the area with flows and showers of fragments *(i)*. Though there is little evidence left of the total thickness of these deposits, near San Joaquin Mountain a section more than two thousand feet thick still remains. As the frequency of the eruptions diminished, the range we now call the Sierra Nevada began to rise along fractures, or faults, chiefly along the eastern margin of the range—a tilting westward of a 430-mile-long, 70-mile-wide block of the earth's crust.

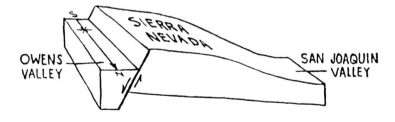

Simplified diagram showing how the Sierra rose along faults that mark the east boundary of the range.

The Ice Age. Early in the uplift of the Sierra, the earth's climate became cooler and more moist. Each winter brought snow that fell on deep snows remaining from preceding seasons. As a result of continuous accumulation, the deeper snow was compacted into ice and finally began to creep or flow slowly down the canyons as glaciers. Thus was the Ice Age born, the time when ice covered half of North America and many other parts of the world.

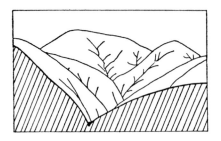 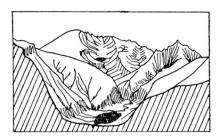

Left, *narrow stream valleys before glaciation.*
Right, *widened by glaciation, valleys become characteristically U-shaped.*

Before the development of glaciers, the Sierra probably consisted of rolling hills separated by rather narrow, shallow stream valleys (left diagram), in contrast to the sharp ridges and deep, wide canyons of today. The stream valleys that guided the first glaciers were widened and deepened by glacial scouring, until the topography eventually resembled that shown in the right diagram. At least four and possibly six times during the Ice Age the glaciers melted back to their sources or *cirques*—theater-shaped basins at the head of glaciated valleys—in response to climatic changes. Following each of the melt-backs, or recessions, the climate apparently became cooler and moister and the glaciers again advanced down the valleys. A record of these retreats is preserved in the forms of the huge arc-shaped piles of rock debris, or *moraines*, deposited by the glaciers at the mouths of the major canyons along the range front (see photo section "Ice!"). Other traces of the glaciers can be found throughout the area—the rounded form of ridges and canyon walls, the grooves and scratches ground into them, and boulders of all sizes deposited by the glaciers as they melted back.

The landscape today. While relentless but slow uplift and glaciation were dramatically changing the landscape, drama of a more catastrophic kind was also contributing to the changing scenery. All along the Sierra front, and especially in the Mammoth-Mono region, volcanic eruptions—many violent—accompanied the faulting along the range front. Although sporadic volcanism along the entire Sierra Nevada had been going on for a long time, local volcanic activity escalated remarkably during the Ice Age. Precursors to the main event were eruptions north and west of Long Valley at Glass and Bald mountains and at San Joaquin Mountain ridge—eruptions of light-colored lava, pumice, and ash (rhyolite and closely related rocks). Evidently the subterranean magma that fed those eruptions grew in size and energy to the point that it could no longer be contained. About 730,000 years ago an enormous eruption centered near Little Antelope Valley exploded through overlying rock, spewing glowing lava and black clouds of ash high into the atmosphere. The estimated volume of glowing pumice and ash disgorged is a staggering 150 cubic miles. (Mount St. Helens disgorged less than one cubic mile.) As the eruption continued and intensified, support was progressively removed from the roof over the entire magma chamber, and it collapsed, leaving the elliptical depression now known as Long Valley Caldera. The caldera extends westward from the east side of Long Valley to Minaret Summit and southward from Bald Mountain to Crowley Dam.

Geophysical measurements, supported by recent drilling, indicate that the original caldera floor sank at least a mile, but the caldera filled rapidly with erupting pumice and ash. Erosion and subsequent volcanic extrusions have blanketed the present floor of the caldera so completely that not even a remnant of the material from that initial cataclysm is exposed inside the caldera today. It is admirably exposed, however, southeast of Long Valley where it forms the broad expanse of the Volcanic Tableland. Its surface has weathered to a rosy tan color. Excellent exposures of the soft, porous, pumiceous, salmon-colored *tuff* can be seen in the roadcuts along US 395 between Toms Place and Bishop. Further evidence of the magnitude of the Long Valley eruption comes from Kansas and Nebraska where, at several localities, ash from the Long Valley event has been positively identified. (*Ash* is a geologic term for dust-size particles of volcanic rock.) Intermittent eruptions within the caldera, but on a vastly reduced scale, subsequently filled much of the western half of the caldera with volcanic domes and lava flows over the next 600,000 years.

Overlapping the younger eruptions within the caldera, a chain of new volcanoes began to propagate along a north-south line extending from Mammoth Mountain for 30 miles, through the Mono Craters to Mono Lake. The oldest and largest of these young volcanoes is Mammoth Mountain, a composite dome built piecemeal by recurring viscous extrusions of gray or reddish lava during an interval of 180,000 years, beginning around 200,000 years ago and ending 50,000 years ago. The lava is sprinkled with tiny clear to whitish feldspar crystals and shiny black flakes of mica.

Beginning 40,000 years ago in the north at Mono Craters and occurring more or less randomly thereafter at various places along the entire north-south line, the chain of young volcanoes erupted sporadically. Unlike the Long Valley eruption, which left a gigantic depression as its signature, the young volcanoes built conspicuous domes to commemorate their activity. The domes represent the latest and most passive phase of the volcanic process. They were preceded by explosive eruptions that propelled clouds of pumice and ash high into the prevailing winds that distributed the debris widely in all directions, but left the thickest accumulations nearby. Ash from one of these eruptions has been identified in meadows as far away as the valley of the Little Kern, 110 miles south. Three of the youngest domes, which are well exposed and readily accessible, are at Glass and Deadman creeks; all three are about 550 years old.

Recent evidence serves to remind us that this *is* earthquake and volcano country. That evidence, gathered since the vigorous earthquake swarms in 1980 and 1983, is based on: the ages of the most recent eruptions at Negit Island and the Deadman domes; geophysical data that can be interpreted to indicate the persistence of a residual magma chamber beneath the caldera and the possible movement of new magma to depths as shallow as 3 kilometers; a 70 cm uplift of the ground surface; and the spasmodic tremors from 1980-83, a peculiar pattern on a seismograph that is believed to indicate the movement of magma. There is no reason to believe that this region's long history of earthquakes and volcanism, extending back into antiquity too remote to comprehend, has abruptly ended. Fortunately, during the present period of relative tranquility, we can enjoy and revel in the beauty created throughout that violent history. And we can feel secure in the extensive network of devices that continually monitors changes that could indicate the beginnings of renewed activity. At the same time, we will do well to remember that this is but an intermission in the ongoing production of high drama!

Rocks

All the rocks that constitute the outer shell of the earth are classified into three great categories: *sedimentary rocks*—those composed of clays, sands and gravels that were once transported by running water, ice, wind or gravity and then accumulated in oceans or in basins on land; *igneous rocks*—once-molten rocks that welled up from the earth's interior; *metamorphic rocks*—those which, because of heat and pressure at great depth, were recrystallized from original sedimentary, igneous or earlier metamorphic rocks. Examples of all three classes abound in the Mammoth region.

Sediments and sedimentary or "layered" rocks

In the area depicted on the geologic map, most of the sedimentary material is unconsolidated. It includes the loose silt, sand and gravel that make up the floors of the large valleys, and also the gravel and boulders comprising the impressive glacial moraines that block the mouths of all the major canyons. Most sediments eventually harden into rocks. A good example of sedimentary rock can be found throughout a large area west of the Alkali Lakes, along the road to Benton Crossing. The area is underlain by sandstone long ago deposited in a lake as sand by streams flowing from the Sierra. The western edge of the sandstone marks the shoreline of a prehistoric lake that filled

Long Valley following the colossal eruption that created the Long Valley caldera during the middle of the Ice Age. The lake basin was similar to the present form of Long Valley, its deepest part near the present course of Owens River as evidenced by the conspicuous mounds of grayish white clay (some of them containing tiny shells of organisms, *ostracoda*, that lived in the ancient lake) near Benton Crossing. The same streams that deposited the sand (now sandstone) close to the shore also carried the clay, but because clay particles are so small and light they drifted out to the deeper, quiet water before settling out. Most of the clay has since been stripped from the valley by erosion; only remnant mounds remain of a once-extensive layer.

The same processes involved in the formation of these ancient lake deposits are active today. If, say, Convict Lake could be sliced in two lengthwise so that a cross-section of the sediments on the bottom could be seen, the coarse gravels would be found near the small delta at its inlet, grading outward into finer material in the deep center of the lake.

Segregation of lake deposits.

Igneous rocks

Igneous rocks occur as two distinct kinds—volcanic and granitic. Though most granitic rocks are commonly called granite, *granitic* refers to a family of related rocks, true granite being only one of its many members. Although many volcanic rocks have nearly the same chemical composition as granitic rocks, their appearance is strikingly different, chiefly because of the size of their minerals. Granitic rocks are composed entirely of interlocking crystals averaging at least one-sixteenth to one-eighth inch long. Volcanic rocks typically contain only a small proportion of such crystals; they consist mostly of natural glass or of material so fine-grained that its particles cannot be distinguished even with the aid of a microscope.

To understand the dissimilar appearance of the two kinds of igneous rocks, granitic rock can best be considered as volcanic rock that failed to reach the earth's surface. Both originated as hot fluid rock—magma—deep within the earth. But unlike the volcanic rocks that erupted on the earth's surface and then cooled quickly as earth and air conducted heat away from the molten, flowing rock, the granitic magma was unable to force its way up through the earth's crust and consequently cooled and crystallized slowly at depths measurable in tens of thousands of feet. The slow cooling process allowed crystals to form and grow until the molten rock was completely transformed into the solid mass of interlocking crystals we see today in granite and other granitic rocks. Laboratory research suggests that the time involved in the cooling process is measurable in millions of years. Granitic rock is visible today only because uplift and consequent erosion eventually removed the great thickness of overlying rock.

Dark-colored volcanic rocks. Most of the volcanic rocks in this area occupy a large area north and east of Mammoth Lakes. Their color often tells much about the nature of their eruption. Dark-colored volcanic rocks are exposed at numerous places along Highway 203 west of US 395. The rough black rock projecting jaggedly above the sagebrush once flowed as lava from vents probably less than a mile from the Post Office, vents subsequently buried under the great thickness of glacial debris that covers most of Mammoth Creek's valley. Lava of this type, called basalt, commonly erupts with less violence than the light-colored varieties. Close inspection of the basalt reveals many features typical of dark-colored volcanic rock. The surface of the flow is full of bubbles, or *vesicles*, and is ropy, like taffy. Many of the vesicles are lined with a hard white material, commonly silica and/or calcium, which was deposited there by gases streaming up through the lava before it cooled completely. On a freshly broken surface glass-clear feldspar crystals, some nearly an inch across, can be seen within a mass of extremely fine-grained material. These crystals grew while the magma was still deep within the earth, long before it erupted.

Light-colored volcanic rocks. The light-colored rocks, which erupted at a lower temperature than the basalt, commonly formed symmetrical protrusions called *volcanic domes* (see photo section "Fire!"). Although many of the domes stand hundreds of feet above the immediate landscape, they are dwarfed by the towering peaks of the Sierra and consequently many of them go unnoticed. Perhaps the best place to examine light-colored volcanic rocks is at the dome about three and three-quarter miles west of US 395, on the Deadman Creek road. This dome, formed of a light gray rock called *rhyolite*, is one of the youngest in the area. Because of its youth, erosion has not yet modified its shape nor has vegetation become established. Rhyolite is lighter weight than basalt, owing partly to its spongelike texture. Some of the rocks look much like solidified froth, while others are solid glass ranging in color from light to dark gray. Some of the glass is black and is called *obsidian*. Including such a dark rock as obsidian in the light-colored group may seem inconsistent. Obsidian, nevertheless, is typically associated with light-colored volcanic rocks and is similar to them in chemical composition; it does not occur with the dark-colored rocks such as basalt. Rhyolite often has a layered or banded appearance, a relic pattern developed when the rock was fluid. Obsidian generally occurs as layers, streaks, or pods in the light-colored, frothy rhyolite. It may have a few very small white or clear crystals of feldspar and clear quartz, and much of the rock may be sprinkled with tiny black flakes of mica.

Unlike basaltic lava, which flows readily from its vent, rhyolitic lava is extremely viscous and is often semiplastic or solid by the time it emerges at the surface, thus readily plugging its vent much like a cork in a bottle. This allows gas pressure below to build up a tremendous head, which may be relieved by violent explosions resulting in showers of pea- to walnut-size pumice fragments and fine ash that may blanket the country for miles. Pumice, found almost everywhere in this area, resembles the frothy rhyolite seen in some of the large blocks around the dome's base, although it is generally lighter weight and will even float for a time on water. During the active life of a rhyolitic volcano, the viscous lava may become sufficiently fluid to flow sluggishly for short distances; much of the light-colored volcanic rock just north of Mammoth Lakes village was formed in this way. Similar stubby flows are associated with the Mono Craters, which are also rhyolite domes. The formation of domes often marks the last activity of rhyolite volcanoes, although sometimes domes succeed each other, the new one destroying the older one by violent explosions. The explosions frequently develop large craters, within which a new dome may arise—as at Panum Crater, the northernmost of the Mono Craters.

The Mono Craters, the Inyo Craters and the young domes in the Mammoth area are in almost perfect north-south alignment. Excluding Mammoth Mountain at the south end of the chain, which is older, all of these domes erupted over a period of about 40,000 years, most of them during the last 10,000 years. The youngest erupted about 1400 A.D., and one small flow on Negit Island may be as young as the late 1700s. Their chemical composition is so similar that, together with their alignment, it is logical to conclude that they probably all came from a common subterranean reservoir. Their remarkable alignment suggests that a large fracture, or a narrow zone of fractures, provided channels through which the fluid rock reached the earth's surface.

Granitic rocks. Granitic rocks are exposed in the canyons of Sherwin, Hilton, and Rock creeks and on Mammoth Crest; they become progressively more abundant toward the west, near the core of the Sierra Nevada. Though exposures of granitic rock in place are not easily reached without hiking, granitic boulders abound in nearly all the glacial moraines and can also be seen around Rock Creek, Toms Place, and along Highway 203. Nearly all the granitic rocks in this area are light gray, some almost white. They are readily distinguished from the light-colored volcanic rocks because they are composed entirely of visible crystals, while the volcanic rocks consist of very fine-grained material and glass, with only a scattering of crystals that can be seen with the unaided eye. The rocks' gray color is caused by a sprinkling of small

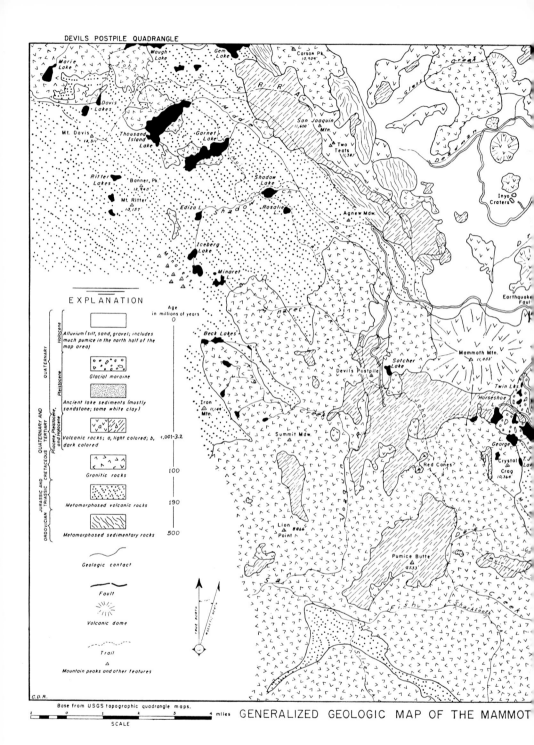

EXPLANATION

Age
in millions of years

QUATERNARY

Holocene

Alluvium (silt, sand, gravel; includes
much pumice in the north half of the
map area)

0

Pleistocene

Glacial moraine

Ancient lake sediments (mostly
sandstone; some white clay)

QUATERNARY AND TERTIARY

Pliocene, Pleistocene, and Holocene

Volcanic rocks; a, light colored; b,
dark colored

<.001-3.2

JURASSIC AND CRETACEOUS

Granitic rocks

100

TRIASSIC

Metamorphosed volcanic rocks

190

ORDOVICIAN

Metamorphosed sedimentary rocks

500

Geologic contact

Fault

Volcanic dome

Trail

Mountain peaks and other features

C.D.R.

Base from USGS topographic quadrangle maps.

SCALE

GENERALIZED GEOLOGIC MAP OF THE MAMMOT

120

Geology of the Mt. Morrison quad by C.D. Rinehart & D.C. Ross, 1955; Devils Postpile by C.D. Rinehart & N.K. Huber, 1958.

121

black crystals of mica and the mineral hornblende, which occur among the cloudy quartz and light-gray to pale flesh-colored feldspar crystals.

Metamorphic rocks

Here, metamorphic rocks—rocks that have been changed (metamorphosed) from their original state—originated from the older sedimentary and volcanic rocks that covered the intruding molten granitic rock and that were subjected for a long time to intense heat and pressure. Most of the metamorphic rocks have been removed by stream and glacial erosion; those that remain appear as islands in a sea of granitic rock. To distinguish these rocks from their younger, unmetamorphosed relatives, they will be referred to below as *metasedimentary* and *metavolcanic* rocks. Most of the metasediments are very fine grained, having been deposited as mud and silt in a shallow seaway covering eastern California and Nevada.

Metamorphic rocks, widespread from McGee Creek to Virginia Creek, form most of the high peaks on the skyline. Many are conspicuously layered, with beds a few inches to several feet in thickness. They range in color from the light gray metamorphosed limestone (marble) of Mammoth Rock, through shades of brown and brownish red as those exposed on the aptly named Bloody Mountain, to the typical dark gray of the metavolcanic rocks that form the southern two-thirds of Mammoth Crest. Although most of these rocks originally accumulated as nearly horizontal layers, enormous forces—preceding and accompanying emplacement of the granitic rocks—metamorphosed and slowly deformed them until the layers now stand nearly vertical. The metamorphic rocks are in two distinct bodies, the metasediments to the east and the younger metavolcanics to the west (see geologic map). To understand why the rocks are arranged so regularly, examine the sequence of cross-sections in the diagrams discussed above. Prior to their last folding, the layered rocks were stacked up very much like a deck of cards. The major effect of the folding was to tilt the entire pile toward the west *(f)* with the top (younger) layers west of the bottom (older) layers. Regardless of where one stands on the metamorphic formations, the younger rocks always lie to the west.

Metavolcanic rocks. The metavolcanic rocks are unlike most of the younger volcanic rocks described above. Very few originated as molten lava. Instead, the material of which they are made exploded from volcanoes and vents and fell to the earth as fine ash laden with small feldspar and quartz crystals and with tiny rock fragments. Much of this material fell into quiet water; many of the resulting rocks are layered, showing the action of gentle currents that winnowed the volcanic material and sorted it into thin laminations of fine and coarse material. Also, beds of limestone a few feet thick, some containing fossil clams, occur here and there within the metavolcanics, further indicating the existence of an ancient sea.

The most common metavolcanic rock is a dark gray fine-grained rock, inset with abundant white or gray feldspar crystals averaging slightly less than a sixteenth of an inch across and with dark rock fragments averaging an inch or less across. Rock of this type is well exposed along the trails to Duck Lake and Shadow Lake. Probably the most spectacular rock in the area, common between Shadow Lake and Lake Ediza, is the metavolcanic *breccia* (pronounced "bretchia") that occurs in beds measurable in tens to hundreds of feet thick. This breccia consists of many angular rock fragments, an inch to more than a foot across, cemented together by a very fine-grained material. It is likely that this fine-grained material erupted explosively as ash while the large fragments were ripped from the throat of a volcano and hurled out. The large size of the fragments suggests that they were deposited near the site of eruption.

Since the changes wrought by metamorphism are often obscure, they can best be seen with the aid of a microscope. The principal change is the growth of new minerals, mostly microscopic in size, in response to heat and pressure; the chemical composition and the general appearance of most of the rocks, however, are essentially unchanged.

Mount Morrison   *Ed Cooper*

Ice!

A land born of fire
and sculptured by ice.

For several million years, fire and ice have played their antagonistic roles, shaping the landscape we see today—the one building and adding, the other quarrying, scouring, tearing down.

During summer when only a few snow patches spangle Sierra peaks, it takes considerable imagination to picture the Ice

Age landscape. It was a time of fluctuating climates that began about two million years ago. During the cooler and moister times, ice built up and glaciers advanced down the canyons as they do in the Arctic today. When the climate warmed, the glaciers melted back. Cold, moist times alternated with warmer, dryer times at least four and possibly six times.

Glacier, Ritter Range   *Tom Ross*

T J Johnston

Broad, theatre-shaped basins—cirques—
form the head of most Sierra canyons.
There, snow accumulated and compacted
into the ice masses that eventually sent
rivers of ice flowing down-canyon, planing,
grooving, and rounding all the rock they
overrode. Small glaciers linger in some
High Sierra cirques today. Shading some of
the higher cirques are ridges that never
were rounded by overriding ice. Their rock,
standing above the ice, and subject to the
effects of alternate freezing and thawing
today as in the past, has shattered into
spires and pinnacles. Thus the Minarets
and other jagged peaks of the Ritter
Range stand in marked contrast to the
lower, rounded glaciated Sierra crest a few
miles east.

Unglaciated peaks of the Minarets   *Ed Cooper*

Glacier-planed bedrock   *Philip Hyde*
below Minarets

Rock grooved and polished   *Philip Hyde*
by glacier

Flat-bottomed glacial valley—Little Lakes Valley   *Ed Cooper*

Mountains sculptured by glaciers are both more forbidding

and more hospitable than unglaciated mountains—forbidding because of steep canyon walls and jagged pinnacles, hospitable because of broad valley bottoms holding chains of lakes and flower-filled meadows. Although the deep canyons of the Sierra have been cut primarily by streams, it is the glaciers that have given the canyons their distinctive U-shaped forms by widening the valley floors and steepening the canyon walls.

On their way down-canyon, the glaciers scooped out many basins in the bedrock. In some of these basins lie alpine lakes. Other basins contain marshes, slowly filling with mud and gravel washed in by streams. As the marshes fill, they dry and grass growing along the margins will steadily advance until the marsh has disappeared. A meadow of grass and flowers will take its place.

U-shaped canyon, Convict Lake   *Stephen H. Willard*

Mountain iris   *Philip W. Faulconer*

Willow catkins   *Don Gibbon*

Glacial moraines, Green Creek

John S. Shelton

Serving as great conveyor belts, glaciers carry rock down

from the high lands, then dump it where they melt in the lower lands. Such dumps, "glacial moraines," are composed of rock debris ranging in size from sand to boulders. Moraines stand hundreds of feet high at the mouth of almost every canyon between Sherwin Summit and Sonora Pass.

Green Creek moraine, a few miles north of Conway Summit, is one of the longer ones (photo above). Its sinuous shape outlines the path of the lower end of the glacier. The huge arc-shaped piles of debris at the

mouths of Laurel and Convict creek canyons (see page opposite) are moraines also. They outline the location of the glaciers' snouts at the climax of the last glacial advance.

The Ice Age ended about eleven thousand years ago—or did it? Are we perhaps enjoying only a brief, warm interlude before the next glacial advance which could be triggered by only a few degrees drop in average temperature? We may not live long enough to know whether the Sierra's small glaciers will melt away entirely, or whether ice will again build up and begin flowing down Sierra canyons.

Moraines at the mouth of Convict Creek Canyon   John S. Shelton

Moraines at the mouth of Laurel Creek Canyon   John S. Shelton

Mono Lake   *Stephen H. Willard*

Tufa deposit, Mono Lake   *Bev Steveson*

Tufa deposit, Mono Lake   *Bev Steveson*

During the Ice Age Mono Lake was three or four times larger,

its water level over six hundred feet higher than at present. Shorelines of the ancient lake may be seen clearly at several places. Tufa towers that formed under water now stand high above the water line.

The knobby white tufa towers are deposits of calcium carbonate that formed under water when the lake level was higher. These limy deposits are clustered around fresh-water springs that bubble up from the lake bottom. A chemical reaction between the calcium in the fresh water and carbonates in the lake water causes calcium carbonate to precipitate.

Climates &
Forest Communities

The Sierra Nevada is one of the world's great mountain ranges, in height as well as length. Its crest towers nearly two miles above Owens Valley, more than one mile above Long Valley. Twelve peaks exceed 14,000 feet, rising almost three miles above the Central Valley to the west. Such a colossal mountain range has not one, but *several* climates.

A basic fact governing climate is that air becomes colder the higher the elevation. At high altitudes ice forms on airplane wings; in the high mountains, rain often falls as hail or snow. Daily temperatures in the High Sierra may be 30 to 80 degrees colder than in the Central Valley. The ground itself is colder, slowing down plant growth. Snow covers the ground seven to nine months of the year, making a short growing season. Rainfall too is affected by the altitude, for as clouds heavy with water vapor are blown eastward from the Pacific, they are deflected upward several miles by the Sierra. Increasing coldness makes more and more of their moisture condense; rainfall increases up the western Sierra slope until it reaches a maximum at about 6500 feet elevation. Above that, precipitation (measured as water content of the snow) decreases, for the clouds have already dropped much of their moisture. As the clouds soar over the Sierra crest and cross the eastern slope, they have little moisture left. Consequently the eastern Sierra slope receives far less water than the western slope. The desert ranges and valleys farther east are said to be in the *rain shadow* of the Sierra. All this causes tremendous climatic variations along the Sierra slope.

Extreme climates—the heat and dryness of the high desert, the cold and snow of the arctic—are only a few miles apart on the Sierra's steep eastern slope. Annual snowfall at the Mammoth ski tows averages 335 inches, or almost 30 feet; nearby Long Valley is lucky to have ten inches of rain. On the first of June it is still winter at the lakes above nine thousand feet—willows bare, lakes frozen and few birds nesting. Yet only twenty minutes east by car and three thousand feet lower in Long Valley, spring has already gone and the hot summer begun—some flowers gone to seed and young birds already out of their nests.

Each climate has its own assemblage or community of plants and animals that can survive only under the special conditions of temperature, moisture, altitude and soil found there. To put it another way, the differences in moisture, soils, topography, geologic history and evolution of species from stock isolated from the main parent—the *biome*—all play an active role in determining the plant and animal community of a given region. (This concept furthers the recognition of the close relationship existing among all living things.)

Conditions range from the sagebrush desert of Long Valley to the alpine cold of the Sierra crest. Among plants there is a regular progression from the heat-tolerant forms at the low altitudes to the cold-tolerant forms at the high altitudes. For example, sagebrush flourishes in the desert, and a four-inch dwarf willow above treeline. One is adapted to heat, the other to cold; neither survives in the other's climate. The progression of climates and plant communities can be recognized easily by the changes of tree species. A generalized profile of the eastern Sierra slope shows the following changes.

Animals too distribute themselves according to climatic conditions. For example, certain mammals such as the antelope ground squirrel and the desert coyote live in the shadscale scrub of Lone Pine and Manzanar—open desert prairie country where summer temperatures are high—but they do not live at higher altitudes. Along Sherwin Grade, where the juniper and pinyon pine grow, typical mammals are the black-tailed jack rabbit, the Panamint kangaroo rat and the Townsend ground squirrel. Look for them again among the pinyon at Casa Diablo. A little higher, among mountain mahogany and in the Jeffrey pine forest lives the least chipmunk.

At the still higher elevations of Mammoth Lakes and June Lake, there will be fir trees, lodgepole pine and quaking aspen. The climate of this lodgepole-red fir forest is ideal for summer camping—not so chilly as the high mountain mixed forest, yet cooler than the sometimes hot and dry Jeffrey pine forest. The greatest variety of mammals occurs in the lodgepole-red fir community—among them the lodgepole chipmunk, golden-mantled

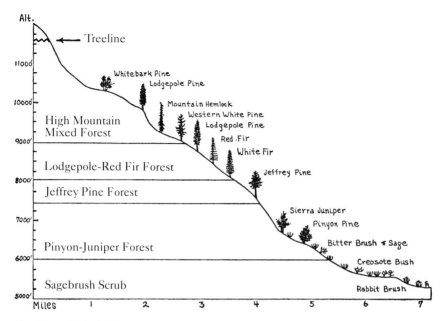

Alt.

← Treeline

11000'

Whitebark Pine
Lodgepole Pine

10000'

Mountain Hemlock
Western White Pine
Lodgepole Pine

High Mountain
Mixed Forest

Red Fir

9000'

White Fir

Lodgepole-Red Fir Forest

Jeffrey Pine

8000'

Jeffrey Pine Forest

7000'

Sierra Juniper

Pinyon Pine

Bitter Brush ↟ Sage

Pinyon-Juniper Forest

6000'

Creosote Bush

Sagebrush Scrub

Rabbit Brush

5000'

Miles   1   2   3   4   5   6   7

Tree Progression in the East Central Sierra

ground squirrel, chickaree, porcupine and the Belding ground squirrel. Actually, more Beldings will be seen in the next higher and still cooler high mountain mixed forest. Stands of lodgepole pine, mountain hemlock, and whitebark pine (which at treeline often consists of only low shrublike thickets) indicate the extent of this forest . Here also live the chickarees, white-tailed jackrabbits, pikas (especially in boulder slopes), marmots, golden-mantled ground squirrels, Inyo mule deer, and the little alpine chipmunks. Above treeline, scattered dwarf plants, seldom over four inches high, grow on the seemingly barren, rocky slopes. This is the coldest region of all and has the shortest growing season; flowers must grow, bloom, and produce seed all in a few weeks. Few mammals can survive in such a rigorous climate. During the summer months the alpine chipmunk, pika, marmot and white-tailed jackrabbit extend their range above treeline. Occasionally the mountain coyote and Inyo mule deer also range into this alpine region. The latter two are wide-ranging species and, on the east slope, range rather freely into and across the lodgepole-fir, high mountain and alpine communities all summer.

There are variations, of course, from the generalized progression pictured. When a slope is as abrupt as in the eastern Sierra, the communities may be so jammed together that one of them is missing. Most communities have fingerlike extensions upward and downward into adjacent communities. For example, in a forest of Jeffrey pine there may be a ribbon of lodgepole and aspen following down a stream. Since lodgepole grow best in a colder climate, they will be among the Jeffrey only if there is a cold pocket within the warmer Jeffrey climate. Such pockets or ribbons are often caused by cold air draining down canyon bottoms or by differences in exposure to the sun. Occasionally the sequence of trees may be upside down when compared with the diagram, as when a shady slope or ravine dominated by hemlock and lodgepole is topped by a sunny slope or ridge of juniper. Each forest community, then, is actually a mosaic of microclimates—small areas having climates that differ from the general pattern because of exposure to the sun, protection from wind, or unusual moisture. Despite these variations, the concepts of tree progression and of forest communities are very useful.

The diagram represents the general elevations where the different trees grow abundantly, though locally some may range higher and lower. Notice in the diagram that the distance from desert to alpine climate is only six miles. The same changes on the more gradual western slope of the Sierra may cover sixty miles. It is the steepness of the eastern Sierra slope that accounts for the diversity and amazing contrast of scenery and vegetation within short distances. The variety of soils and climates accounts also for the great variety of flowers and the wide range of growing and blooming seasons. Growing seasons vary from six months at 6000 feet to two months or less on the high slopes, and the length of the flowering season often depends on how long snow remains in spring.

Trees

The ten most common trees of the eastern Sierra are grouped below as they are found from lower to higher altitude, as on the preceding diagram. Since the cones are quite distinctive, you will have little trouble recognizing these common trees. Most cones are easy to find. Along the short, steep Fern Lake trail you can find nine of these ten. Other trees that you may discover in the region are: copper birch and cottonwood in the lower altitudes near water; mountain mahogany on hot, dry slopes; limber pine near treeline.

Pinyon-Juniper Forest

Trees 10–30 feet high, scattered. The ground covered with desert shrubs.

Pinyon or piñon pine, *Pinus monophylla*. Pine family. Needles single, about one inch long. Cones up to 3 inches long. Of all North American pines, only the pinyon has a single needle; other pines have 2 to 5 needles bundled together.

As you drive north from Bishop, there are few trees except along streams or near houses. But as the road climbs Sherwin Grade, you will notice some short, squat, gray-green trees—the pinyon pine. They signal a bit more rain-fall and cooler temperatures—the high desert. In the low hills east of US

395, east toward Benton and south toward the Volcanic Tableland, you can discover extensive stands of pinyon pine. Their delicious nuts, sold locally in late fall, were the food staple of the Paiutes. Each group had its own pine-nut territory. Trespassing was resented and was the most common cause of quarreling among otherwise peaceful Paiute groups. Pine-nut crops vary from plentiful to scant, however; a poor crop meant a hard winter and even starvation for the Paiutes. In good years, some of the Paiutes moved from the valleys up to the pinyon forest to live during fall and winter, unlike most mountain Indians who *descended* to the valleys in winter.

Utah juniper, *Juniperus osteosperma.* Cypress family. Leaves scalelike, bark light silver gray to dark gray, berries reddish brown. Grows along the base of the Sierra and east across the Great Basin, scattered among the pinyon pine.

Western juniper, *Juniperus occidentalis.* Cypress family. Leaves scalelike, ⅛ inch long. Bark reddish brown, stringy. Berries ¼ inch, blue-black with grayish bloom. Does not fit neatly into one of our forest communities; instead, grows in isolated stands on dry, rocky sites, locally up to about 9000 feet in the Sierra.

On exposed slopes where it has no protection against windstorms, its trunk is often exceedingly large for its height, its top splintered and its thick limbs grotesquely twisted and broken, with only a few tufts of green showing that it still lives. A stand of tall, symmetrical junipers grows about 3 miles up the Valentine Lake trail, beautiful examples of this tough, rugged tree.

Quaking aspen, *Populus tremuloides.* Willow family. Light green leaves that tremble in the slightest breeze. Bark white and smooth, though rough and black at the base of old trees.

This is the tree that comes into its glory in late September, when its leaves glow red and golden. Lundy, McGee, Hilton and Rock Creek canyons have particularly extensive displays of brilliant color. The French trappers of the West's early days had a legend that the Cross was fashioned from aspen wood and that aspen have trembled ever since. Botanists explain the aspen's quaking in the nature of its leafstalk. Besides being longer than the leaf, it is flattened perpendicular to the leaf's plane, thus acting as a pivot and causing the leaves to quiver in the gentlest wind. Aspen prefer damp areas, but since they can tolerate a variety of climates, they are not good indicators of altitude or forest progression. From the sagebrush country, where they grow large and straight along streams, they range to the upper limit of the lodgepole-red fir forest, where usually they are scrubby and bent from heavy snows. Near campsites, their bark may be rough and black with irregular scars, rather than shining white—the trees' attempts to heal the wounds inflicted by pocket knives. Aspen have a peculiar ability to reproduce by means of root suckers, which gives them a temporary advantage when a forest is swept by fire.

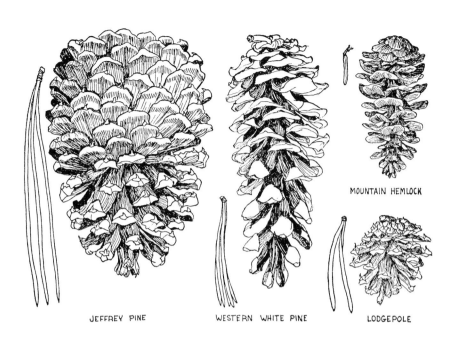

JEFFREY PINE   WESTERN WHITE PINE   MOUNTAIN HEMLOCK

LODGEPOLE

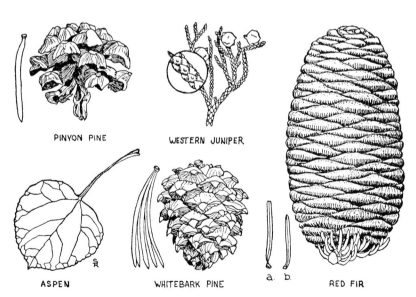

PINYON PINE   WESTERN JUNIPER

ASPEN   WHITEBARK PINE   a. b.   RED FIR

Jeffrey Pine Forest

Open forest of very tall trees. The trunks of mature trees are clear of branches for many feet above the ground. Little underbrush.

Jeffrey pine, *Pinus Jeffreyi.* Pine family. Needles 3 in a bundle, up to 6 inches long. Cones measure 6–10 inches. Bark of mature trees cracked into irregular reddish brown plates, like very large jigsaw pieces.

The vanilla-bark pine, as the Jeffrey is called sometimes, is the three-needle pine of the eastern slope; its counterpart on the western Sierra slope is the ponderosa or yellow pine, abundant in Yosemite Park . A few ponderosa grow on the eastern slope—along lower Rock Creek, for example—but most of the 3-needle pine are Jeffrey. The differences between the two are slight: the bark of the Jeffrey has a distinct vanilla or pineapple odor and its cone is larger. Holding both hands around a cone provides a simple test. If the prickles hurt, it is a ponderosa cone; if they curve in and do not prick, it is a Jeffrey cone. Many summer campers find the climate of the Jeffrey pine forest most to their liking. It is cooler and greener than the lower sagebrush country, yet warmer than the sometimes nippy red-fir climate.

White fir, *Abies concolor.* Pine family. Needles single, usually more than one inch long. Cones upright on top branches, up to 5 inches long. Bark of young trees silvery; of older trees, ashy gray.

Comparison of white fir needles, left, and red fir needles, right.

White fir are not abundant east of the Sierra crest. Here they are scattered among Jeffrey pine and blend into the red fir forest around 7500 feet. If the trees are old, the two are easily distinguished. Break off a small piece of bark; if the fresh surface is tan it is white fir, if deep red it is red fir. Determining young firs requires close examination of their needles. A white-fir needle has a half twist at its base, where it joins the twig; a red fir needle is curved but not twisted at its base.

Lodgepole-Red Fir Forest

A dense forest, with crowded young trees shouldering their way up toward the sunlight.

Lodgepole pine, *Pinus Murrayana.* Pine family. Also called tamarack pine. Needles 2 in a bundle, broad and stiff. Cones up to 2 inches long. Bark thin. The only two-needle pine in the area. Grows from 7500 feet to treeline.

Because dead lower branches remain on the trees a long time, a lodgepole forest looks scraggly. For the same reason, it is usually easy to find dry lodgepole wood even in wet weather. The Plains Indians used young lodgepole for their tipi poles; the pioneers for their log cabins. Lodgepole pine were preferred because the trunks are usually straight, taper little, have few large branches and their thin bark is easy to peel. Since lodgepole cones are pitch-free and small, they are ideal for decorating Christmas packages.

Red fir, *Abies magnifica.* Pine family. Needles single, up to 1¼ inches long. Cones upright on top branches, up to 8 inches long. Bark of mature trees up to 6 inches thick, deep red inside, red-brown outside.

Beware of camping under a dead fir-snag, for firs are very susceptible to rot. A little wind may topple over a thirty-foot length. Foresters sometimes refer to fir snags as "widow-makers" and make a point of clearing them out of campgrounds. A dead pine is much less dangerous; its pitch helps resist decay. During violent storms, pines may crash down roots and all, but they very seldom break off as do the firs. Fir cones (red and white) seldom are found on the ground. If chickarees do not get them first, they disintegrate on the tree in fall, the scales peeling off and the seeds dropping down; the center stems remain upright on the top branches, looking like candles. To distinguish red from white, see "White fir" above. The red fir is prized as a Christmas tree and often called silver-tip, after the silvery green new growth on the tips of its branches.

High Mountain Mixed Forest

Much of the ground bare, occasional low shrubs and flowers. Near treeline, most trees are twisted and stunted by wind and snow.

Western white or silver pine, *Pinus monticola.* Pine family. Needles 3–5 in a bundle, slender, 2–4 inches long. Cones up to 8 inches long.

This pine is most easily identified by its cones, which hang from the tips of its branches like bunches of bananas. On a mature tree, it is often impossible to get a sample of the needles, for the trunk is clear of branches for many feet above the ground. In the eastern Sierra, the western white pine intermingles with lodgepole and red fir and is not abundant.

Mountain hemlock, *Tsuga mertensiana.* Pine family. Needles single, up to ¾ of an inch long. Cones 2–3 inches.

Above 9500 feet the mountain hemlock is in its glory. Occasionally it is found lower, but then always on shaded north slopes or in cold canyons. It can be identified by its bent and drooping tip; fir and pine tips are stiff and erect. Hemlock limbs grow down to its base, and the ends of its branches droop. It is a fascinating experience to see a young hemlock in June, bent over at right angles under the packed snow of winter, suddenly released from the weight as the sun melts the snow, straighten up in a few hours.

Whitebark pine, *Pinus albicaulis.* Pine family. Needles 5 in a bundle up to 1½ inches long. Bark silver, or reddish silver if wind-whipped, except at the base of old trees where it is rough and black. Cones on the trees purple, up to 3 inches long, with conspicuous drops of shiny pitch. Mature cones are seldom found on the ground intact, for nutcrackers and chipmunks shatter them while they are still on the tree. But you can find their remains littering the ground beneath—single, thick, thumbnail-size scales.

This is the creeping pine of treeline, often dwarfed and misshapen, yet surviving in a climate where few other trees and only a few small plants can grow. It usually grows in a cluster, with several trunks coming from a common center. Its flexibility helps it survive storms and snows that would break the branches of a less pliable tree. If you choose to camp or sleep under a whitebark's low branches, which can give amazingly good protection in high, wind-swept country, treat it kindly. The foot-long twig you snap off carelessly may have taken twenty years to reach its stubby length. Covered with snow seven months or more, withstanding gale winds, and blessed with few days warm enough for growth, a whitebark may grow less than half an inch a year.

Wildflowers & Shrubs

More than one thousand kinds of flowering plants have been collected in this region. Thirty-eight of the more common and colorful flowers are described here. From May through September, by following spring up the mountain slope, you can find flowering plants somewhere, beginning with the bright pink flowers of the desert peach along US 395 and ending with the deep blue gentian in the high meadows and the yellow buckwheat on the high ridges. Flowering periods vary considerably from summer to summer, and from place to place. To make identification easier, they are grouped according to their color—white, yellow, red, lavender, blue. The scientific plant names in this book conform to Munz and Keck's *A California Flora* (1968).

With each new parking area, each new condo development, each new campground, living places for plants are reduced. The meadows have fared the worst; most have been ditched, drained, grazed, filled, paved or drowned. The Valentine Reserve encompasses the only remaining pristine, extensive, mountain meadow in Mammoth. Watch for its annual open house, usually late July; the broad slopes of grass and flowers are unforgettable. To make up for all the flowers lost to acres of asphalt, perhaps we can give greater care to those remaining. Mountain plants are sturdy, surviving ice, snow and winds; but they cannot survive constant trampling and picking. Many are perennial, needing several summers free from disturbance to reach maturity and bloom. As a sign reads in the Missouri Botanic Garden, "Let it be said of these flowers that they died with their roots on." If we remember that high-mountain gardens are even more vulnerable than our home gardens, we are more likely to step *over* small plants and go *around* wet flower-jungles. Fortunately we have miles of wilderness at our back door, and there you can still discover magical meadows and carpets of wildflowers.

White flowers

Corn lily or false hellebore, *Veratrum californicum.* Lily family. This plant with its 3–6-foot stem and large leaves dominates the marshy meadows where it is common. The tall stems resemble cornstalks and are more often seen without the bloom, for they do not bloom every summer. When this plant first comes up in the spring, it resembles the "skunk cabbage" of the Northwest.

Mariposa lily, *Calochortus Leichtlinii.* Lily family. These one-inch flowers have creamy-white petals with a dark spot at their base. They grow in dry areas (6000–8000 feet) and bloom from late June to early July. *Mariposa* is Spanish for *butterfly.*

White bog orchid or Sierra rein orchis, *Habenaria dilatata var. leucostachys.* Orchid family. The thick, hollow stem, 10–15 inches long, is sheathed in plain slender leaves. The ½-inch flowers have a delicate sweet-spicy perfume. Though few people expect to find orchids in the mountains, this one grows in damp meadows (6500–9500 feet) throughout the region, blooming in late July.

Thistle poppy, *Argemone munita* ssp. *rotundata.* Poppy family. Flowers 3–4 inches broad, showy, white with yellow center and fragile, papery petals. It is named for the stiff spines that cover the entire plant except the petals. The stems are 1–3 feet long, several arising from the base of each plant. Common along edges of roads (5500–8500 feet).

Nude buckwheat, *Eriogonum gracilipes* ssp. *nudum.* Buckwheat family. Very small flowers grouped into compact round heads up to ½ inch in diameter; blue-green stems. Leaves, sometimes red, cluster in a circle at the base of the plant. Common in dry places up to 9000 feet.

Cow parsnip, *Heracleum lanatum.* Parsley family. What appears to be a 6–10-inch flower actually is a group of umbrella-like heads of tiny white flowers. An unpleasant odor is characteristic of the plant. Stems are coarse and hollow, 4–6 feet tall. Grows in damp meadows and along stream courses up to 8500 feet.

Swamp whiteheads, *Sphenosciadium capitellatum.* Parsley family. A robust plant 2–5 feet tall, blooming in wet meadows in July and August. Pinhead-

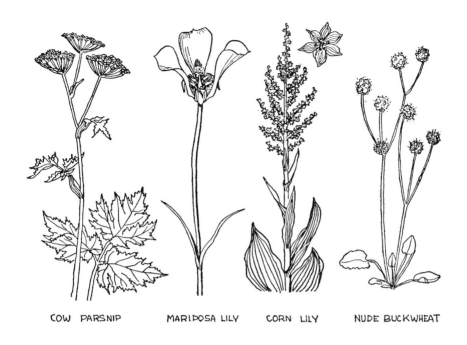

COW PARSNIP   MARIPOSA LILY   CORN LILY   NUDE BUCKWHEAT

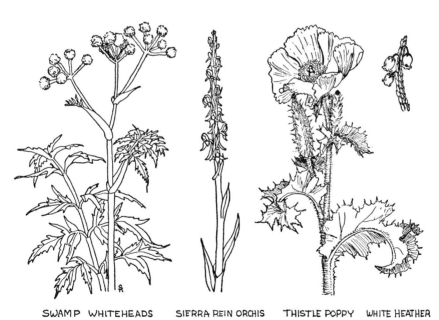

SWAMP WHITEHEADS   SIERRA REIN ORCHIS   THISTLE POPPY   WHITE HEATHER

size flowers make up marble-like balls arranged in open, round clusters.

White or bell heather, *Cassiope mertensiana.* Heath family. Bell-shaped flowers less than ¼ inch across nod on red threadlike stems. Grows in low, dense mats, 2–4 inches high, only at elevations above 9000 feet in forest areas. This plant has close relatives in arctic regions throughout the world.

Prickly phlox, see under purple flowers.

Yarrow, *Achillea lanulosa.* Sunflower family. Flowers ⅛ inch or less, dull white with greenish centers, forming flat-topped clusters. Stems 1–2 feet tall; leaves finely divided, resembling carrot leaves. Foliage and flower both have a strong acrid odor. Common in dry areas.

Yellow flowers

Little tiger lily, *Lilium parvum.* Lily family. Flowers 1–2 inches across, yellow-orange with purple spots and delicate sweet scent. Sometimes the curved outer part of the petal is red-orange. The stems sometimes exceed 6 feet in height and support one to twenty-five flowers on a stalk. Grows in wet, boggy places from 6500 to 10,000 feet.

Sulfur flower, *Eriogonum umbellatum* ssp. *polyanthum.* Buckwheat family. Flowers a brilliant sulfur yellow to chartreuse, fading to deep orange or brick-red, many very small flowers forming spherical clusters. Small gray to reddish leaves form a mat around the base of the plant. Flower stalks 3–9 inches long. In full bloom, sulfur flowers make a colorful display on dry hillsides from 6000 to 9500 feet. Several smaller close relatives with yellow, white or pink blossoms grow at higher elevations.

Western wall flower, *Erysimum capitatum.* Mustard family. Bright lemon-yellow fragrant flowers. The slender stem unbranched, 1–2 feet high.

Cinquefoil, *Potentilla gracilis* ssp. *Nuttallii,* see sketch (a). Rose family. The yellow roselike flowers are ½ inch or more across. Two or more types of this plant grow commonly in the dry woods and drier meadows throughout the area. The yellow variety is more often found in meadows; its creamy white relative, *Potentilla glandulosa* (b), in forests, especially lodgepole.

Evening primrose, *Oenothera Hookeri.* Evening Primrose family. Flowers 2–3 inches, lemon-yellow, that open toward evening and close during the day. Stems tough, 2–5 feet long; leaves strongly influenced by light direction, following the sun throughout the day. Very common along streambeds and in sandy meadows from 4000 to 8000 feet.

Mullein, *Verbascum thapsus* (not pictured). Figwort family. Flowers ½ inch across, light yellow-gold, many of them crowded on a single robust stalk, 3–5 feet long. Woolly leaves sheath the tall heavy stalk. A mass of leaves forms a rosette at the base. New England ladies used to rub mullein leaves on their cheeks to make them pink. Very common along highways at lower

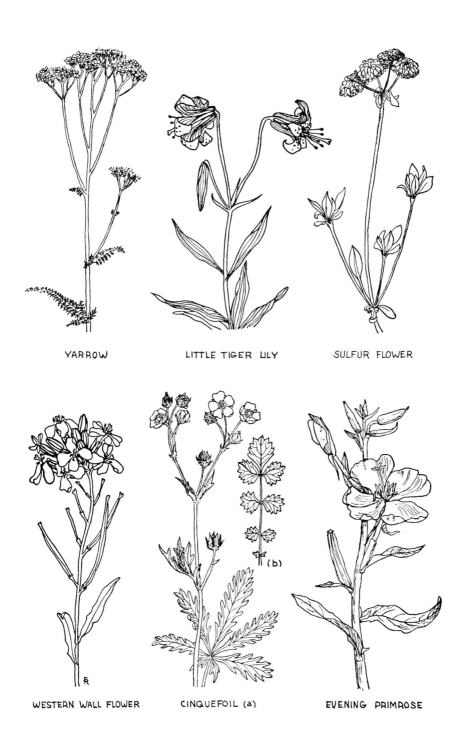

YARROW   LITTLE TIGER LILY   SULFUR FLOWER

WESTERN WALL FLOWER   CINQUEFOIL (a)   EVENING PRIMROSE

147

elevations, especially near Mono Lake; conspicuous in August. This plant's seeds were used by Indians for food.

Common monkey flower, *Mimulus guttatus.* Figwort family. Flower one inch across, brilliant yellow with brown spots in the throat. Stems fragile, leaves delicate, wilts almost immediately when picked. Grows in or near running water from 7000 to 10,500 feet. A very tiny yellow monkey flower is found in meadows, and a miniature rose-purple one grows on dry slopes at high elevations. A larger sturdier plant, with a pink flower striped yellow and white, grows in damp places, *M. lewisii.*

Woolly wyethia or mule ears, *Wyethia mollis.* Sunflower family. The flower head is 2–3 inches across, showy, composed of deep-yellow flowers arranged in a circle around the outside of the head; the inner flowers are greenish. Several flower stalks 1–2 feet long rise from among large woolly leaves. Conspicuous in sagebrush areas, especially in late June when they are in full bloom.

Golden groundsel or old-man's-beard, *Senecio triangularis.* Sunflower family. Deep-yellow flowers, ¼–½ inch across, cluster to form ragged looking heads. Common in meadows at all elevations, blooming by late August.

Pink and red flowers

Red columbine, *Aquilegia formosa.* Buttercup family. Flowers one inch broad, red with yellow centers, hang on slender stems. These bright flowers are great favorites of hummingbirds. Common in drier parts of meadows in the lodgepole-hemlock woods. A rare relative, *A. pubescens,* is a delicate flower with creamy white petals tinted yellow, pink or, less commonly, blue. A true alpine plant found in rocky areas above 8500 feet.

Red heather, *Phyllodoce breweri.* Heath family. Rose-pink flowers, ½ inch across, are held on delicate threadlike stalks. Evergreen leaves that look like pine needles cover the low-growing stems. Grows in low dense mats in pine forests (9000–10,000 feet). It may be confused with the bog laurel described below.

Alpine or bog laurel, *Kalmia polifolia* var. *microphylla.* Heath family. Soon after snow melts from high mountain meadows, this plant blossoms with pink, ½-inch flowers. When the flower opens the tips of the pollen sacs are lodged in tiny pits at the center of the petals. When an insect lights on the flower to get nectar, the stamen springs up, and pollen is dusted over the body of the insect, which then transports the pollen to another flower.

Scarlet penstemon, *Penstemon Bridgesii.* Figwort family. Bright red, tube-shaped flowers line stalks 10–15 inches long. Many stalks grow from one root crown, making a flash of color along rocky banks and roadsides (7000–9000 feet). Several other members of this group are common to the area—a larger, bright blue penstemon on dry slopes, magenta pride-of-the-mountains in high, rocky places, and a tall delicate pink penstemon in the sagebrush flats.

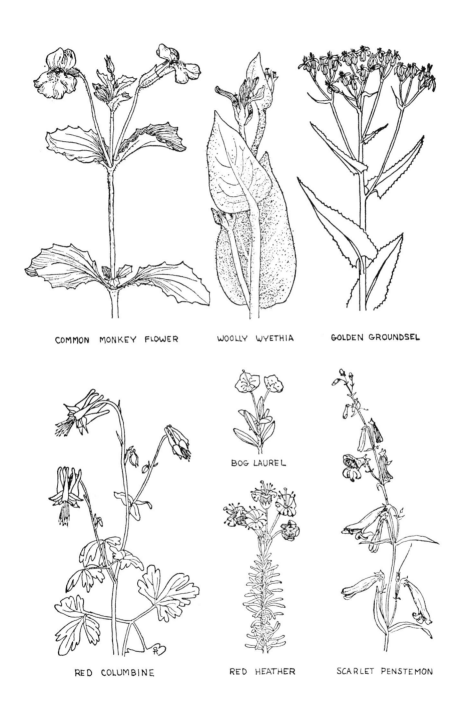

COMMON MONKEY FLOWER   WOOLLY WYETHIA   GOLDEN GROUNDSEL

BOG LAUREL

RED COLUMBINE   RED HEATHER   SCARLET PENSTEMON

149

Scarlet gilia, *Ipomopsis aggregata.* Gilia family. Flowers brilliant, 1–2 inches long. Numerous blossoms line a single stem, 8–20 inches long. Though the gilia's tube-shaped flower opens into a five-pointed star, it may be mistaken for the scarlet penstemon described above. Slender, finger-like leaves form a rosette at the base; many of these rosettes may be seen among blossoming plants, for this plant grows one year, then blooms the next. Common on dry hillsides (6500–9000 feet). A color variation in rich salmon pink is sometimes seen in meadows (6500–7500 feet).

Indian paintbrush, *Castilleja miniata.* Figwort family. Vivid red-orange dense cluster, 1–1½ inches long, at the end of the stem. The actual flower is a green tube hidden inside the colorful bract. Common in moist places. Several other varieties—including one deep pink, one light yellow, and one light orange—grow on dry hillsides. A brilliant purplish-red, short paintbrush grows in moist alpine meadows. A smaller, paler variety grows on high, rocky slopes.

Lewis' monkey flower, see common monkey flower under yellow flowers.

Lavender flowers

Wild onion, *Allium validum.* Lily family. Small flowers are packed into a flat cluster atop a leafless triangular stalk 1–3 feet long. The entire plant emits a distinct onion odor; it is an excellent substitute for domestic onions, although much stronger. Common in wet meadows, especially above 8000 feet. Different varieties may occasionally be found on dry sagebrush slopes.

Pussypaws, *Calyptridium umbellatum.* Purslane family. Rose-lavender flowers, smaller than ¼ inch, are sandwiched between two white papery structures that persist long after the flower has gone, making the round heads look like soiled white fur. These clustered heads resemble the bottom of a cat's paw. The stems radiate out from a circle of dark leathery leaves that lie flat on the ground. Grows in dry, open places above 8500 feet.

Fireweed, *Epilobium angustifolium.* Evening Primrose family. Many rose-purple flowers less than an inch across line a single red-stemmed stalk. The leaves turn bright red in fall. In many areas fireweed is the first plant to grow on a burned-over area, hence its name.

Prickly or Douglas phlox, *Phlox diffusa.* Gilia family. Cushions of light lavender to white catch the eye on dry hillsides in early summer. The small flowers, less than ½ inch across, bloom all at once, obscuring the prickly leaves of the plant. Common on dry slopes from 7000 to 11,000 feet. Many forms of phlox occur in the Sierra.

Sierra shooting star, *Dodecatheon jeffreyi.* Primrose family. Lavender petals with a yellow band at the base turn back from black anthers, forming the point of the shooting star. Ruddy stalks 1–2 feet tall. Common in moist meadows above 7000 feet in spring. Later in summer as the snow disap-

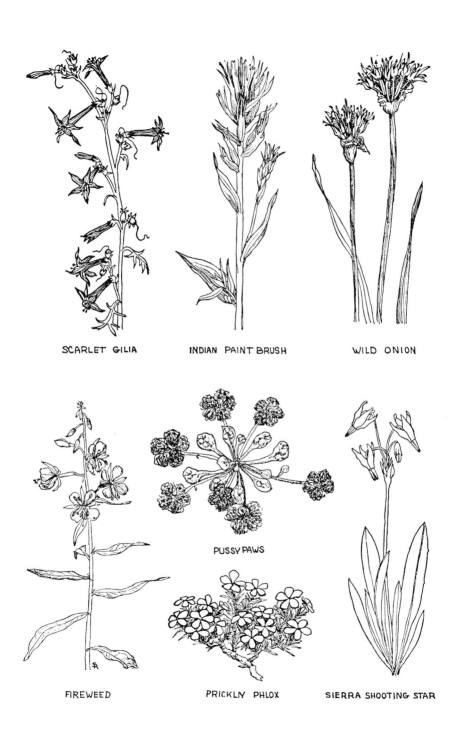

SCARLET GILIA   INDIAN PAINT BRUSH   WILD ONION

PUSSY PAWS

FIREWEED   PRICKLY PHLOX   SIERRA SHOOTING STAR

pears from high meadows, the related miniature alpine shooting star, *D. alpinum*, can be seen.

Mustang mint or pennyroyal, *Monardella odoratissima* ssp. *parvifolia.* Mint family. Many very small lavender flowers form rounded clusters on stalks less than a foot high. The leaves give off a pungent minty smell. Grows on dry hillsides at 6500–9500 feet.

Elephant heads, *Pedicularis groenlandica.* Figwort family. The deep-red-dish-purple flowers, less than ½ inch across and resembling the heads of elephants, are crowded along the stem. Blooms in the higher meadows (7500–10,500 feet) in July and August. Elephant's ears or snouts, *P. attollens,* a near relative, can be distinguished by its lighter color. Its petals do not form an elephant's head but are more like ruffles.

Subalpine or mountain daisy, *Erigeron peregrinus* ssp. *callianthemum* var. *angustifolia* (not pictured). Sunflower family. Flowers 1–2 inches broad with yellow centers grow singly or in twos and threes on slender leafy stalks. It is common in drier meadows and shaded forests (7000–10,000 feet). There are numerous other daisy-like flowers in the region, but this is by far the most common.

Blue flowers

Western blue flag, *Iris missouriensis.* Iris family. Flowers 3–4 inches broad, sky-blue with yellow ribs on the inner petals. This flower, also called mountain iris, blooms early; in June meadows from 6000 to 8000 feet may turn blue with its blossoms.

Larkspur or delphinium, *Delphinium* species. Buttercup family. One larkspur of the region, *Delphinium glaucum*, is a magnificent plant up to 7 feet tall, which blooms in late July and August (6000–9000 feet). Stalks with medium-blue flowers crowded along them rise 2–4 feet above masses of leaves. Another larkspur, *D. polycladon*, is smaller, 2–4 feet high. It has several stalks of deep-blue-violet flowers, less than an inch across. Lush, round, many-lobed leaves form a bushy growth around the base of the plant. It is frequently found along watercourses (7000–10,000 feet). A much smaller variety is found in forests and dry hillside areas.

Monkshood, *Aconitum columbianum.* Buttercup family. Monkshood is often mistaken for the delphiniums described above, but close examination reveals the distinctive shape of the flowers, which are like the hoods of monks. In all other respects the plants are similar, but monkshood is much less common.

Lupine, *Lupinus* species. Pea family. Five or more similar species of lupine are common in the region. The flowers are like small, deep blue sweet peas crowded together on erect stems. The most common species, illustrated here, grows in damp meadows. Others prefer the shaded forests, some the

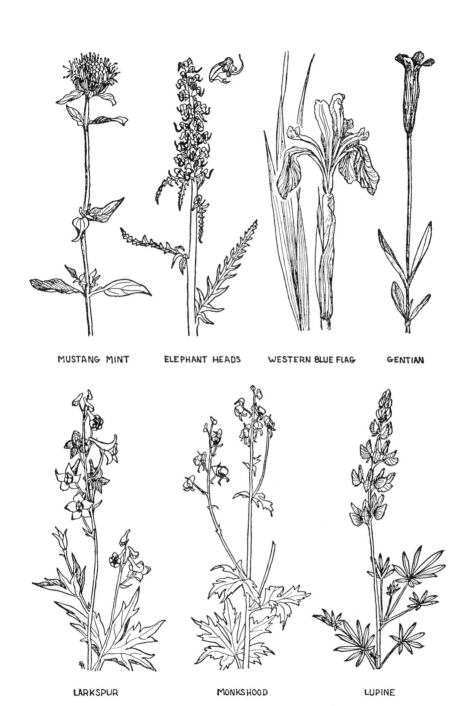

MUSTANG MINT   ELEPHANT HEADS   WESTERN BLUE FLAG   GENTIAN

LARKSPUR   MONKSHOOD   LUPINE

dry hillsides, and still other small, compact lupines grow on wind-swept ridges. All are long-blooming.

Sierra gentian, *Gentiana holopetala*. Gentian family. The common species is a deep blue flower on a short stem, often hidden among the taller grasses in damp meadows in early autumn. Two other types of gentian are occasionally found in the region—one a much larger plant with two-inch brilliant blue flowers, the other a tiny white one restricted to high mountain meadows.

Blue stick-seed or forget-me-not, *Hackelia floribunda* (not pictured). Borage family. Flowers are sky-blue with white centers, ¼ inch across. Small clumps of this plant are common along the edges of forests (7000–9500 feet). The name comes from the fact that the seed is covered with tiny hooks that cling to anything with which they come in contact. Occasionally a group of plants will have pure pink blossoms. A relative with much smaller, lighter blue flowers grows in meadows.

Blue penstemon, see scarlet penstemon.

Shrubs

Mountain alder, *Alnus tenuifolia*. Birch family. This shrub is 4–10 feet high and grows above 7000 feet. The flowers are like tiny pine cones, persisting on the branches long after the seed is shed. The smooth bark varies from silver to rich brown. Dense stands grow in wet places and form nearly impassable thickets.

ALPINE WILLOW

Willow, *Salix* species. Willow family. There are a number of willows in the region, typically growing where there is an abundance of water. Large ones, reaching tree proportions, line creeks at lower elevations; smaller bushy forms cluster in thickets at higher meadows; above treeline, the dwarf alpine willow carpets the moist ground near snowbanks. The characteristics

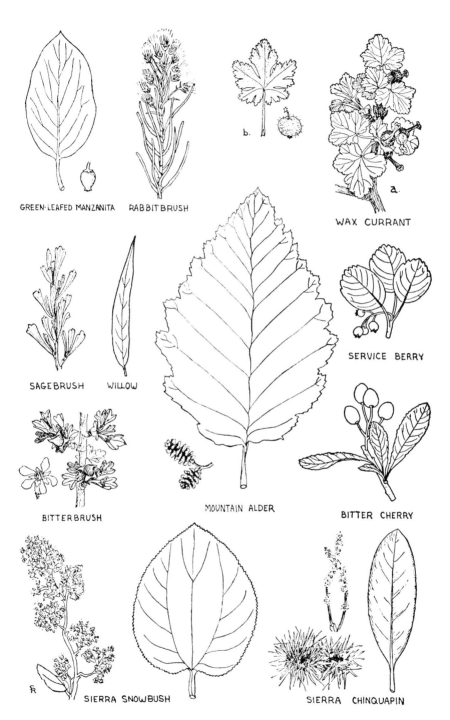

GREEN-LEAFED MANZANITA   RABBITBRUSH

b.

WAX CURRANT   a.

SAGEBRUSH   WILLOW

SERVICE BERRY

BITTERBRUSH

MOUNTAIN ALDER

BITTER CHERRY

SIERRA SNOWBUSH

SIERRA CHINQUAPIN

155

of all are similar, despite their great variation in size. The leaves are long and narrow, the stems covered with a smooth golden- to rose-toned bark that is especially striking in winter after the leaves have fallen. The typical catkins, showing just as soon as the snow frees the branches, are not often seen by visitors.

Wild rose, *Rosa woodsii* var. *ultramontana* (not pictured). Rose family. This scraggly shrub is common in lower meadows (6000–8000 feet). In late May and June it is covered with delicate pink blossoms having a rich perfume. The fruit turns scarlet in August, and in late autumn the leaves turn a rich red-brown.

Bitterbrush or antelope brush, *Purshia tridentata.* Rose family. Forms dense masses 1–4 feet high in sagebrush country and in open parts of Jeffrey pine forests. It is a preferred food of deer, antelope and sheep. In some places it is conspicuously angular in form owing to intense browsing. Only a certain portion of each year's tender young shoots can be eaten without seriously damaging the plants. If they are overbrowsed they die, and the range becomes virtually useless. When the population of any deer herd exceeds the capacity of its winter range, three things may happen: 1) many deer may die of starvation, especially a large proportion of fawns; 2) some may migrate into unaccustomed and often inhabited areas, where they can cause serious damage to orchards and crops; or 3) the deer barely manage to survive, mainly on the food stored as body fat, but the vigor and well-being of the herd decreases markedly.

Bitter cherry, *Prunus emarginata.* Rose family. A graceful shrub with a red-brown, glossy bark. In spring it is covered with delicate white, sweet-scented flowers. Small bright red cherries, bitter and inedible, ripen later in the summer. Its habitat is similar to that of bitterbrush.

Service berry, *Amelanchier pallida.* Rose family. Known in some regions as "sarvus berry." Resembles the bitter cherry and grows in similar localities, but has round rather than slender leaves.

Tobacco brush, or Sierra snowbush, *Ceanothus velutinus.* Buckthorn family. Often called "wild lilac," a name shared by some forty plants in California. The name snowbush comes from the mass of white, sweet-smelling flowers that blossom in early summer. Grows up to 5 feet high, forming dense hillside stands, especially in the Jeffrey pine and red fir forests (6500–9000 feet). The evergreen leaves are sticky and appear freshly varnished on the upper surface. When broken, they give off a strong, spicy odor.

Green-leafed manzanita, *Arctostaphylos patula.* Heath family. Often mixed with the Sierra snowbush, manzanita is distinguished by its smooth red-brown bark, round, leathery evergreen leaves and very gnarled branches. It is said that a reward of one hundred dollars was once offered to anyone who could find a piece of straight manzanita branch 12 inches long—and that the reward has never been claimed. In late June, bunches of delicate pink, bell-shaped flowers blossom. The early Spaniards named this plant *manzanita* (little apple) for its small apple-shaped berries. Above 8000 feet a smaller relative, *A. nevadensis*, carpets the forest floor.

Wax currant, *Ribes cereum*. Saxifrage family. This relative of the domestic currant lives on dry hillsides from 7000 to 9000 feet elevation. It is 3 to 5 feet high, covered with small, toothed leaves having a waxy surface (a). The stems are without spines and have a smooth silvery bark. The small red fruits which ripen late in August are pithy and quite unpalatable. In moist shaded places *R. montigenum* is found, sometimes in large, nearly impenetrable patches. This "gooseberry currant" (b) has many stiff yellow spines on its branches. Its juicy, tart fruit makes excellent jelly.

Sagebrush, *Artemisia tridentata*. Sunflower family. Although large expanses of the eastern Sierra are covered with this common shrub, nearly to the exclusion of all other plants, its growth stops abruptly at the edge of forested areas, for it cannot survive the forest's moisture and lack of sun. The name and odor of sage are deceiving, for this plant is not at all related to seasoning sage of the mint family, but is more closely related to goldenrod. In late fall, slender flower stalks bear tiny, greyish yellow blossoms.

Sierra chinquapin, *Castanopsis sempervirens*. Oak family. Grows in localities similar to those of manzanita and Sierra snowbush. Its evergreen leaves are backed with rusty fur. Clusters of spine-covered fruits remain on the plant for several years.

Rabbitbrush, *Chrysothamnus nauseosus*. Sunflower family. This 2–5-foot shrub, common on sagebrush flats, is easily mistaken for sagebrush because it is the same color, except in fall when masses of brilliant golden-yellow blossoms cover the tops of the plants. A smaller species of rabbitbrush, known as ragweed, grows along roadways at higher elevations.

≈≈≈≈

Other interesting plants found in the region—such as mountain mahogany, grass of Parnassus, western roseroot, Labrador tea, mountain penstemon, Sierra primrose—are described and illustrated in *Deepest Valley: Guide to Owens Valley*.

Mammals

Following are brief descriptions of some of the more conspicuous mammals of the region. Although they are grouped roughly according to the forest communities which they prefer, there are no sharp lines or boundaries between the communities, and animals will range into higher or lower communities whenever they can find food and suitable habitat. The accompanying diagram illustrates the progression of forest communities and some typical mammals to look for.

Sagebrush Scrub

White-tailed antelope squirrel, *Ammospermophilus leucurus.* A small ground squirrel about the size of a chipmunk, but has a shorter tail and seldom climbs trees. Has a single white stripe down each side. Total length about 8½ inches.

A small chipmunk-like ground squirrel with conspicuous white tail arched over its back may scamper in the early morning or evening across Highway 395 between Lone Pine and Independence or on Sherwin Grade. Beyond the highway shoulder, it may stop beneath a shrub to take a quick look before going on. This desert squirrel feeds on grains, seeds and green plants—and on meat when it is available (animals and insects killed on the highway).

Pinyon-Juniper Forest

California ground squirrel, *Spermophilus beecheyi.* Larger than a house rat, about the size of a gray squirrel but the tail not bushy as in a tree squirrel and only about three-fourths of the body length. General coloration dull yellowish brown with grizzled white patches on the sides of the neck and shoulders. Total length about 17 inches.

In Inyo-Mono the California ground squirrels are not abundant, as they are in the foothills of the San Joaquin and Sacramento valleys. Primarily ground dwellers, single squirrels may be seen atop fence posts, rocks, or even in the low branches of the brush just south of Casa Diablo. Look also for these "digger" or Beechey squirrels and their workings in the dry sandy ground beneath sage and bitterbrush at Rush Creek Ranch and just north of Lee Vining. Like other ground squirrels their diet is varied—seeds, grains, green plants, insects, meat, and the eggs and young of birds when available.

Black-tailed jackrabbit, *Lepus californicus.* A large slender yellowish brown rabbit with upstanding ears about 5 inches long; upper side of the tail black. About the size of a small house cat. Total length about 22 inches.

In the early morning or evening, jackrabbits are commonly seen in Long Valley. If you see one ahead of you along the highway, slow down for a better look; chances are that if you stop he will dart into the sagebrush cover. Occasionally, one will race beside the road ahead of the car, leaping into the air in a characteristic spy hop to get a better look at the whole situation. Pressed harder, he will stretch out—into a speedy overdrive—until overtaken, then dash for cover. Jackrabbits feed on grains, seeds, grasses, green plants and some shrubs. Apparently they can exist for long periods without water, obtaining enough for their needs from their food, though they take water readily and regularly when it is available. It is reported that jackrabbits are quick to find and use guzzlers, devices for collecting and storing rain water below the ground in arid regions. A built-in ramp enables mammals, birds and even reptiles to use this kind of water supply.

Panamint kangaroo rat, *Dipodomys panamantinus.* Smaller than a common rat; very small front feet and large kangaroo-like hind legs and feet; coat silky soft; tail longer than head and body, with a pronounced hairy tuft. General coloration light brown above and pure white below. Total length about 12 inches. Near Casa Diablo the Panamint kangaroo rat can often be seen at night in the beam of headlights hopping jerkily across the highway.

160

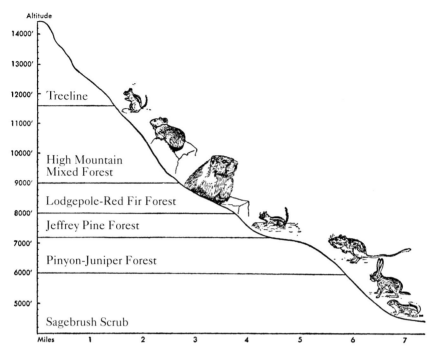

Progression of Mammals in Eastern Sierra Forest Communities.

Bottom to top, white-tailed antelope squirrel, black-tailed jackrabbit, Panamint kangaroo rat, least chipmunk, yellowbellied marmot, pika, alpine chipmunk.

Striped skunk, *Mephitis mephitis.* About the size of a house cat but very chunky, with short stocky legs and a big bushy tail almost as long as the head and body. The general color is black, with a broad white patch across back of head and nape which splits into a very wide stripe down each side of the back and onto the base of the tail. Total length 28 inches.

Look for the striped skunk in early morning, at dusk, or at night shuffling across 395—particularly just south of Mammoth Creek, at Convict Creek or at Rock Creek below Paradise Camp. Often its tail will be arched behind. If you stop the car and attempt to press him he'll hurry up to a point, then raise his tail stiffly like a warning flag, the tail appearing much broader as the hair also stiffens. He will stand his ground in partial reverse, ready for action if further pressed. If not, the flag will slowly descend as he ambles off for cover with no harm done.

Skunks are valuable mousers; they also eat pounds of insects and their eggs and larvae each season. Their diet also includes small mammals, frogs, snakes, birds and their eggs, and carrion from highway kills. In sum, skunks are widely and beneficially omnivorous.

Jeffrey Pine Forest

Least chipmunk, *Eutamias minimus.* A typical chipmunk but very small, only a little larger than a house mouse. Shoulders and top of head gray, sides reddish brown, body with nine alternately light and dark brown stripes. Total length about 7 inches.

In large open sage and bitterbrush flats, as in Long Valley, virtually any chipmunk dashing across the highway or scampering about the brushy cover will be the least, or painted chipmunk. If he is badly frightened, the dash may be accompanied by a staccato call as he heads for a dense brushy clump in which to hide. As he travels, he often holds his tail nearly vertical or with a slight arc forward. Foraging and alert spying regularly takes individuals to the very tips of sage or bitterbrush twigs; there they may perch quietly feeding with tail draped over foliage or hanging downward. If alarmed, the chipmunk may utter a single call at short intervals with frequent flicks of the tail. Since least chipmunks hibernate for only a short period, they can be seen from about mid-February until mid-November. The usual chipmunk diet of seeds, grains, green herbage and browse, and petals of flowers is varied from time to time with meat. One least chipmunk at Gull Lake in late winter fed avidly on bits of cooked beef remaining on a bone placed in a bird-feeding station.

Lodgepole-Red Fir Forest

White-tailed jackrabbit, *Lepus townsendii.* A large jackrabbit with white feet and large fluffy, all white tail. In summer light brownish gray above with mostly white underparts; in winter the coat is pure white except for the black-tipped ears. Total length about 25 inches.

In winter or early spring along Highway 395 north of Rock Creek you are almost certain to see at least one of these beautiful snow-white jackrabbits (or Sierra hares). In spring, during the change to summer coat, any large grayish jackrabbit with pure white tail along the highway will be a white-tail. The best time to see them is in the late evening or at night. The normal summer range of the white-tailed jackrabbit is from lodgepole-red fir forest to above treeline. In late fall, severe frosts and snow drive the rabbits to better habitat at the lower elevations, hence their relative abundance during the winter months. These jackrabbits are often, but incorrectly, called snowshoe rabbits. The true snowshoe does not occur in Mono County.

Porcupine, *Erethizon dorsatum.* Larger than a house cat, with a long wiry brownish and yellowish black coat overlying many sharp yellowish white spines on the upper parts of the tail, body and head (except the face). Total length about 36 inches.

Occasionally streamside campers near aspen and willows are awakened at night by the sound of paper rattling or something shuffling about. A flashlight beam reveals not a cub bear but a fat, woolly (and spiny) rodent snooping about, possibly for the vegetable sack. If he finds a sweaty shoe or belt, a porcupine will gnaw such items for their saltiness. Undisturbed, porcupines are generally harmless; but if aroused, they will quickly bristle, and if pressed hard will attempt to strike with flicks of the tail. Porcupines cannot throw their quills, but many a dog has felt the pain of a cluster of barbed spines driven hard into its muzzle by the tail of a porcupine he molested. Look for them slowly shuffling across the highway in fall and again in spring when they are migrating. Many are killed by cars, especially in the evening.

There are occasional cries of alarm about damage done to forests by the porcupine's habit of eating bark and often girdling a tree in the process. The alarm is caused by an old, but dying, human habit of trying to classify animals according to how good they are or how bad. The ecologist knows that many of the natural forces which man has chosen to call destructive are in reality constructive. Predators, for example, although lethal to individuals, enhance the vigor of the herd as a whole upon which they prey. Fire, through the ages, has been a forest-building force, favoring fire-resistant species and thinning out fire-vulnerable species, which, because they have certain other advantages, would otherwise take over a range. Disease weeds out mutations toward weakness.

Thus it is probably fire that has made it possible for man to look upon—and enjoy—a slope of aspens, golden in the autumn. It is probably the lodgepole needle miner that has kept the lodgepole from taking over much of the forest and has given the graceful mountain hemlock a chance instead. Mountain lions and other predators kept the deer population in balance with the range. All these are fairly obvious examples and natural cycles that exist in nature, that led to John Muir's observing that when you try to pick out something by itself you "find it tied to all the universe." Aldo Leopold put it this way: "Who but a fool would ask, What good is it?" And so the porcupine, among other things, may be one of the forces that tend to keep a forest an open forest rather than a thicket.

Perhaps the porcupine is like the termite, which has the scavenger role of eating, or cleaning up wood that has been attacked already by some fungus. Perhaps the porcupines single out trees that need singling out. Whatever their role may be, they played it for millions of years before man began to fret about it, and the forests survived nevertheless—and *perhaps even improved.*

Belding ground squirrel, *Spermophilus beldingi.* About the size of a common rat, with a short tail (less than half the length of head and body) and small ears. The general coloration is light yellowish brown above, the underparts lighter.

These ground squirrels are known also as picket pins, undoubtedly from their habit of sitting or standing stiffly erect, with forelegs pressed closely to their chests, in mountain meadows or open flats. Persistent watching will reveal that they often pivot in place or melt to the ground as individual squirrels resume feeding. They eat succulent bits of grass, herbs, seeds, a little browse where it can be reached from the ground and meat (animals killed on roads). Each season hundreds of Belding squirrels are themselves killed crossing the highway. They are an important prey of hawks, badgers, coyotes and weasels. Belding squirrels appear from hibernation usually about mid-March and are active until November.

Lodgepole chipmunk, *Eutamias speciosus.* The lodgepole chipmunk is slightly larger than the least chipmunk, and has more reddish brown and dark brown in its body color and less gray. It is distinguished from the golden-mantled ground squirrel by its smaller size, larger ears and more pointed nose, and the white stripes on its head as well as on its body. Total length 8½ inches.

The lodgepole chipmunk is predominantly arboreal and is most abundant in the Inyo-Mono region about lodgepole pines, and in forests in which lodgepole, western white pine and hemlock are mixed. Like most chipmunks, it is very active and alert. When frightened, it will often dash for the nearest tree, ascending on the far side out of sight. Alarmed or angry, it will often scold sharply from a limb, flicking its tail with each call. Seeds, grains, nuts, and often meat (insects, eggs, nestling birds) are among the foods lodgepole chipmunks eat.

Golden-mantled ground squirrel, *Spermophilus lateralis.* A small, brilliantly colored ground squirrel, resembling a chipmunk except that its body is stockier, the nose blunter, and the tail shorter. Head and neck rusty red. There is a broad white stripe on each side sandwiched between two dark stripes. This white stripe extends from the hip to the neck, but never onto the head as in chipmunks. Size a little smaller than a house rat; total length 9½ to 11½ inches.

Although predominantly terrestrial, these ground squirrels will climb trees and shrubs for short distances. They are common in sun-swept rocky areas. Campgrounds are often their food centers; various and sundry items including meat are crammed into their bulging cheek pouches, then stored in burrows or buried in odd places in the forest duff. Many of the seeds planted then germinate, adding to the forest cover. Look for golden-mantled ground squirrels from late February until November.

Each year dozens of squirrels and chipmunks are captured or handled by campers, and attempts made to tame them. The State Department of Public Health earnestly cautions against this hazardous practice, for these animals may carry the germs of relapsing fever, bubonic plague or even rabies. Feed them if you must, but do not fondle or touch them lest a scratch or sharp bite cause injury or serious illness.

Chickaree, *Tamiasciurus douglasii.* A small, dark brown, tree-climbing squirrel, about the size of a common rat; brushlike tail, about two thirds the length of head and body; buff-colored beneath. Total length about 12½ inches.

Also called pine squirrel and Douglas squirrel, this is the little tree squirrel of the high mountain forests, ranging to treeline. It seldom lingers for long on the forest floor, except to travel between widely spaced trees, to water, to investigate, or to "work" and scale a cone it has severed from aloft. Few travelers get by without being seen by a watchful and vocal chickaree, who will sound off the alert with his calls. The approach and position of many a hunter has been quickly revealed by the chickaree. Chickarees are active the year-round and, helped by their stored supplies, are able to find food throughout the long winter. Probably their most feared enemy is the pine marten, who is able to pursue them relentlessly through the tallest trees.

Shasta beaver, *Castor canadensis shasta.* A large, husky, and powerfully built mammal, largest of North American rodents; broad flat tail; short inconspicuous ears on a rather boxy head with squarish muzzle. Color usually rich chestnut brown above, somewhat lighter beneath. Total length 43 inches; tail 4½ inches wide, 16 inches long; adult weights from 30 to over 70 pounds.

The first trial transplant of Shasta beaver from Modoc County was made in August 1941, when five animals were placed in Robinson Creek near Bridgeport. Basic purposes were water conservation, formation of a lake for fishing, and more beaver for fur. Later, other transplants were made. The resourceful beaver took hold and, with ideas of their own, individuals began "bud colonies." Beaver will eventually explore and settle an entire drainage; and a really eager beaver will follow water courses and even cross over into other drainages twenty-five to thirty miles away. This was the origin of the Mill Creek colony above Lundy Lake, which, though viable for years, is now gone.

Five beaver were planted in the shallow lake on McGee Creek in July, 1946. The colony thrived for more than twenty years, but is now gone. Evidence of their work will linger for decades—gnawed aspen stumps and limb cuttings, cut willows and other plant debris. Remnants of an old beaver lodge may persist for many years.

Though these remarkable rodent engineers, wherever found, are wary, watchfulness in early morning, at dusk or on cloudy days will likely reward the patient observer. Preferred foods of beaver include stems and roots of aquatic plants, bark, twigs, and wood of cottonwoods, alders, willows and es-pecially aspen. Because of the limited groves of fine aspen and streamside cover along Inyo-Mono streams, serious question has been raised repeatedly regarding the value of beaver introductions in this area. At colony after colony beaver eventually destroy most of the aspen trees within their forage range; many other trees, such as lodgepole pine, and much streamside cover is killed by flooding. Monumented by an impenetrable tangle of dead standing cover and criss-crossed downed debris, the entire area will be abandoned. Fisheries and wildlife biologists have known for years that to plant beaver is to plant a whole watershed; and beaver on the move will travel long distances in their quest for suitable habitat. Beaver were not na-tive to Inyo-Mono and area conditions were never really suitable for them; meantime, history has shown in the long term their introduction was re-source policy ill-advised.

Inyo mule deer, *Odocoileus hemionus.* In summer, tannish or tawny above, grayer in winter. The rump is white to buffy; the narrow tail constricted at the base, white with prominent black tuft. Fawns are generally light chest-nut with buffy spots. Length up to 5½ feet, weight up to 200 pounds.

The Inyo mule deer of the eastern Sierra, the California mule deer of the western slope, and the black-tailed deer of the Coast Ranges are all races of the same species with differentiating characteristics. The Inyo mule deer—which ranges from Walker Pass as far north as Yosemite, and east to the White and Inyo Mountains—is slightly larger and heavier than its close relative on the western slope. Deer you see in the eastern Sierra south of Mono Lake and vicinity of the Mono Craters may be either Inyo or Rocky Mountain mule deer, since range overlap and race intermingling occurs there. North of Mono Lake only Rocky Mountain mule deer are present. Deer migrate with the seasons, to the high country in summer and back down to the snow-free valleys in late fall. Since their foods are chiefly tender herbs, grasses, new twigs, buds and leaves, they follow spring as it advances up the mountain slopes. Thus they are found at various times of the year in the Jeffrey pine, lodgepole-fir and high mountain forests, and occasionally even above treeline. Their fawns are born in June and July, in a healthy herd often as sets of twins.

The size and health of the Sherwin/Buttermilk deer herd (named after its winter ranges) is a subject of continuing heated controversy. The issues change. What does not change is a disregard for some basic facts about deer.

Fact 1. Above all else, deer need cover and deer need food. They need them on their winter range, on their summer range and on their migration routes between the two.

Fact 2. Summer range for this herd poses no problems. In late spring most of the herd migrates over the Sierra crest to canyons and ridges on the western slope where wilderness designations permanently protect their habitat and where feed is ample.

Fact 3. Winter range—particularly the condition of bitterbrush, the preferred food—is one of the critical factors in a herd's health. In the eastern Sierra, where drought years are common, bitterbrush in drought years produce little new growth, the nutritious shoots that the deer depend on to carry them through the severe winter cold. It is part of the natural cycle that in drought years, when winter range is poor, some deer will starve, the does will bear fewer fawns, and the herd will decrease. In wet years, when winter range is good, more deer will survive, the does will bear more and healthier fawns and the herd will increase.

Fact 4. Well-meaning proposals to improve the winter range are floated time after time. The hard fact is that, despite numerous attempts and experiments, to date no one has yet discovered how to make bitterbrush grow in arid country on command. When bitterbrush receive several years of ample rain *at the right times,* and if at the same time browsing is light, young plants will sprout and old plants will grow new shoots. Lacking rain, bitterbrush simply refuses to grow.

Fact 5. On their migration from Round Valley north along the base of the Sierra, the deer encounter numerous hazards. Some of them are natural hazards, such as predation by coyotes and mountain lions. To these natural hazards we have added others: noise, dogs and traffic. Crossing 395 and 203 can be fatal. Add up the acres now used for roads, the airport and subdivisions; food and cover available have decreased by that much.

Fact 6. The condition of the *staging area* is another critical factor in a herd's health. This is an area where the deer in late spring gather to rest and feed and gain strength after their trek from the winter range. Even in the best of years, many deer are in poor shape at the end of winter. The does are heavy with fawns. All need two to six weeks to rest and to feed on the young, nutritious spring growth—to recover from the hard winter and to gain strength for their push over the high passes to summer range. If cover and feed here are decreased, if the deer are stressed by noise or dogs or human presence, they may not regain the strength they need to bear healthy fawns.

For your own protection, do not feed or try to touch the deer. They are easily frightened; an enraged deer can tear deep gashes with its sharp front hooves. *Never pick up a fawn because it seems to be an orphan.* Forest rangers are often brought young animals by well-meaning people who think them abandoned. The mothers are only hiding—watching and waiting for the humans to leave, to resume care of their young. Since it is usually impossible to find the place from which the baby was kidnaped and to return it there, it must then be raised artificially, which is often unsuccessful.

High Mountain Mixed Forest

Alpine chipmunk, *Eutamias alpinus.* About the size of a house mouse; smallest of the Sierra chipmunks, with head and body about 4 inches long, tail barely 3 inches long. Typical chipmunk color pattern but much paler, tail more buff than black.

The agile alpine chipmunks are characteristic of the more rocky areas of the high mountain forest. You will see them snooping about scrubby, treeline pines, often with short quick movements punctuated by a flick of the tail. One might think that at the higher elevations chipmunks would be relatively safe; this is not the case. Their arch enemies are least weasels and pine martens; occasionally they fall prey to sharp-shinned, Cooper's, and red-tailed hawks.

Yellowbellied marmot, *Marmota flaviventris.* A large woodchuck about the size of a broad house cat, heavy set, with short legs and bushy tail. Dark brown above grizzled with white; underparts yellowish; a narrow white cross band in front of eyes. Total length 22 to 28 inches.

Other common names for the marmot are rock (or granite) chuck, mountain chuck, or whistler (from the sharp whistling note often uttered by an alarmed marmot from his boulder lookout). This big fellow often sprawls flat atop a sunny promontory or a large boulder. As you approach he may flatten even more, with just the head and shoulders showing. If closely approached, he will appear to slither or slide from his lookout into the talus out of sight. If surprised while feeding on tender grass in a small meadow patch, he will hastily gallop like a small roly-poly bear to the safety of his rocky home, stopping squirrel-fashion for a last look before disappearing. Coyotes, eagles and red-tailed hawks are among its common enemies. Although typical of the high mountain mixed forest, marmots descend into rocky areas to their liking in the lodgepole-red fir forest and even the Jeffrey pine forest, as in the basaltic lava near the junction of the Mammoth Lakes highway with US 395.

Pika or cony, *Ochotona princeps.* Resembles a small guinea pig, or a tiny gray rabbit with very short ears. Total length 7½ inches.

You may be traveling a high mountain trail near a talus slide when suddenly a pika sounds off with a sharp series of calls echoing among the rocks (sounding a little like two rocks struck together) and difficult to pinpoint. Careful scrutiny of every boulder in the general direction of the calls may reveal what appears to be a little rock rabbit, which may betray itself as it runs from its vantage point toward its den beneath the talus. Usually near the entrance, the cracks of the rocks will be crammed with various kinds of hay brought in for curing by the busy pika. Enough is stored during summer to last the winter. Enemies of the pika include weasels and martens.

WHITE-TAILED JACKRABBIT

SHASTA BEAVER

GOLDEN-MANTLED
GROUND SQUIRREL

CHICKAREE

BELDING GROUND SQUIRREL

YELLOW-HAIRED PORCUPINE

CALIFORNIA GROUND SQUIRREL

STRIPED SKUNK

Above treeline

All the mammals characteristic of the high mountain mixed forest also range upward above treeline. Generally speaking, the higher one travels the fewer individuals will be seen, owing to the increased severity of living conditions. The most common mammal will probably be the alpine chipmunk. The marmot probably ranges the highest; marmot signs have been found at the very top of Mount Ritter.

Fish

Two general types of fish are found in the east-central Sierra region—game fish and rough fish. Rough fish are nongame species, most of which contribute to the habitat in which they live, often by providing forage in one way or another for the game species. Several kinds of rough fish have been used for many years in Inyo-Mono waters as bait for large trout; lake chubs, a species of minnow, are perhaps best known. Other kinds of rough fish are dace, suckers, sticklebacks and carp. The latter two were introduced many years ago into certain Inyo-Mono waters and, fortunately, have never become widely distributed. Carp, especially, have frequently destroyed important game fisheries by competing for food and muddying the water. Many thousands of dollars have been spent by the Department of Fish and Game in rough-fish control work directed primarily at carp. The work is done most economically with chemicals that suffocate the carp as well as all other fish. The fishery is restored by replanting when the chemicals have disappeared from the water, usually after several weeks.

The most important game fish in the Inyo-Mono area are the trouts. Some are native to California and some were introduced many years ago from the eastern United States. Prior to settlement of the area by white men, there were no trout fisheries south of Conway Summit on the east side of the

Sierra crest. To the north, in the East and West Walker River drainages, there were cutthroat trout in abundance. It is believed that these were introduced in the Mono Basin and the Owens River drainage shortly after 1850, the trout having been carried over the summit in water barrels fastened to freight wagons. Abundant cutthroat trout fisheries were present in Rush Creek and Bishop Creek by 1900.

Golden trout, which are native to waters at the head of the South Fork of the Kern River, were first introduced into Inyo-Mono waters in 1893 by cattlemen. A few of the trout were carried from Mulkey Meadows in a coffee can and planted in the Cottonwood Lakes. From these lakes have since come most of the golden trout stock planted in hundreds of High Sierra lakes and streams. The other nonnative trouts—rainbow, eastern brook and brown—were introduced soon after 1900 and were planted from state hatcheries established on Oak Creek near Independence and on Fern Creek near Silver Lake. Nearly all the high lakes and streams accessible from Inyo-Mono were originally planted with fingerling trout raised in these hatcheries.

As the number of anglers fishing the more accessible waters increased, the resident stocks of trout were rapidly depleted. The fisheries were supplemented with larger and larger hatchery fish. Thus was developed the catchable rainbow—a special hybrid trout of fast growth and high egg yield that could be produced in great numbers at such tepid volcanic springs as Hot Creek, Black Rock, and Fish Springs, where ample water of fairly constant temperature was available. Plants are made at intervals throughout the fishing season in order to distribute the trout as equitably as possible and, at the same time, prevent excessive drain on the resident fisheries. Catchable rainbow are planted where a return to the angler of at least fifty percent may be expected. In one Inyo-Mono stream, returns of ninety-two percent from catchable rainbow planting were recorded. The four-year average recorded return was eighty-five percent. In 1988 it cost about sixty-five cents to produce and plant a catchable rainbow.

Prior to 1947 back-country lakes were planted by pack train or back pack. Since then, more and more such waters have been planted by airplane. Fingerling trout are released in free fall 200–600 feet above the water surface. The little trout sound like heavy raindrops as they hit the water. They are momentarily stunned, but quickly recover and disappear. Within a few minutes hundreds of them may be seen swimming about the margin as they get acquainted with their new home. Tests have shown the accuracy of planting to be about 99 percent; the loss of fingerlings in planting is usually less than 2 percent. Airplane planting takes only a fraction of the time and expense of the old method.

By far the greatest effort in management of California fisheries is devoted to rainbow trout, for several reasons. First, rainbow trout are the predominant native species of California. Second, experimental culture from 1930 to 1940 revealed that more could be obtained economically in terms of growth rate, egg production, flexibility of stock, and desirable sporting qualities than from any other species. And third, rainbow trout could be used in greater numbers over a much wider range of habitat than any other species. Over the years two principal strains have been used—spring-spawned and fall-spawned. From spring-spawned stock come the fingerlings planted in High Sierra lakes and streams where fisheries have been depleted through natural causes. Rainbow spawn naturally in spring, when nursery areas are provided with ample water of favorable temperatures for eggs and young fish emerging from the gravel. Fall-spawned stock were developed in order to provide large numbers of catchable rainbow trout for planting in the lower-altitude roadside waters just before and during the summer fishing season. Usually the "aged" trout are planted in greatest numbers just ahead of the principal holiday periods in order to offset seasonal peaks of angling pressure.

The golden trout is the state fish. Anglers prize it for its brilliant coloration, fighting qualities and delicate taste (stemming from rich body fat). For these reasons, golden trout have been reared and planted to maintain the species within its present range. The major part of at least one entire drainage in the central Sierra has been dedicated to golden trout. In a number of other drainages where other trout species predominate, it has been the aim of fish management to maintain where possible one or more good golden trout fisheries in order to provide a degree of variety for fishermen. Still, since comparatively few alpine waters are really suited to golden trout, their distribution will probably always be somewhat restricted.

Trout of the Central Sierra

Rainbow trout, *Salmo gairdnerii.* Planted throughout Inyo-Mono in nearly all heavily fished roadside streams and lakes as catchables averaging eight inches. Fingerlings are air-planted in back-country lakes where natural propagation is insufficient to maintain the fishery. Irregular black spots on the upper half of head and body, and on back and tail fins; bluish green to gun-metal gray back, silvery sides to pearly white belly and chin. Often conspicuous reddish band extending midway along sides from gill covers on head to narrow part of body in front of tail.

In large, deep, clear lakes (Lake Mary, Duck, Garnet and Thousand Island lakes) steelhead-like rainbow trout are frequently caught. In these the upper half of the body is deep bluish or gray-blue, the lower half silvery to white. There are few spots and no reddish band, except for male trout in spring at spawning time. A granite-type rainbow has developed in certain high montane glacial lakes where the margin and bottom are mostly granite talus or rubble. Such rainbow have a pale grayish to silvery white ground color and are profusely spotted over the head, body and fins.

Golden trout, *Salmo aguabonita.* Originally from headwater streams tributary to the South Fork of the Kern River; now most abundant in alpine regions of Fresno and Tulare counties. Good golden trout fisheries also found in upper Fish Creek and in alpine Inyo-Mono waters from the Cottonwood Lakes near Olancha northward to Sonora Pass, as in the Shadow Creek drainage. Some golden fisheries sustained by annual or biennial air-plants of fingerlings. Many waters self-sustaining and no planting required since suitable spawning areas provide ample new stock.

A brilliantly colored trout with olive green on the upper areas of the body giving way to pale lemon-yellow sides, then golden yellow and vermilion or cherry red on the lower sides and belly. Gill covers and lower body fins often bright red. Large back fin, belly and anal fins are often white-tipped bordered with black. Relatively few round black spots are generally confined to the back fins and tail with a scattering of spots forward onto the head. A typical golden has a row of roundish blotches, called parr marks, on the sides from the head to the tail through which extends a bright red band. Golden and rainbow trout cross readily in nature, and where the two have intermingled every variation may be found between the typical rainbow and the typical golden.

Lahontan cutthroat trout, *Salmo clarkii henshawi.* Once widespread in Inyo-Mono; now restricted to a few rather isolated waters. A large number of cutthroat fingerlings are planted each year in Crowley Lake, where perhaps the largest number of Inyo-Mono cutthroat exist. Elsewhere only a few persist in waters where they are isolated or not driven out by other species. Like golden, the cutthroat does best where not mixed with other trout. Body usually yellowish olive with a wide ruby band along each side from gill covers to tail. Gill covers are usually ruby to rose red. Body and unpaired fins typically covered with numerous black spots, hence the common name, black-spotted trout. Look for two bright red stripes, one on each side of the midline beneath the lower jaw.

Eastern brook trout, *Salvelinus fontinalis.* Probably more widespread and more abundant than any other species, owing to hardiness and adaptability to rigors of high mountain lake and stream habitats. Planted in High Sierra lakes and streams from Haiwee north to Sonora Pass and eastward to certain small streams in the White Mountains. Prefers relatively shallow, weedy, timbered lakes with mud or silt bottoms; has done fairly well in a few large, deep, clear rockbound lakes. Chiefly a marginal or shoal feeder and readily rises to a wet or dry fly cast from shore; therefore more easily caught than any other species. Spawns in the fall from late September to December. Eggs refrigerated by a blanket of winter ice and snow, hatching from March to May, when the spring thaw occurs. Back and sides usually dark olive green with the back, head, back fin and tail marked by wavy lines. Sides punctuated by round light spots with scattered red spots or small red spots with blue halos. Paired and unpaired belly fins have conspicuous white edges bordered with black. Black markings or blotches inside mouth. At spawning time the lower sides and belly in male eastern brook are bright orange to cherry red, while lower sides and belly of female are opalescent silvery.

Brown trout (loch leven), *Salmo trutta.* Widely distributed from stock cultured at Mount Whitney Hatchery near Independence. Many high mountain streams and lakes planted with them but they prefer lower altitude. Now common to abundant only in such waters as the Owens River, Crowley Lake, Convict Lake, Bridgeport Reservoir and Grant Lake. In Grant Lake they quickly crowded out the former cutthroat fishery and for years supplied enough eggs for planting throughout the Inyo-Mono area. Good self-sustaining brown trout fisheries still persist in many high lakes and in several lower streams such as Rush and Lee Vining creeks. The brown trout is more wary and less easily caught than any other trout; a fisherman can be justly proud of catching one. Spawns from October to December. Eggs lie dormant in the gravel, under snow and ice, and hatch from March to May or soon after spring thaw.

Color usually dark brown or olive brown on the back, more golden brown or bronzed on the sides and lower fins; yellow or yellow to white on the belly. Large, dark spots on head and gill covers, upper part of body, back fins and tail. In the so-called loch leven variety, red spots along the sides of the body are set off by a light halo and there are relatively fewer large dark spots on the body. Brown trout from the large lakes mentioned above are often silvery on the sides and belly.

Birds

In the High Sierra, where winter temperatures go below freezing and the ground is snow-covered for six to nine months, few birds are able to find food year-round. Some that are not ground feeders—such as chickadees, nuthatches, nutcrackers, and dippers—remain in the mountains in winter, but even they come down from the high country they frequent in summer. Most birds come to the mountains in late spring, nest, raise their young during summer while insects are abundant, then in fall migrate back to lower altitudes and warmer climates where their particular foods—berries, seeds, worms or insects—are more plentiful during the winter.

Following are descriptions of fifteen easily identified, common birds. Other common mountain birds in this region are the fox sparrow, pine siskin, and several varieties of warblers, woodpeckers, and hummingbirds. If you are particularly interested in birds, explore the desert marshes and lakes east of US 395. Ducks, grebes, terns, avocets, willets and phalaropes are among the water birds there. The sagebrush country has its birds also—shrikes, nighthawks, Brewer's sparrows, thrashers, magpies, horned larks, towhees, kingbirds, harriers (marsh hawks) and kestrels (sparrow hawks).

Sage grouse, *Centrocercus urophasianus.* Chicken size. Upper parts mottled brown and gray, under parts whitish, belly black.

The sagebrush country east of the Cascades and Sierra is the home of the sage grouse. Look for it in sage flats and swales, usually less than a mile from water. When startled, the birds take flight with the loud whirring of wings characteristic of grouse, pheasant and quail. The sage grouse can be distinguished in flight from the quail by its larger size and long tail of stiff, pointed feathers; the quail has a rounded tail. The female grouse is smaller than the male and has a shorter, pointed tail. Her nest is a shallow depression in the ground hidden under shrubs. The half-grown, scrawny young, seen in early summer, resemble young turkeys. In March and April, male grouse gather at traditional strutting grounds to court the females. DFG biologists sometimes conduct guided tours to watch the cocks' unusual courtship displays; inquire locally.

Mountain quail, *Oreortyx picta.* Twice the size of a robin. Plump, blue-gray body; sides barred with black and white, throat red-brown. Straight black plume on its head.

Mountain quail live in open country, often in the sagebrush, nesting on the ground in dense brush. An unforgettable sight is a brood of quail chicks, up to fifteen of them, scurrying after their mother, their legs moving so fast they seem to be on wheels. In fall, flocks of mountain quail migrate downhill to avoid the deep snows that cover the berries, seeds, leaves and flowers they feed on. They travel chiefly on foot, seldom flying except to escape danger.

California gull, *Larus californicus* (not pictured). Gray above, white below. Wing tipped with black. Yellow bill, greenish legs.

Thousands of California gulls fly inland in March and April to nest on Mono Lake islands, returning to the coast in late July. In the 1970s the falling lake level due to Los Angeles water diversions raised fears that Negit Island, which for years had harbored the main colony, might cease to be an island. Those fears were realized in 1979 when the water separating Negit from the mainland became so low that coyotes waded to the island and devastated the gull colony. Not a chick fledged on Negit that summer, compared to the thousands (perhaps as many as 17,000) in previous years. The colony was so disrupted that it wasn't until 1986 that gulls returned in any numbers to Negit. Coyotes invaded two other islets used by gulls in 1982 when the lake level fell even lower, to 6372 feet.

Lower lake levels pose a different threat to the migratory birds that use the eastern Sierra flyway. At least 900 thousand birds—eared grebes and two phalaropes, Wilson's and red-necked—depend on Mono as a stopover for resting and feeding on their long flight south in fall. A healthy lake with abundant brine shrimp is critical to these migrants. (See "Mono Lake" in Roadsides and History chapters.)

SAGE GROUSE

MOUNTAIN QUAIL

STELLER'S JAY

HERMIT THRUSH

MOUNTAIN CHICKADEE

DIPPER

CLARK'S NUTCRACKER

MOUNTAIN BLUEBIRD

WESTERN TANAGER

CASSIN'S PURPLE FINCH

DARK-EYED JUNCO

WHITE-CROWNED SPARROW

Gulls are among the predator birds, which eat the eggs and young of other birds. While predation seems a violent way of life—seeing one animal kill another is never a pretty sight—we are learning that it is one of nature's vital mechanisms to prevent any one animal from becoming too abundant and out of balance with its food supply. Since predators often catch the crippled, the sick, the slow and the old, they also may contribute to the health of a species by encouraging the survival of the most alert and vigorous. Perhaps predation among animals would be less abhorrent to us if we remember that man is the greatest predator of all, killing animals not only that he may eat, but also for sport and for the trophies, furs and feathers he displays. Nature is prolific, producing each year many more young than there is food or shelter for. This is her insurance that species will survive, despite the death of many individuals. Should all young water birds, for example, survive and reproduce for only a few years, the lakes of the earth would be crowded with birds who could find neither room to swim nor food to eat. Remove the predators—such as hawks, coyotes, and mountain lions, as we have done in many regions—and in only a few years mice, rabbits and deer will multiply out of all proportion to their natural food supply. When that happens they will continue to eat until they have denuded the land, and then many will starve.

Steller's jay, *Cyanocitta stelleri*. Slightly larger than a robin. Wings, tail, and most of body deep blue, foreparts and crest blackish.

Jays, crows and magpies are all members of the family that includes some of the most intelligent birds. The bold, saucy Steller's jays frequent campgrounds and resorts, where they have learned that picnic scraps are plentiful. Their calls are many and varied, the most common one being harsh and raucous. But near their own nests, which they build of twigs and mud, they are quiet and secretive. They will rob other nests when they can, but their main foods are nuts, grains and insects. One female jay, killed while foraging for her five nestlings in Sequoia Park, was found to have twenty-two pine beetles in her mouth and throat. With nestlings demanding food many times an hour, you can see how many insects destructive to trees just one family of birds will eat in a season. No wonder many foresters consider birds among trees' best friends!

Clark's nutcracker, *Nucifraga columbiana*. Slightly larger than a robin. Head and body light gray, tail white with black center-feathers, wings black with conspicuous white patches, bill black.

The sleek, gray nutcracker, like its relative the Steller's jay, is noisy, conspicuous and smart. During nesting season you may see a nutcracker flying to the top of a tree, pursued by a dozen or so scolding, excited small birds. They are mobbing him, defending their nests against a supposed or real attack. Small birds (and nutcrackers too) similarly mob hawks and owls.

Nutcrackers have some unusual behavior patterns, all associated with their preference for pine seed. During late summer most nutcrackers feed near tree line on the whitebark pine, exchanging raucous calls with each other and whacking open the cones with their sturdy, black bills. Then in fall they begin to store seed. Each bird, filling its throat pouch with over a hundred seeds, makes many trips a day to storage sites, where it buries small caches of seed in the ground. (If you watch them working among the whitebark in fall, you can clearly see their bulging throat pouches.) In late fall nutcrackers continue storing seed but at lower elevations, seed from the Jeffrey and pinyon pine. These lower-elevation, snow-free caches enable them to nest during late winter and feed their young in early spring, months earlier than other Sierran birds. By mid-summer most nutcrackers have returned to tree line, feeding on seed they stored the previous fall until new cones are ripe. Some of the buried seeds are never eaten and eventually sprout. Although most pine seeds have large "wings" to catch the wind, whitebark seeds are wingless and must be scattered some other way. It is the nutcracker, caching seeds, that is the primary agent in scattering as well as planting whitebark pine seed.

Mountain chickadee, *Parus gambeli.* Smaller than a sparrow. Black cap and throat, gray back and tail, underparts grayish-white.

This small, friendly bird may be found almost everywhere in the forests above 7500 feet, constantly hopping from twig to twig, often hanging upside down as it hunts for tiny insects and their eggs on leaves and in the cracks of bark. Its strong feet, a bit large for its size, enable it to perform the acrobatics necessary to foraging. Imitating the chickadees' call is fun, for they respond readily. Learn to whistle their simple call—tsee-dee-dee—keep repeating it, and usually several will answer and come close.

American dipper or water ouzel, *Cinclus mexicanus.* Slightly smaller than a robin. Dark gray all over, yellowish feet. Easily identified by his plain color and his habit of constantly bobbing up and down.

The dipper is a most unusual bird, for he lives his whole life in and near plunging, foaming streams, often near waterfalls. He nests in rock crevices along streams, sometimes in the cliffs behind falls. Water insects and larvae are his main food, which he obtains by diving and walking under water. Yet the dipper is a songbird, related to the wrens and thrushes, rather than to any of the water birds whose habits he has adopted. Though he does not have the webbed feet and long bill characteristic of most water birds, he does have other specialized equipment that enables him to live in an environment of constantly dashing water: large, strong legs and sharp-clawed feet for gripping slippery rock and walking under water; dense plumage; an oil-gland ten times larger than that of related land-birds, which enables him to keep his feathers pliable and water resistant; a cover over each nostril that he can close under water; and a silvery white inner eyelid whose function seems to be wiping spray and water away from his eyes. The dipper sings loudly and joyously no matter what, even when covered with spray in the midst of a frothy stream. He seems oblivious to bad weather, warbling amid sleet and snow just as brightly as in the crisp evenings of Indian summer.

Hermit thrush, *Catharus guttatus.* Sparrow size. Grayish brown head, back, and wings; rusty tail; speckled throat and breast.

This shy bird of the deep woods is more often heard than seen. His is one of the most beautiful of all bird songs, clear flute-like notes that seem to hang in the stillness of dense forests. During the nesting season in June and July (seldom in August), he repeats the two phrases of his song over and over—the first consisting of three high notes, the second a slur down the scale. This is his warning to other thrushes to stay away from his nesting and feeding territory. Hermit thrushes can almost always be heard in the woods east of Horseshoe Lake, along the Crystal Lake trail, and elsewhere in red fir forest from about 8500 to 9500 feet. They are hard to see because they spend much of their time in the shade, near cover. They can be identified by their large eyes and slender bills, their habit of frequently raising and lowering their tails slowly, and their robinlike behavior—running a few steps, then drawing themselves up and cocking their heads as they look for food. They usually nest in deep shade in small trees. Insects supply half their diet, seeds and berries the rest.

The hermit thrush might be confused with the fox sparrow, because their coloring is similar. But the sparrow can be distinguished readily by its short, broad bill and its habit of jumping forward and scratching back vigorously with both feet at once in loose leaves.

American Robin, *Turdus migratorius* (not pictured). Breast rusty-red, head and tail blackish, back gray, bill yellow.

The handsome rusty-breasted male and the lighter-colored, duller female come to the mountains usually in June. They build their nest of twigs, grass and mud, often in the fork of a tree branch. Robins are common around many of the lower mountain lakes and in meadows, wherever worms are plentiful and the grass not high enough to hide them. They feed also on berries and on insects such as caterpillars, beetles and grasshoppers. In August look for young robins with speckled breasts and fluffed-out feathers, almost as big as their parents but still following them and begging for food.

Mountain bluebird, *Sialia currucoides.* Slightly larger than a sparrow. Rich azure blue all over except for whitish belly. Female paler.

The bluebird is one of the few brightly colored mountain birds. Watch for the male in flight, his rich sky-blue flashing in the sun. Bluebirds are common in lower meadows, sitting on fence posts or hovering in the air as they hunt for food. You will also find them 3000 feet higher, at tree line. Insects make up 90 percent of their diet. Often they nest high in dead snags, in old woodpecker holes or natural hollows.

Brewer blackbird, *Euphagus cyanocephalus* (not pictured). Glossy black, pale yellow eye. Female more brownish than black, dark brown eye.

This is the common blackbird of farms, city lawns, and parks. It walks, rather than hops, as it forages for insects and seeds and scavenges scraps in campgrounds. Blackbirds usually flock and prefer marshy places, where they nest in dense thickets of brush and small trees. Look for them near the springs and ponds along the road to Benton Crossing, where there are also red-winged and the rarer yellow-headed blackbirds.

Western tanager, *Piranga ludoviciana.* Larger than a sparrow. Orange-red head, bright yellow body; wings, tail and middle of back black. Female dull greenish above, yellowish below.

The tanager is the most colorful bird of this region, a flash of bright yellow and black flying among the trees. It lives in the forest from about 7500 to 9000 feet and builds its nest toward the tips of branches. It is relatively un-afraid of people and is quick to come to feeding trays. Watermelon, placed out of reach of ground squirrels, will attract them.

Cassin's purple finch, *Carpodacus cassinii.* Sparrow size. Rose-red patch on top of head; neck, back, wings and tail brown; rump, throat and breast pale rose. Female brown streaked with gray.

Small flocks are common in the forests from about 8000 to 9500 feet. They often build their nests at the tip of pine branches. They forage for buds, seeds and insects in trees and bushes as well as on the ground. Since they are not ground-feeders exclusively, they can live in the mountains even in winter, though they will go down to the lower slopes. They may be mistaken for the house finch or linnet because their colorings are similar, but the lin-net is never found at such high altitudes.

Another finch, the gray-crowned rosy finch, inhabits the higher altitudes of tree line and above. Its coloring is less bright, its head is dark brown with a gray patch, and rump, shoulder and lower belly are washed with a deep pink. It nests in the crags and feeds on insects frozen on high snowfields. It has spectacular flight habits, sometimes diving a hundred feet before open-ing its wings.

Dark-eyed junco, *Junco hyemalis.* Sparrow size. The "Oregon junco" of the west has head and breast black, bill whitish, back and wings rusty brown, underparts gray, tail black with white borders, legs and feet pink.

This chunky little bird seems to mind his own business as he hops about on the ground, picking up the seeds that form the major part of his diet. Juncos are one of the more successful kinds of birds; in most of the Sierra they out-number every other bird species. The junco is most easily identified in flight by the conspicuous flash of white on the outer sides of his tail. He nests on the ground, in shrubs, or in low branches of trees such as mountain hem-lock. In June and July he often hops about on snowbanks, picking out in-sects that have landed there and frozen. In late summer and fall, juncos usu-ally flock together.

White-crowned sparrow, *Zonotrichia leucophrys.* Upper parts grayish brown, underparts clear, light gray; three prominent white stripes on head, separated by black.

This cocky sparrow is found commonly in the willows near mountain mead-ows and lakes, from about 7500 to 9500 feet. He nests on the ground or in the low branches of willows. In summer, his chief food is insects; in winter, seeds and weed sprouts.

Historic waterwheel *T J Johnston*

Silver!

The discovery of blue-black silver ore at the Comstock

in 1859, east of Lake Tahoe, brought a torrent of men flooding east across the Sierra into lands the gold-seekers had passed by without a look. Among miners at the played-out placers of the Mother Lode, news of the Comstock's incredible riches spread like wildfire.

Stamp mill, May Lundy Mine   *Frasher's Photo*

Lundy about 1900   *Frasher's Photo*

Hotel, Benton   *Genny Smith collection*

On to Washoe!
Silver at the Comstock!

By tens, by hundreds, across the Sierra to Washoe they surged, answering the cry of Silver at the Comstock! Rumors and dreams spurred them on farther, east into the desert ranges and south along the Sierra to prospect its eastern slope. And right behind the prospectors came hundreds of teamsters, merchants, cattlemen and farmers to supply them.

The Paiutes and Washoes east of the Sierra had lived undisturbed longer than most western Indians. The massive Sierra effectively barricaded them from all the trappers, traders, padres, soldiers, and ranchers west of the mountains. But the torrent of white men lured by the Comstock disrupted their lives and overran their lands almost overnight.

News of gold near Mono Lake in 1859 brought several hundred men racing to Monoville the first summer. Other strikes followed quickly. Aurora, northeast of Mono Lake, mushroomed into a camp of five thousand people. Silver was discovered at Blind Springs Hill near Benton, gold at the May Lundy, both silver and gold at Bodie, the wildest camp of all.

Prospectors *Eastern California Museum photo*

Pack train early 1880s *Laws Railroad Museum photo*

Freighting for the California-Nevada Canal Water & Power Company *Billy Young*

Church, Bodie   *Philip Hyde*

Boom, bust,
ghost town, oblivion—

this is the story rusted wheels and weather-beaten boards tell us at hundreds of old mining camps. For some the boom was brighter and lasted longer; for others the bust came sooner. But even the richest camps such as Bodie and Aurora, each producing thirty million dollars in gold and silver, had only brief years of glory. Few traces remain of most camps. Though fire destroyed much of Bodie, what survived is now preserved as a state historic park—not a restored tourist attraction, but a true ghost town.

Bodie   *Philip Hyde*

House, Bodie   *Philip Hyde*

Mammoth Camp in the 1920s *H. W. Mendenhall, Adele Reed collection*

Old Mammoth took its name from the Mammoth Mine,

one bonanza that never materialized at all. In 1878 General Dodge, a prominent San Francisco mining investor, and associates bought five claims on Mineral Hill east of Lake Mary. Their Mammoth Mining Company built a flume, tramway and 40-stamp mill. The mill was powered by the six-foot Knight wheel (similar to a Pelton) pictured on the first photo page. It's said a thousand people flocked to Mammoth that first summer (it was touted as the "largest bonanza outside of Virginia City") but they soon flocked elsewhere. Barely two years later,

the mill shut down and company property was sold at a sheriff's sale.

Twenty years later, young Dr. Guy Doyle from Chicago hauled the old wheel up the hill to power a 10-stamp mill he built closer to the mine tunnels. But the bonanza eluded him too, and another twenty years later, its mining days over, the old wheel was sledded down to the meadows. There it generated power for Mammoth's first resort, the Wildasinn Hotel. Later, pioneer cattleman Charlie Summers hooked it up to the new hotel and rooming house he built in 1918, Mammoth Camp.

Doyle mill, early 1900s   *Stephen H. Willard, Adele Reed collection*

Mammoth Mining Company mill   *Genny Smith collection*

Hauling logs to Mammoth sawmill, about 1919   *H. W. Mendenhall, Adele Reed collection*

Mono County Courthouse, built in 1880   *Julius Shulman*

Mono County's first choice for county seat was the booming camp of Aurora. When Mono and adjacent Esmeralda (Nevada) counties were established in 1861, no one knew exactly where the state line was. Both counties claimed Aurora and both named it county seat. In fact, in a most unusual election in 1863, Aurorans voted twice, for two full slates of county officers—one for Esmeralda, one for Mono. But Mono lost its claim when the boundary survey determined that Aurora lay east of the state line; its voters then chose Bridgeport. The courthouse, built in 1880, continues to serve Mono County today.

History

For all the newness the high country promises, there is oldness to think about too. Every so often you have the feeling—once you leave the roads—that you are walking where few have walked before. Chances are good that you will be right in thinking so, but those chances aren't improving. In the 1930s dozens of Sierra peaks had not yet been climbed. No longer. But there are still slopes and woods and streamsides where you will find no evidence of human passage—until you discover a fragment of obsidian arrowhead.

Suppose, for example, you have chosen the trail that crosses McGee Pass. You are dropping down the west side into a high granite world, with colorful peaks piling up around you in their metamorphic colors, spacious meadows sloping up to them, crags, snow fields, flowers, a meandering stream, clean wind—all these things telling you about what *is*—when unexpectedly you stumble upon a fragment of obsidian, dozens of them, hundreds of them, *thousands* of them! Telling you about what *was*. They lie along the trail. They spread out into the meadow, everywhere! Suddenly, then, you find your alpine world shared—shared by people who found this place as wonderful as you do, brown-skinned Paiutes who came to this special place century after century, to chip and exchange obsidian for something else, something that time would not treat so well. Now you look at the great peaks differently, see them in a new dimension, think of those others who shared this same cool, fresh, sage-perfumed air that promises a moon or two of balmy days before winter again swirls in.

The obsidian you saw is *pre*history, and we can't tell you much about that here. But it does help to look at the record that has been written, to glean from it the bits of condiment that can flavor our *today* and give it perspective.

The First People: The Paiutes

East of the Sierra and west of the Rockies, encircled by high mountains, lies a high desert land—the Great Basin. Its rivers never leave the basin, never reach the sea, but sink into sand or drain into ever-saltier lakes. Its climate is harsh, its water scant, its forests scrubby, its animals scarce. Along the western edge of this inhospitable land—in eastern Oregon, western Nevada and eastern California—lived the Northern Paiutes, related by language and culture not to the Indians west of the Sierra, but to the Shoshoni and Bannock and other Great Basin peoples. *Paiute* (spelled also Piute, Pah Ute, Payuches, all names related to *pah*, meaning *water*) was the name early white explorers bestowed upon many Great Basin Indians. Paiute groups consisted of families living near each other, too loosely organized to be considered tribes. Their customs varied slightly, their dialects considerably. No one knows how many hundreds of years the Paiutes have lived in the Great Basin. It is believed that their ancestors migrated to this continent from central Asia via the Bering Strait twenty or thirty thousand years ago and fanned out through the Americas, some descendants eventually locating east of the Sierra and developing the customs and languages we have labeled *Paiute*.

The Kuzedika, the Paiutes of Mono Lake. Among the Paiutes living along the eastern base of the Sierra was a small group near Mono Lake. These Indians called themselves neither Paiutes nor Monos, but *Kuzedika*, meaning *kutsavi eaters*. Kutsavi, brine-fly larvae collected in late summer from Mono Lake's shore and dried, was a food staple and a trading article. The words *Mono* and *Monache* come from their western neighbors, the Yokuts; it is derived from a Yokut word meaning *flies*. To the Yokuts, the people at Owens and Mono lakes were the fly people. Among the Kuzedika's neighbors were a Paiute group at Benton whom they called *ütü' ütü witü* (hot-place people) and a group in Owens Valley, *pitana patü* (south-place people). Among other nearby Paiutes were the *salt-place people* in Deep Springs Valley, the *alkali-eaters* in Soda Springs Valley and the *fish-eaters* at Walker Lake, Nevada.

Paiute groups were generally at peace with each other and with their eastern neighbors, the Shoshoni, sometimes intermarrying. The squabbles that occurred usually resulted from one group's trespassing on another's pine-nut or hunting territory. Most often they were settled by shouting and hurling stones at the intruders; killings were rare. Each group had a headman who settled disputes and organized the few communal activities such as pine-nut trips.

Paiute customs. A young boy learned to hunt lizards and mice and smudge out gophers and ground squirrels. He also caught fish with small bone hooks or shot them with willow arrows. Later the men would teach him hunting secrets; he would learn also to respect his elders and not to boast. An older boy would be awakened very early one morning, just after the morning star had risen. After special songs had been sung to him, he would bathe in a creek, asking the Great Power for blessing and guidance. This was his initiation into manhood, which allowed him to join the hunts for big game. His first kill he must neither skin nor eat, lest he have bad luck and poor hunting in the future.

Though the word *Indian* often evokes a picture of a feather-bonneted, war-whooping creature, the Paiutes little resembled this stereotype. They wore no feathered headdresses, rode no horses. They often were barefoot; in good weather the men and children went naked. There was no emphasis on warfare—no war paint or war dances.

Food, clothing and shelter. In this land of extreme temperatures and scarce food, the ingenious Paiutes managed to survive by using tools of wood, stone and bone and utilizing what few materials were at hand for food, clothing and shelter. They built circular shelters of bent poles covered with grass, small branches, and sagebrush bark. Their summer shelter was essentially a sun shade, a roof of branches supported by four willow posts. They hunted deer and mountain sheep occasionally, but subsisted mostly on small game, insects, pine nuts, and seeds. *Piüga (pee-ag'-gee)*, caterpillars that live part of their lives in Jeffrey pine, were an important food. They collected them in steep-sided trenches encircling the trees, cooked them in a fire pit with hot coals, and then dried them. Traces of these trenches can still be discovered in the Jeffrey forest. The women gathered many kinds of seeds, which they added to a mush of ground pine-nut meal, a staple to which might be added a handful of kutsavi, piüga or meat. Surviving a bitterly cold winter often depended on the year's pine-nut crop.

They made bows from juniper wood or, occasionally, mountain mahogany; arrows from willow, with greasewood foreshafts and obsidian points wrapped on with sinew and glued with a sticky substance from sagebrush. They made traps for small animals from looped willow stems . They wove fiber into nets for fishing and rabbit drives. During these drives, the old men would hold the nets in a long crescent to catch the rabbits the others drove in and clubbed. The rabbit skins they wove into capes and robes. From local clays they made smoking pipes and a little pottery. They wove beautiful willow baskets of many sizes and shapes—food containers, cooking baskets, hats, cradles, seed beaters, winnowing trays and pitch-coated water bottles.

The Kuzedika regularly crossed the Sierra over Mono Pass to trade with the Miwoks in Yosemite. The men traveled with buckskin bundles slung over their shoulders, the women with large baskets on their backs, tumplines pulling against their foreheads. The baskets were crammed with pine nuts, obsidian, red and white powder for paint making, kutsavi, smaller baskets, and salt that had been scraped up from saline lakes and patted into flat cakes. These they traded for shell beads, acorns, manzanita berries and elderberries.

Celebrations and stories. Despite hardships, the Paiutes had their pleasures. In the fall, after seeds were gathered, Paiutes gathered at traditional places for week-long celebrations, with dancing and gambling. Gambling, their favorite amusement, took many forms—wrestling, running, ball games, throwing spears, and most popular of all, the hand game. In this game four small bone sticks, two marked, were hidden in the hands of two partners; an opponent guessed in which hands the unmarked sticks were, betting large amounts of shell beads or goods. On winter evenings story telling often focused on their favorite characters, Coyote and Hai'nanu, who got themselves into all sorts of scrapes. Hai'nanu was a rascal and a rogue; Coyote a trickster—greedy, disobedient, and boastful. As related by Jack Stewart, a very old Paiute from Big Pine, "The evil in the world came from Coyote. Wolf and Coyote settled things so that there would always be evil along with good. Evil is clever and talks well, always trying to get you. It makes people dishonest and lazy. But by following a good life, being kind, helpful, and generous, you have great power, as I have had."

Discovery and Exploration

For three hundred years after the Spanish explorer Cabrillo discovered California in 1542, the Paiutes continued living in their traditional ways, with no interference from white men. The ships of the Spanish explorers, the rush of fur ships to the northwest for sea otter pelts, the chain of missions established by the padres, the great ranchos of the Spanish land grants, the beaver trade developed by the Hudson's Bay Company in the Oregon Territory, the ships which took the rancho's cowhides and tallow to New England's boot and shoe factories—all these activities were confined to a few coastal pueblos and valleys, for ships were California's sole tie with the rest of the world. By 1825, when about seven thousand Spaniards and Mexicans (plus a few British, Americans, and Russians) had settled in California, no white man had yet crossed the immense mountain barrier of the Sierra Nevada nor the deserts of Nevada and Utah. During the next twenty-seven years, the trails of the mountain men and the explorers and even the forty-niners—all headed for California—barely touched Mono country.

Which explorer first set eyes on Mono Lake and which white men first trod the Mammoth country have long been tantalizing questions. Because misinformation on these matters, although long ago discredited, still lingers, let us examine in some detail who really deserves these honors.

The mountain men, trail blazers of the far west

When fashion decreed that the well-dressed man of the early 1800s should wear a high-crowned hat made of beaver-felt, the demand for beaver skins sent their price soaring. Lured by the profits to be made—prime furs brought four to six dollars a pound in St. Louis—the adventurous and the enterprising set out to trap beaver in the vast wilderness west of the Missouri, roaming the Rocky Mountains and the far west wherever their search led them. These American fur trappers, the *mountain men*, were the first to travel the immense distances separating coastal California from the frontier towns along the Missouri River. It was they who explored the west and blazed the first trails, and who later served as guides and scouts.

Jed Smith. One of the most daring was Jedediah Smith, still in his twenties when in 1826 he led the first trapping party to California overland. His route lay far south of the Sierra, following the Inconstant River (the Mojave) and finally reaching Mission San Gabriel. He was also the first white man to cross the Sierra, from west to east, on his return trip the next summer to the fur trappers' rendezvous in Bear Valley near Salt Lake.

You may still read, in otherwise reliable books, that Jed Smith was the first white man to visit Owens Valley and that he found gold at Mono Lake. Since Smith's diaries and maps had disappeared, for many years his routes were debatable. It was not until 1934 that Maurice Sullivan tracked down and published a transcript of Smith's lost diary and an 1839 map based on Smith's sketches. Then in 1954 Carl Wheat and Dale Morgan published another copy of a Smith map (the Frémont-Gibbs-Smith map). Remarkable historical detective work lay behind both discoveries. Smith's journal and the maps shed new light on his achievements and his routes. None of them led to Mono. On his heroic Sierra crossing, Smith started from the north bank of the Stanislaus River in the Sierra foothills, crossed the mountains near Ebbetts or Carson pass, passed Walker Lake and headed east toward Gabbs Valley. He and his two men barely survived the desert crossing that lay ahead.

Peter Skene Ogden. It is possible that the first white man to traverse the length of the eastern Sierra was not an American but a British fur trapper, Peter Skene Ogden of the Hudson's Bay Company. You probably never heard of Ogden, for American history books have neglected British trappers' remarkable feats of exploration in North America. Ogden's epic 1829–30

Sixth Expedition explored for beaver from the Columbia River south to the Gulf of California. Unfortunately all of his journals were lost and nine of his men drowned as they crossed the Columbia River on their return trip, so we will never know his exact route. But, from a brief report he wrote, we know that he followed the Unknown River (the Humboldt) to its sink, and then set a course south and southwest, which could have taken him to the Walker and then the Owens river.

Joe Walker. Of Joe Walker we know a bit more, although he too left sketchy records. Joseph Reddeford Walker, an experienced mountain man, was employed by Captain Bonneville in 1833 to explore for beaver west of Salt Lake. Walker, with his party of fifty, crossed the desert by following the Humboldt River, then struck south to Bridgeport Valley. They crossed the Sierra divide in late fall through deep snow by one of the southern tributaries of the East Walker River. On his return trip the following year, Walker discovered the pass in the southern Sierra that Frémont later named for him, struck north and followed the Owens River. From the northern end of Owens Valley to the Humboldt River, the account of his route is so garbled that we likely will never know exactly where he went. Perhaps his route led from Benton Hot Springs to Walker Lake or the Walker River. However, a lake and a hot spring described in clerk Zenas Leonard's account of the expedition present tantalizing puzzles.

> In the evening we encamped on the margin of a large lake formed by a river which heads in this mountain. This lake...has no outlet for the water....The water in this lake is similar to lie, and tastes much like pearlash....There is also a great quantity of pumice stone floating on the surface of the water, and the shore is covered with them.

> At length we arrived at some springs which presented a really remarkable appearance, and may be called boiling, or more properly Steam Springs, situated near the base of the mountain, on or near the banks of a small river. These springs are three in number, and rise within a short distance of each other, one being much larger than the other two. The water constantly boils as if it was in a kettle over a fire, and is so hot that if a piece of meat is put under the water...it will cook in a few minutes....(*Adventures of Zenas Leonard, Fur Trader*)

Can you think of any lake that fits this description besides Mono? And any hot spring besides Hot Creek? If Walker's party did pass Mono Lake and Hot Creek, then his route is even more puzzling.

Mountain men returning to the frontier towns were lavish in their praise of California—its temperate climate, game, fertile soil, the easy life on the ranchos. Sailing men, too, spread tales of the wonders of the Pacific coast. Adventurous pioneers were already settling west of the Missouri River; stories of the far west beckoned them on farther. Pioneer migration steadily increased during the 1840s, most of the settlers going to the northwest over the well-established Oregon Trail, a few to California. The first pioneers reached California in 1840, the thirty-some members of the Bidwell party. No one had discovered a wagon route across the Sierra and neither did they.

Traveling was so difficult, they abandoned their wagons in northeastern Nevada and walked the rest of the way to the Sacramento Valley, crossing the Sierra near Sonora Pass with their goods strapped to oxen and mules. In 1843 Joe Walker guided the first wagon train over his eastern Sierra route, but that too proved to be an impossible route. The wagons mired down in the sand and had to be abandoned, somewhere near Owens Lake. The party proceeded on foot, the women and children on horseback, over Walker Pass.

Three years later Walker guided the first expedition charged officially with exploring Inyo-Mono country, Captain John Frémont's Third Expedition. Among the group were the mountain man, Kit Carson, and two whose names are immortalized on Sierra maps, Dick Owens and Edward Kern. Frémont and a small group crossed the Sierra by following the Truckee River up stream. The larger group he sent south with Walker, to map and explore the eastern Sierra route over Walker Pass. From Walker Lake the group headed south to the Adobe Hills, probably camped in Adobe Valley, and then followed the Owens River to Owens Lake.

Discovery of Mono Lake

The pioneers' steady parade westward was interrupted in 1848 by the spine-tingling news that gold had been discovered near John Sutter's Sacramento Valley rancho. Californians dropped whatever they were doing and raced to the Sierra foothills. As the news spread that miners were panning out $100 in gold a day and that a lucky one had found a twelve-ounce nugget, men streamed in from neighboring Mexico and Oregon. By the following year California's magic name had crossed both oceans, and men from everywhere were embarking for the land of gold. But while all the world knew of the Mother Lode on the Sierra's western slope, for a few more years no one even thought about the eastern slope.

Lt. Tredwell Moore, 1852. Mono Lake was discovered quite by accident. As late as 1852, maps showed only empty white space for most of the lands east of the Sierra Nevada. During the next twenty years that white space diminished markedly. It was left to a soldier, not a mountain man looking for beaver nor a prospector looking for gold, to discover and name Mono Lake. Lt. Tredwell Moore and his troopers, bent on finding and punishing Chief Tenaya and some Miwoks who were suspected of killing three white men in Yosemite, pursued the Indians as they fled east across the mountains. Moore pushed on over Mono Pass, following a long-used trail down to the camps of the Kuzedika. If Chief Tenaya was there, hidden by his friends, Moore never found him. Instead, he found an astonishingly large lake that he named after the Indians who lived there, and he picked up some gold specimens. Moore's discoveries, of the lake and of placer gold there, were publicized in Stockton and San Francisco newspapers in August 1852, and on his return trip to Mariposa and Fort Miller (Millerton), the gold samples he displayed stimulated others to prospect this previously unexplored region. In 1853, as a result of Moore's information, Mono Lake was depicted for the first time on a published map of California.

The first prospectors. Leroy Vining and some friends, excited by the samples, wasted little time. With one of Moore's scouts as guide, they headed for Mono Pass and prospected near Mono Lake that very fall. Over the next few years, other prospectors looking for new placers drifted south from the Mormon settlement of Genoa in Carson Valley. In 1857 rumor had it that Mormon miners were washing out gold at Brown's Creek (a tributary of Virginia Creek, also known as Dog Creek, Dogtown Diggings), the general location still marked by the remains of stone cabins, about six miles north of Conway Summit. Two years later it was reported that Dogtown had a store, and that up to a hundred men were working the placers. It is ironic that the first sizable group of miners on the east side should be predominantly Mormon, for of all groups the Mormons were among the few who did not heed the siren song of gold. Brigham Young threatened the Saints in Salt Lake Valley with damnation if they did.

Boom and Bust: Mining Comes to Mono

Gold at the Mono Diggings, 1859. By the spring of 1859 rumor had it that placers had been discovered in Mono Gulch, the large wash north of Mono Lake. Local legend credits Cord Norst, a Dogtown miner, with the find. In any case, Dogtown miners rushed to the new diggings, and soon western-Sierra miners were racing over Sonora and Mono passes. That summer, perhaps two hundred men in the new camp of Monoville were washing out an average of $12 to $20 dollars a day; by the next summer there may have been a thousand or more. In the fall of the same year, W. S. Bodey and companions located placer ground while prospecting the hills northeast of Monoville but caused no excitement.

Silver at Esmeralda, 1860. The same year as the Monoville strike, fabulously rich silver ore was discovered east of Lake Tahoe—the Comstock Lode, the biggest bonanza of them all, which produced about $700 million worth of gold and silver. Thousands of miners who had only recently come to California now poured back across its borders to Washoe, as Nevada was then called. The next summer three prospectors, who had been at the Comstock long enough to learn a little about silver, located rich quartz veins several miles east of Bodey's find. The miners there organized the Esmeralda District and named their wildly speculative camp *Aurora*. In their best days, the mines supported sixteen mills and a prosperous community of about five thousand people. Hopelessly infected with "Washoe fever" and the

"Esmeralda excitement," men surged to the new camps, each one hoping to strike it rich. With them went almost as many merchants and sawyers and suppliers to furnish them with food, liquor, clothing, tools, horses and hay and to furnish the mines with fuel, lumber and machinery.

The Aurora boom stirred up demands for a wagon road across the Sierra. Supplies from the coast for Monoville and Aurora had to come via Carson Valley or over Mono and Sonora passes by pack train—long, precarious and expensive routes. Construction of the Sonora Pass Toll Road started in 1863; it was completed in 1868. But, ironically, in those few years Aurora passed her peak and was on the way to becoming a ghost town.

The Paiutes' land was theirs no longer. Cattle grazed on the best wild-seed plots, sheep on the deer's brush slopes. Pinyon trees were cut for fuel. Game and fish, never abundant, became even more scarce. Some of the Paiutes fought back; many began working for the white man.

Creation of Mono County, 1861. The sudden influx of people into the land east of the Sierra, then eastern Calaveras County, led to a petition asking the California legislature to create Esmeralda County. The bill was amended to read Mono County and passed in 1861, with Aurora the county seat. Nine years later Mono County had its first census. Such are the fluctuations of mining prosperity, however, that instead of thousands, Mono County had only 430 inhabitants! Of the two sizable communities existing when the county was created, by 1870 Monoville was deserted and correction of the state boundary line placed Aurora in Nevada. Bridgeport replaced Aurora as the county seat. According to the 1870 census, sixty farms and ranches had been settled and over nine thousand acres were producing wheat, oats, barley, hay and potatoes; 35,000 pounds of butter and 4,000 pounds of cheese, besides local beef and pork, were produced yearly for local consumption.

Mining districts: unofficial self-government. In the absence of any effective local or state government in the scattered mining camps, anarchy was effectively avoided by calling a meeting of miners in the area and formally declaring a *District*, naming it and electing a committee to draw up a set of regulations governing claims. The formalities over, a liquid celebration usually rounded out the evening. Regulations might specify, for example, that a miner could hold only one claim of a given length, that he could hold it only as long as he worked it, that he could add to his holdings by buying others, and might specify a procedure for resolving disputes, such as calling a mass meeting or choosing arbiters. A district recorder was elected to register claims and make transfers of title. Sometimes a simple but effective criminal code was also adopted, such as: thieves were to be whipped in public, horse thieves and murderers hanged. Banishment was another common punishment (Git on yer horse an' git!). Justice was immediate, for there were seldom jails to hold the accused. The district served its purpose remarkably well, though if the recorder was careless, claims might be recorded incorrectly or the whole book of claims lost. The district became superfluous when the federal government assumed the regulation of mining on public land.

The Lost Cement Mine. In 1864 several mining districts were formed southeast of Aurora, the only one of importance being the Blind Springs Mining District and its camp of Benton. Over a period of twenty years, this district produced about $4 million worth of silver. For the next thirteen years the center of excitement shifted south to Cerro Gordo in the Inyo Mountains and east to silver strikes in Nevada.

Prospecting continued in Mono County during the '60s and '70s, however, much of it stimulated by widely spread tales of the Lost Cement Mine. Lumps of gold "like raisins in a pudding" had been found in a reddish "cement" somewhere on the headwaters of the Owens River, according to one version. Another version told that a prospector in San Francisco, who was very ill and knew he could never make it back to Mono, gave to a Dr. Randall (as payment for services) some ore, a map, and a detailed description of the mine. Arriving at Monoville in 1861, Dr. Randall hired men to go with him to Pumice Flat, 37 miles south of Monoville, and there located a quarter-section of land. The next summer Dr. Randall returned to his location and employed eleven men, with Gid Whiteman as foreman. They found some reddish lava, *cement*, and though the story is vague on whether it contained any gold, hundreds of prospectors began searching for the red cement. Indians who brought gold to Benton, never saying where they got it, were suspected of knowing the mine's whereabouts. Whiteman searched for over twenty summers, believing until his death in 1883 that he was near the lost mine.

Possibly the golden-studded cement was found but kept a secret; possibly the whole story was the raving of a deranged prospector; possibly the tale was true and the reddish cement is there still, waiting to be uncovered. Whatever the case, the legend lives and prospectors still search for the Lost Cement Mine.

The Mammoth Mines, 1878. In the late 1870s mining excitement returned to Mono County as new discoveries were made, one after the other. Four men prospecting for the Lost Cement Mine in 1877 located the Alpha claim on Mineral Hill (now known as Red or Gold Mountain). Others located the Mammoth, the Head Light, Monte Cristo, Last Chance and dozens more. All joined to organize Lake District. The next spring General George Dodge, a prominent mining investor, and other financiers from San Francisco came to visit the new district. Pronouncing it "good enough for a stock deal," Dodge bought five claims for $10,000 in cash and $20,000 in company stock and organized the Mammoth Mining Company. The company began construction that July of a 20-stamp mill, four tunnels into Red Mountain, a tramway to move ore to the mill, and a flume to bring water to power the mill's machinery. The rush to Mammoth was underway; including the nearby districts of Prescott, Mountain View, Laurel and North Fork, during the summer of 1879 perhaps 2500 people flocked to the new mines. Mammoth's boom also stimulated toll-road building, routes important to later settlers and stockmen—the Sherwin Road southeast to Bishop, a wagon road east to Benton, and the French Trail that led west across the Sierra to Fresno Flats (today's Oakhurst).

But the Mammoth bonanza never materialized. Within two years the company was having financial problems, stockholders did not pay their assessments, and in October 1880 the mill closed for good. The inglorious finale occurred on July 6, 1881 at a sheriff's sale in Mammoth City. Some of the mill's machinery was shipped to Bodie, some disappeared or deteriorated through the years, and scrap dealers finally took just about all the metal that was left.

Bodie, 1878. A few months after making his placer find in 1859, Bodey perished in a blizzard on his way to Monoville for supplies. Other prospectors staked quartz claims nearby over a number of years. Companies succeeded each other but all failed financially, including one headed by Governor Leland Stanford. An accidental cave-in uncovered a rich ledge, which was bought by the newly organized Standard Company in 1877. The company erected a mill, the ore proved to be very rich, and within a year the rush was on to Bodie. (Bodey's name suffered a series of misspellings.)

Bodie's production record far surpasses that of any other Mono County mine, an estimated $30 million in gold and silver. To approximate today's values, multiply by at least 15 or 20. The Standard Company paid almost a million dollars in dividends to its stockholders during a single year. Bodie also boasted more gambling, drinking and shooting than any other lawless mining camp. A favorite story is of a child on her way to Bodie who prayed, "Good-bye God! I'm going to Bodie." A Bodie editor replied that the little girl had been misquoted, that what she really said was, "Good, by God! I'm going to Bodie." High living and speculation dominated the camp of eight (possibly ten) thousand people, until the stock market crash of 1881. One by one Bodie's mines closed until by 1888 only four or five hundred people remained. Bodie's notorious days were over, though the two most profitable companies—The Standard and The Bodie—merged and operated successfully for a number of years.

Promoters' heyday. It was along streambeds that the early prospectors searched, for they were looking for placers—stream deposits of sand and gravel containing particles of gold. Placer mining is essentially a settling process, washing away the sand and mud and retaining the heavier gold. And since placer mining required few tools, anyone became a miner simply by outfitting himself with a pick, shovel and gold pan. Some of the placers were phenomenally rich; in seven weeks, fifty hired Indians washed out two hundred and seventy-three pounds of gold at the Feather River diggings. But panning proved to be slow, back-breaking, and profitable only on the richest placers. Crude wooden devices were invented—rockers, sluices and long-Toms—that enabled several men working together to wash much larger amounts of river sand.

During the twenty years separating Dogtown and Bodie, mining methods had changed dramatically. Prospectors no longer explored only streambeds. Instead they tramped the mountains looking for gold-bearing quartz veins. Few prospectors worked their claims; instead, they looked for a company to sell to. Most "miners" were day laborers working for companies at about four dollars for a ten-hour day; few remained as independent as the forty-niner with his burro and a few tools.

These changes were due to the exhaustion of the rich placers and to the nature of quartz mining, called hard-rock mining. Extracting gold from quartz requires blasting, hauling, crushing and finally separating the gold from the crushed rock. To do all this by hand yields little gold. To be worthwhile, quartz mining requires large-scale construction: tunnels and shafts driven hundreds of feet, tramways and railroads to move the ore, three-story stamp mills for crushing it, and water or steam power for running the mills. Skilled men, expensive machinery, buildings, roads—all required thousands of dollars of capital.

As numerous small companies organized to raise the necessary capital, promoters and financiers came into their own. Many made fortunes not by producing gold, but by buying and selling mining stock at the right moment. Stock in the Bodie Mining Company jumped from 50 cents to $54 a share; Hale and Norcross Mine (Virginia City) stock slid from $2900 to $41.50 a share in six months. Promoters of 1870 were much like those of today—some honest, some frauds, their mine always a sure thing. Many were the gullible investors who bought stock on the high assay value of one small ore sample.

Production figures for the early mines are impossible to obtain. Records were lost, destroyed or never kept in the first place (the income tax had not yet been invented). Local rumor and promoters' inflated reports, quoted in newspapers, were as unreliable then as they are today. All production figures quoted in this book are estimates taken from correspondence with or publications of the State Division of Mines. Its estimates are based on statistics of the U.S. Mint (gold received) and the U.S. Customs House (gold shipped).

The Lundy and Tioga mines. In 1879, the year of feverish excitement both in Bodie and Mammoth City, veins of ore were also discovered in Mill Creek (Lundy) Canyon and the Homer Mining District formed there. The small town of Lundy lived on for a number of years, the May Lundy Mine producing an estimated $2 million in gold. Lundy's editor, Lying Jim Townsend, published one of the most unusual and entertaining camp newspapers, the *Homer Mining Index*. Jim's wit and his best tales matched anything Mark Twain wrote. In 1884 the Lundy mines closed and the paper ceased printing for a few years. But then Jim was hired by a con man who had gone to London, organized the Homer District Consolidated Gold Mines Ltd., and was trying to raise $5 million in order to sell some worthless claims that he did not have clear title to. Jim's contribution to the scheme was to resurrect the *Index*, describe the Lundy mines as if they were active and paying, and send the papers to London for the benefit of the potential investors. Among Jim's stories during this time, one concerned a monster that lived in Mono Lake and another described a group of large boulders that trembled and flashed in the night. According to Chalfant (*Gold, Guns and Ghost Towns*), the *Index* also printed ads for two imaginary banks, three large groceries and a timetable for a nonexistent railroad.

In 1882, the Great Sierra Consolidated Silver Mining Company was organized to develop the Tioga Mine on a ridge just east of Tioga Pass. Two years and $300,000 later, financial disaster closed the mine abruptly. But during its brief life, men and mules performed some incredible feats. Routes to the mine were spectacular. Accessible at first only by the Bloody Canyon-Mono Pass trail, later an even more precipitous trail was built from Lundy. An engine, boiler, compressor, drills, pipe—16,000 pounds of machinery in all, impossible to pack in by mule—were hauled over this route on sleds in winter. A quote from the *Index* of March 1882 (this time probably not exaggerated) makes vivid the difficulties miners faced before the days of trucks and tractors.

> The first ascent, from Mill Creek to the mouth of Lake Canyon, is 990 feet, almost perpendicular. From that point to the south end of Lake Oneida...is a rise of 845 feet....The machinery will probably be hoisted straight up to the summit of Mount Warren ridge...an almost vertical rise of 2,160 feet. From the summit the descent will be made to Saddlebags Lake....It is being transported on six heavy sleds admirably constructed of hardwood...a pair of bobsleds accompany the expedition, the latter being laden with bedding, provisions, cooking utensils, etc. The heaviest load is 4,200 pounds. Ten or twelve men, two mules, 4,500 feet of one-inch Manila rope, heavy double block and tackle, and all the available trees along the route are employed in "snaking" the machinery up the mountain....

Farming and Ranching Succeed Mining

Since Bodie's decline, gold and silver mining in Mono County has been small-scale only. Some thousands of dollars were taken out by working tailings and by small mills. But the big bonanzas were elsewhere—Cripple Creek, the Klondike, Tombstone—and other minerals took center stage. For a brief period (1953) the Black Rock Mine southeast of Benton was the second largest tungsten producer in California. But prospecting continues, and there's always someone looking for the Lost Cement Mine. Today Mono County's most important mineral products are pyrophyllite, pumice, stone, clay, sand and gravel.

The mines had drawn thousands of men east of the Sierra and had stimulated farming, ranching and lumbering. When they closed, many miners packed up and headed for the next bonanza; a few stayed on, ranching and operating small sawmills. For the next thirty years, about a hundred farm families worked some 50,000 acres, grazing cattle, diverting streams to flood some of the bottomlands, and raising hay, wheat, and barley. The severe droughts of 1863–64, '71, and '77 caused terrible losses of livestock in other parts of California. Animals died of thirst and starvation, for deep wells and irrigated pasture were then not common ranching practice. In 1877 alone, southern California sheepmen lost about 2.5 million head. Spurred by these repeated droughts, ranchers from the west and the south began driving their animals into the eastern Sierra, where sagebrush slopes and mountain meadows offered dependable summer feed.

Ranching declined drastically during the 1920s and 1930s because of depressions and the lack of nearby markets, then increased as cattle raising became profitable once again. A few sheepmen still bring their sheep to the mountain meadows in late summer, though what used to be a month-long drive from Bakersfield and Lancaster is now a one-day truck ride. Today Mono County has about 110 ranches, ranging in size from small ranchettes to thousands of acres. Farm products produced, in order of their value, are: beef cattle, row crops and seed crops, alfalfa and hay, and sheep. Production of carrots, seed garlic and seed potatoes is increasing, especially in Hammil Valley. Conditions in Mono—isolation from the pests and diseases of other agricultural areas and cool nights in summer—seem to favor these crops. In the two fertile valleys covered by this guidebook, Long Valley and the Mono Basin, ranching today consists largely of grazing on City of Los Angeles leases.

The Los Angeles Aqueduct Reaches into Mono

During the early 1900s, the growing city of Los Angeles began looking for water; the Owens River, draining more than a hundred miles of the Sierra Nevada's eastern slope, had lots of it. Although 233 miles away, Owens water was high quality and could flow by gravity all the way to the city. The long fight over water rights and groundwater pumping between Owens Valley citizens and the city's Department of Water and Power (DWP) is not the subject of discussion here. *Deepest Valley*, the companion book to *Mammoth Lakes Sierra*, will discuss that controversy in a coming new edition. Today's 338-mile-long Los Angeles Aqueduct has delivered over the past twenty years an average 65 percent of the city's total water supply—about 450,000 acre feet per year of the city's roughly 700,000 total acre feet. In past years about 13 percent of that total came from the Mono Basin. All in all, on average, the aqueduct has delivered 550 million gallons of water a day to Los Angeles.

The project did not affect Mono County until DWP began pushing the aqueduct north of Owens Valley. In 1932 DWP purchased Los Angeles Mayor Fred Eaton's Long Valley ranch and started construction of Crowley reservoir at the lower end of Long Valley. To control the streams that are tributary to the Owens, the city then began buying more Long Valley ranches and their water rights. To pick up the waters north of the Owens River drainage—waters of the Mono Basin, whose streams all drain naturally into Mono Lake—DWP filed claims on water from several streams, purchased water rights and began buying ranches and their water rights around Mono Lake. To connect these northern waters with the Owens River system, DWP tunneled through the Mono Craters and began diverting Mono waters in 1941. (Within the craters, much to their surprise, the tunnel builders encountered steam, hot water, volcanic gases, and ground cavings that doubled the cost of the tunnel.)

Then, with ever more people, the city in 1970 completed a second aqueduct, increasing total capacity by 48 percent. To fill this *second barrel*, the city increased its groundwater pumping in Owens Valley and diverted almost the entire flow of the four major Mono Basin streams—Lee Vining, Walker, Parker, and Rush creeks. Between 1941 when diversions started and 1970, the lake level dropped 28 vertical feet. In just the next twelve years, from 1970 to 1982, as the second barrel diverted 90,000 acre feet on average from Mono Lake's tributaries, the lake dropped another 17 feet. Between 1941 and 1982, the lake's volume decreased by half, and its salinity doubled. The lake and all its creatures seemed headed straight for disaster.

The Future of Mono Lake. If diversions were continuing at the past rate and if the lake were continuing to drop one or two feet a year, it would reach the critical level of 6350 feet in twenty or thirty years. Critical because at that level salinity would increase another 50 percent, the lake's volume would decrease by another 30 percent, alkali flies and brine shrimp would be unable to reproduce, and there would be little food for the birds that now depend on Mono as a nesting site and as an important stopover during their migration.

But diversions will not continue at the past rate and the grim scenario just outlined may never occur, thanks to Sally and David Gaines and a handful of friends who in 1978 formed the Mono Lake Committee. Today the committee boasts 20,000 members, a staff of 14, and programs of legislation, education and litigation. In the state and federal legislatures the committee successfully sponsored bills to fund research and to establish the Mono Basin National Forest Scenic Area and the Mono Lake Tufa State Reserve. In the courts, the committee and its allies—notably the National Audubon Society and California Trout—have been winning significant victories. Temporary court-ordered minimum flows in Mono's tributaries have increased the water flowing into the lake, lessening—but not halting—its decline.

In the famous *public trust* suit, the California Supreme Court in 1983 upheld the claim that Mono Lake's public trust environmental and recreational values must be protected "as far as feasible." In another suit, the Third District Court of Appeals in 1989 ruled that DWP's water diversion licenses are illegal and that the State Water Resources Control Board must reissue them with conditions that comply with the Fish and Game Code, which mandates a healthy fishery below dams. It also ruled that the historic fishery must be restored. The State Supreme Court refused to review the case, thus letting the decision stand. The Water Board is currently writing an Environmental Impact Report in its process of reissuing DWP's licenses so that they comply with the Fish and Game Code and also with the public trust doctrine. In the interim, while the EIR is being written, the El Dorado Superior Court has granted preliminary injunctions to keep the lake and its streams from deteriorating further. In two separate rulings in 1990, the Superior Court ruled 1) that the lake level must not drop below 6377 and 2) set minimum streamflows for Rush, Parker, Walker and Lee Vining creeks. The Superior Court is also overseeing the work of restoring the streams to the pre-diversion conditions that provided a healthy fishery.

The lawsuits are far from over. In 1992 and 1993, DWP went back to court repeatedly with objections. For news of the lawsuits, the EIR, and of other possible solutions to the controversy, stop in at the Mono Lake Committee headquarters in the center of Lee Vining or write PO Box 29, Lee Vining, CA 93541. Mono Lake's shrimp, flies, gulls and grebes *need* you—please consider joining and supporting the Committee's efforts.

Year-round Vacation Land

Summer camping. The eastern Sierra has natural attractions in abundance—dramatic mountains, high peaks, hundreds of lakes, dozens of streams, fish, game, and amazing variety. These scenic resources long ago replaced mining as the area's major attraction and the base of its economy. The trend began in the early 1900s, when people came from the mining camps and from Owens Valley to enjoy the scenery and the fishing and the cool mountains. But before 1930, few came long distances. Most people worked fifty hours a week, six days a week; furthermore, it was a rugged two-day trip from Los Angeles. Automobiles were still a novelty, and anyone venturesome enough to drive the eastern Sierra had little more to follow than tracks through the sagebrush. Boiling radiators demanded quantities of water, and cars sank to their axles in the sand and pumice.

As California's people voted many millions for highways, a share was spent on El Camino Sierra, now known as US Highway 395. At the same time, wages began going up, hours going down, automobiles going faster, and vacations getting longer. The growth of southern California during and after World War II resulted in millions of people who lived only six hours away—people with the time and money and desire to camp, hike, fish, hunt and ski. And come they did, more and more of them.

Winter skiing. In the late 1930s, a few local people caught ski fever. They built small portable ski tows, powered them with old Ford or Chevy engines and set them up wherever the snow was suitable—on the slope of McGee Mountain, at Deadman Summit, June Lake or Conway Summit—usually close to Highway 395, for no side roads were plowed. In 1941 an eager skier named Dave McCoy set up his first rope tow on Mammoth Mountain. The *Inyo Register* of 20 November 1941 reported that "over 250 skiers visited Mammoth Mt. over the Thanksgiving weekend. The portable tow, operated by Dave McCoy, was run overtime to accommodate the enthusiastic crowd!"

After World War II, as skiing caught on in many parts of the country, McCoy moved portable tows here and there and up to a hundred weekend skiers might show up at Mammoth Mountain's rope tows, sometimes hiking several miles if the road was snow-blocked or riding the army-surplus weasels that McCoy acquired. The completion of an all-weather road to Mammoth Mountain's north slope in 1954 and the construction of a double chair lift in 1955, more lifts, more runs, a gondola system, more base lodges and the opening of the June Mountain ski area in 1961 put Mammoth Mountain/June Mountain on the skier's map. In 1986 McCoy bought the June Mountain Ski Area and began major improvements. Besides downhill skiing, winter sports today include cross-country skiing, ski mountaineering, snowboarding, snowmobiling and sleighriding. The two ski areas together average well over a million skier-days per year. Snowfall averages about 335 inches a year; the biggest winter ever was 1983–84 with 567 inches of snow. A minimum six-month ski season, dependable snow, wonderfully variable terrain, and the proximity of two huge population centers—in southern California and around San Francisco Bay—have made Mammoth one of the country's outstanding winter resorts.

Tourism and year-round recreation, with snow sports half of the year and camping and hiking the other half, are Mono County's number one industry, generating eight to ten times the value of mining, ranching and lumbering combined. The Inyo National Forest, consistently among the five most heavily used forests in the nation, counted close to 8.5 million recreation visitor days in 1992. Of that, the Mono Lake and Mammoth ranger districts together accounted for 6.6 million visitor days. (The Forest Service measures recreation use in visitor days—one visitor for 12 hours equals a visitor day.) These figures do not include all the people who used motels, condos and other facilities on private land, nor those who hiked the adjacent back country west of the Sierra crest, which is administered by Yosemite National Park and the Sierra National Forest.

Land trades. For years, June Lake and Mammoth Lakes had grown slowly and steadily, every year bringing a few more cabins and maybe a new lodge. But a change in land ownership beginning about 1960 opened a new chapter in the area's growth. The Forest Service entered into a series of land trades that continues today, trading national forest land in Mammoth to private developers in return for land elsewhere that the Forest Service wants to acquire. Then in 1977 the Arcularius family sold their ranch in Old Mammoth meadows. Advertising and marketing fired up a real estate boom that continues today, encouraged speculation in condos and second homes and led to a wide array of summer and winter recreation developments.

Yours for Discovering

Mining was the key that unlocked the treasure chest of the eastern Sierra, one of the last regions of California to be settled. The Spanish-Mexicans and the men of the trading ships, so important to the state's early growth, left no mark east of the mountains. Vast deserts on three sides and an immense mountain barrier on the other kept white men away until relatively late in California's history. Then ranching succeeded mining. Today it is the magnificent mountain scenery, the long snow season, and the back-country wilderness that bring city folk flocking to the eastern Sierra.

However, in spite of all the developments and the weekend traffic and overflowing campgrounds on three-day holidays, pay no attention to those who tell you the Sierra is too crowded. Discovery and wildness are still the essence of much of the Mammoth Lakes Sierra. Just a few minutes off US 395, or midweek or off-season, you can still find wild places and wild things, solitude if you want it, and peace and quiet. You may have to hunt for them, because we haven't told you about many of those special places. But we can assure you that they are there and that you will find them if you try. Miles of joy and endless days of wonder are yours for discovering.

Contributors & Acknowledgments

About the authors and photographers

We have written this guide from very personal points of view, for all of us have lived east of the Sierra for a portion of our lives. While each of us has tried to present facts objectively, our deep affection for the eastern Sierra can't help but shine through. We wouldn't want it otherwise, for we care about this magnificent region and its wild flowers and wild creatures.

Each author is an acknowledged authority in his field. Dean Rinehart, with other members of the US Geological Survey, mapped the geology of the Mount Morrison, Casa Diablo, and Devils Postpile quadrangles during seven summers. Elden Vestal, first Regional Fisheries Biologist for Inyo-Mono with the California Department of Fish and Game, lived and worked in the area for thirteen years. Dr. Bettie E. Willard, daughter of Beatrice and Stephen Willard and raised in Mammoth Lakes, is an alpine plant ecologist. Susan Rinehart, who drew all of the illustrations but one, lived summers in Mammoth with husband Dean, snatching moments to sketch between caring for their two small children. Genny Smith, writer, editor and publisher has been a summer resident of Mammoth Lakes since 1955.

We are privileged to publish photographs from the life work of the land-scape photographer, Stephen Willard, 1894–1966. He and his wife Beatrice opened the Willard Studio at Mammoth Lakes in 1924; she kept the studio open until her own death in 1977. Prints were made by Rick Warner of Whittier. Many of our other photographers live in the eastern Sierra. Edwin C. Rockwell was on the staff of the Inyo National Forest from 1951 to 1980, first in Mammoth Lakes, then in Bishop. T J Johnston has long been a photographer for Mammoth Mountain Ski Area. Tom Ross, well-known mountain climber, lives in Bishop. Bev Steveson has lived summers at Mammoth since 1974. Some of the historic photographs are by the late Harry Mendenhall, who operated a photo studio in Big Pine from about 1910 until 1952. He may have taken his first photographs of Old Mammoth in the early 1900s; his signature is in the Wildasinn Hotel register of 1908. Other historic photos come from the collections of Adele Reed and Billy Young. Adele, author of books on local history, and her husband Bill lived at Mammoth from 1927 to 1948 and then in Bishop until their deaths. The late Billy Young worked for the power company out of Bishop from 1910 to 1953.

Acknowledgments

Thanks to Mike Hamilton, this is the most handsome of our six editions by far. For making this edition the best ever, I am ever grateful to all the following. Consultants: Dr. Carolyn Tiernan of Bishop, board-certified in emergency medicine and nationally ranked in cross-country marathon ski racing; geologist Roy Bailey, USGS; biologists Tom Kucera, Phil Pister, Denyse Racine, Terry Russi, Emilie Strauss, John Wehausen. The eastern Sierra residents who helped with trail scouting: Carole Gerard, Maria and Richard Grant; Peggy & Ray Gray, Mary & Ira Hanson, Tom Klimowski, Paul Kluth, Louise & Dean Lemon. Inyo National Forest staff members: Bill Bramlette, Cynthia Krell, Molly McCartney, Mike Morris, Gary Pingle, John Roupp, Bob Wood. And Gen Clement, Louise & Bill Kelsey, Jim McAllister, George Milovich, Bill Murphy and Mary Roeser who, among many, many others over the past thirty years, helped in some way or other.

Genny Smith
Mammoth Lakes, July 1993

For More Information

You will find many eastern Sierra titles locally that you won't find in the big cities. Bookstores in Bishop and Mammoth Lakes, most ranger stations and the information center in Lee Vining—all specialize in books on the eastern Sierra, including hard-to-find items. The Interagency Visitor Center, at the junction of Highway 136 and US 395 just south of Lone Pine, also stocks an outstanding selection of books.

Catalogs available

Trail guides and natural history books are flooding off the presses at such a rate that a listing here would soon be out of date. Send for the free current catalogs of these publishers. Mentioned below are a few unusual and outstanding books of each publisher.

Artemisia Press (Sally Gaines), PO Box 119, Lee Vining 93541. Books on field ornithology and on Mono Basin's geology and pioneer history. *Birds of Yosemite and the East Slope* by David Gaines; a wealth of information published nowhere else, a joy to read. *Paiute, Prospector, Pioneer* by Thomas Fletcher; admirably researched 19th-century history of the Mono Basin, including Bodie.

California Dept. of Fish and Game, Conservation-Education, 1416 Ninth St., Sacramento 95814. Copies and a publications list may also be obtained from the department's regional offices (Rancho Cordova, Long Beach, Fresno, Yountville, Redding). Authoritative, superbly illustrated booklets, fishing guides and wildlife leaflets.

Angler's guides. Ehlers, Robert R. *Angler's Guide to the Lakes and Streams of the Mono Creek Area;* description of 47 waters of the Mono Creek Area, Fresno County. Vestal, Elden H. and R. Ehlers. *Angler's Guide to the Fish Creek Area;* description of 53 waters of Fish Creek. Creel-size, folded angler's maps 18 x 27 with text.

Species booklets on the following subjects: waterfowl, upland game and golden trout. *Outdoor California.* Wildlife magazine; bimonthly, illustrated. For subscriptions write: PO Box 15087, Sacramento 95851–0087.

Chalfant Press, PO Box 787, Bishop, CA 93514. Chalfant publishes booklets and books on Inyo and Mono counties, mostly on local history. *Desert People and Mountain Men: Exploration of the Great Basin 1824–1865* by Fred Phillips; a small book about Smith, Ogden, Walker and Frémont. *Gold, Guns and Ghost Towns* by W. A. Chalfant; mining tales by the long-time editor of the *Inyo Register. Life among the Paiutes* by Sarah Winnemucca. *The Album* is an historical quarterly.

Friends of the Library, Mammoth Chapter, PO Box 1468, Mammoth Lakes, CA 93546. Mail order service on eastern Sierra books published by Genny Smith Books. See last page of this book for a listing of books in print.

Mono Lake Committee, PO Box 29, Lee Vining, CA 93541. Specializes in books on the Mono Basin. *Mono Lake Guidebook* by David Gaines; elegant guide to Mono Lake's natural history and 50-year-long water crisis; includes a self-guided auto tour.

Sierra Club Store, 730 Polk St., San Francisco 94109. *Starr's Guide to the John Muir Trail and the High Sierra Region;* a classic, updated. *A Climber's Guide to the High Sierra;* the authoritative peak-climbing guide. Stephen Whitney's *A Sierra Club Naturalist's Guide to the Sierra Nevada;* a marvelous contribution to understanding the web of life in the Sierra Nevada. Beautifully illustrated. And unlike most books about the Sierra, it includes the *eastern* Sierra. *Walking Softly in the Wilderness,* a guide to backpacking. *Simple Foods for the Pack;* a guide to delicious natural foods for the trail.

Wilderness Press, 2440 Bancroft Way, Berkeley 94704. High Sierra hiking guides are reliable, accurate and include 15-minute topographic maps with updated roads and trails. Updated topographic maps, printed on tear-resistant plastic, may also be purchased separately. Among the many titles Wilderness Press publishes: *Place Names of the Sierra Nevada* by Peter Browning; *Backpacking Basics* by Winnett and Findling; *Ski Tours in the Sierra Nevada* by Marcus Libkind. *Sierra South, Sierra North* and the two-volume *Pacific Crest Trail,* maps included, are backpackers' bibles.

University of California Press, 2120 Berkeley Way, Berkeley 94720. Two classics that are a joy to read and a scholar's delight: Francis Farquhar's *History of the Sierra Nevada;* and William H. Brewer's *Up and Down California in 1860–1864.* William Kahrl's *Water and Power* is the definitive account of Los Angeles' efforts to obtain and control the waters of the Owens River and the Mono Basin. Another book on western water is John Walton's *Western Times and Water Wars,* 1991. The authoritative, pocket-size California Natural History Guides are crammed with detailed information. Among them are Mary Hill's *Geology of the Sierra Nevada* and *California Landscape: Origin and Evolution.* Others cover Sierra wildflowers, native shrubs and native trees. New guides include *Natural History of the White-Inyo Range, Eastern California* ed. by Clarence Hall and *A Natural History of California* by Allan Schoenherr (you need big pockets for these two—both are well over 500 pages). Philip A. Munz's *California Desert Wildflowers* and *California Mountain Wildflowers* are knapsack-size books that include plants of the eastern Sierra; well illustrated with both sketches and color photographs.

University of Nevada Press, University of Nevada, Reno, NV 89557–0076. If your discoveries in the Mammoth Lakes Sierra spur you to explore farther east, into the desert ranges and valleys of the Great Basin, some recent books by the University of Nevada Press will help you on your way. Long neglected by natural history writers, today the Great Basin is beginning to receive the attention it deserves. The press is now publishing a Great Basin Natural History Series—very handsome books, beautifully illustrated. George and Bliss Hinkle's *Sierra-Nevada Lakes* weaves geography and pioneer history around the major eastern Sierra lakes: Donner, Honey, Pyramid, Mono, Truckee and Tahoe. In *Survival Arts of the Primitive Paiutes*, Margaret Wheat documents the ingenious ways the northern Paiute peoples found food and made shelters in an arid land.

Also highly recommended

If I could have only one book about the eastern Sierra, *California's Eastern Sierra: A Visitor's Guide* by Sue Irwin, 1991, Cachuma Press, would be my choice. A handsome book with stunning color photographs, describing more than 100 scenic and historic points of interest between Olancha and Bridgeport. If I could have another book, I'd choose Stephen Trimble's *The Sagebrush Ocean: A Natural History of the Great Basin*, 1989, University of Nevada Press, even though it is less about the eastern Sierra and more about the Great Basin. An incredibly beautiful book in every way.

Reisner, Marc. *Cadillac Desert*. Penguin Books, 1987. True story of rivers moved, lakes drained and millions made. The glory and the folly of western water policies.

Geology

A wealth of geologic material on this area has been published, but most of it is available only from scientific libraries. It is technical and requires some acquaintance with geologic jargon. If you can handle technical literature, these three publications are basic to understanding the area and also contain valuable bibliographies: *Geology and Mineral Deposits of the Mount Morrison Quadrangle* by C. Dean Rinehart and Donald C. Ross, US Geological Survey Professional Paper 385, 1964; "Volcanism, Structure, and Geochronology of Long Valley Caldera" by Roy A. Bailey, G. B. Dalrymple, and M. A. Lanphere in *Journal of Geophysical Research* 81:725-44, 1976; *Geologic Map of the Long Valley Caldera, Mono-Inyo Craters Volcanic Chain, and Vicinity, Eastern California* by Roy A. Bailey, US Geological Survey, 1989.

California Geology. Division of Mines and Geology, PO Box 2980, Sacramento 95812. A monthly that will keep you informed of geologic events and of current research and new publications.

Huber, N. King and W. Eckhardt. *Devils Postpile Story*. Sequoia Natural History Assoc. Three Rivers, CA 93271, 1985. Exceptionally well illustrated story of the Postpile's origin.

A wealth of reliable easy-to-understand information is available in the General Interest Publications of the US Geological Survey. Sample titles are: "Prospecting for Gold," "Glaciers," "Water Dowsing," "Volcanoes," "Natural Gemstones," "Water use in the United States." Send for a listing of titles available: USGS, Box 25286, Federal Center, Denver CO 80225.

John Muir

Teale, Edwin Way. *The Wilderness World of John Muir*. Boston: Houghton Mifflin, 1954. Cloth and paper. My first choice of John Muir books. Brief biography of Muir plus the best of his writings.

Fishing

Cutter, Ralph. *Sierra Trout Guide*. Portland: Frank Amato Publ., 1991. Outstanding, comprehensive distribution list, with name, location and trout status of nearly all Sierra trout waters based on visitations and DFG survey records.

History

Bean, Betty. *Horseshoe Canyon: A Brief History of the June Lake Loop*. June Lake Loop Women's Club, PO Box 281, June Lake 93529. Excellent historic photos.

DeDecker, Mary. *Mines of the Eastern Sierra*. Glendale: La Siesta Press, 1966. True stories of the booms and busts.

Dwyer, Richard A. and Richard E. Lingenfelter. *Lying on the Eastern Slope*. Florida International University Press, 1984. The misadventures and wise-cracking journalism of Lundy's editor, "Lying Jim" Townsend. An important contribution to mining camp history.

McGrath, Roger D. *Gunfighters, Highwaymen & Vigilantes*. UC Press, 1984. An outstanding study of violence on the frontier, focused on what *really* happened in the mining camps of Bodie and Aurora. The conclusions may surprise you.

Plants

Hickman, James C., Ed. *The Jepson Manual: Higher Plants of California*. Berkeley: UC Press, 1993. Botanists have been waiting for years for a new edition of Willis Linn Jepson's *Manual*, first published in 1925. Finally, here it is—1424 large pages.

Native American Basketry

Bates, Craig D. and Martha Lee. *Tradition and Innovation: A Basket History of the Indians of the Yosemite-Mono Lake Area*. Yosemite Natural History Association, 1990. The Paiutes were noted for their exceptional basketry. Fine photographs of some outstanding baskets.

– G. S.

216

Index

Genny Smith offers these other books about California's magnificent Eastern Sierra...

■ *The Lost Cement Mine* by James W. A. Wright.
Edited by Richard Lingenfelter and Genny Smith. Illustrated by Nina Kelley. 1984. 120 pages, cloth and paper.

The original story of the Lost Cement Gold Mine "somewhere on the headwaters of the Owens River," exactly as published in the San Francisco *Daily Evening Post* in the fall of 1879. Includes historic maps and accounts of Monoville and Mammoth City mining camps. Reproduces Mark Twain's story of his midnight expedition to locate the legendary mine (with drawings from the 1872 first edition of *Roughing It*).

■ *Old Mammoth* by Adele Reed.
Edited by Genny Smith. 1983. Two-color, 192 pages, cloth only.

Memories and stories from Mammoth Lake's earlier times. Superb collection of maps, documents and 160 historic photographs.

■ *Doctor Nellie: The Autobiography of Helen MacKnight Doyle.*
Foreword by Mary Austin. Reprinted 1983. 364 pages, cloth only.

Vivid descriptions of pioneer life east of the Sierra from 1887 to 1920.

■ *Mammoth Gold* by Gary Caldwell.
Edited by Genny Smith. 1990. 192 pages, paper only.

The tumultuous years from 1877 to 1881, when hundreds of prospectors raced to Lake Mining District and the boom town of Mammoth City.

Coming Soon

■ *Earthquakes and Young Volcanoes* by Robert Tilling and others
■ *Deepest Valley* edited by Genny Smith

For retail prices and mail order information, write:
Mammoth Friends of the Library, P.O. Box 1468, Mammoth Lakes, CA 93546

Book dealers, write the distributor:
Marketing manager, University of Nevada Press, Reno, NV 89557-0076

See front cover for upper half of map.

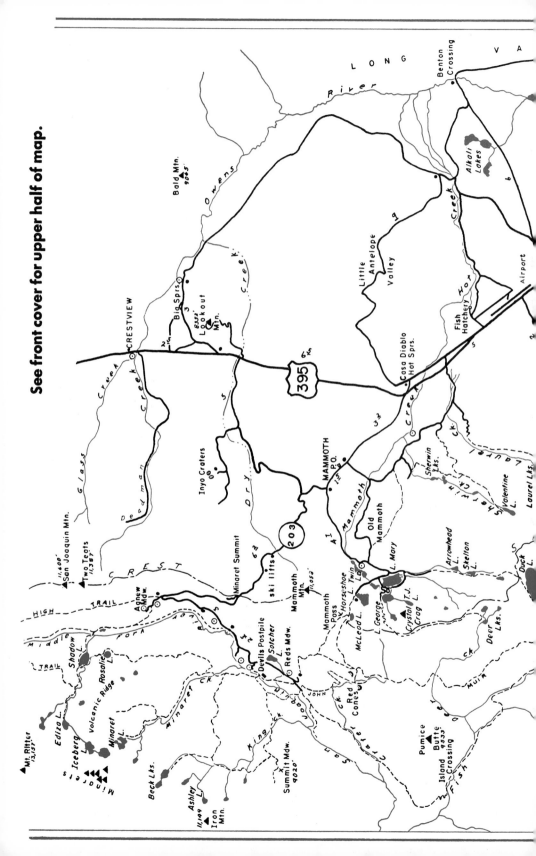

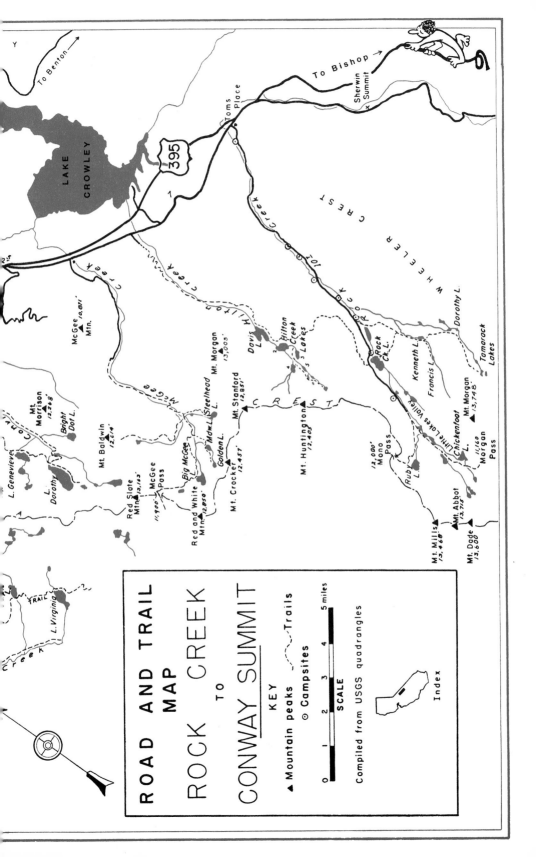